God and the Excluded

Visions and Blind Spots in Contemporary Theology

Joerg Rieger

FORTRESS PRESS
Minneapolis

GOD AND THE EXCLUDED
Visions and Blind Spots in Contemporary Theology

Cover image: *Raigo,* Stanton Macdonald-Wright, 1955. Smithsonian American Art Museum.
Cover design: Marti Naughton
Book design: Ann Delgehausen

Library of Congress Cataloging-in-Publication Data

Rieger, Joerg.
God and the excluded : visions and blind spots in contemporary theology / Joerg Rieger.
p. cm.
Includes bibliographical references and index.
ISBN 0-8006-3254-0 (alk. paper)
1. Theology, Doctrinal. 2. Marginality, Social–Religious aspects–Christianity. I. Title.

BT78 .R48 2000
230'.01–dc21 00-04253

The paper used in this publication meets the minimum requirements of American National Standard for Information Sciences–Permanence of Paper for Printed Library Materials, ANSI Z329.48-1984.

Manufactured in the U.S.A. AF 1-3254
05 04 03 02 01 1 2 3 4 5 6 7 8 9 10

To Rosemarie—

companion in the resistance against exclusion

Contents

Preface

Doing theology in the tension between God and people who are excluded goes against the grain. For centuries theology has assumed that connections to people who are excluded from the mainstream on the grounds of class, race, gender, and other marks of difference are optional. In the contemporary North American context, middle-class theology continues to act as if interaction with impoverished people is optional; white theology acts as if interaction with African Americans and other ethnic minorities is optional; male theology assumes that interaction with women is optional; and similar attitudes are perpetuated in many other places of privilege around the globe. Why should theology as a whole be reconsidered in relation to God and people at the margins now? In this book I take up four major modes of contemporary theology and develop this question into a new constructive theological vision.

At the beginning of the twenty-first century, more so than ever before, it seems that we have managed to render invisible both people at the margins and the powers that hold them there. Although the boom of the economy and other recent success stories may have passed many of us by, most mainline theologians and church people are not forced to face the recesses of suffering at the margins of the global economy and in the ghettoes of our cities. My position as a tenured theologian at a major theological school, as well as the fact that I am male, white, middle class, and from a European background, seems to ensure that I can avoid seeing—let alone being among—the excluded. It also seems to entitle me to continue to do theology as usual.

But what if the growing pain and suffering of large parts of humanity, both at home and around the globe, affect all of us, including the way we do theology? What if we are already located somewhere between God and the excluded, even though we may never realize it? And—and this is the crucial question for the theological task—what if our blindness toward other people also produces a tragic blindness toward God, the Other? If this is the case, reconnecting with people who are excluded, as well as resisting the powers of exclusion, is no longer optional. Rather, it becomes key for developing more adequate theological guidelines and for reconnecting and reshaping the various theological camps. At this point, trying to reactivate theology simply out of the goodness of our own hearts or the beauties of the tradition, roads frequently taken in contemporary theology, are easily co-opted. Unless we begin to engage our blind spots, no new vision can emerge.

In this book I deal with exclusion at various levels, beginning with economics. Exclusion based on gender (and in this context extended to issues of race) is another major concern, discussed in chapter 4. Like the study of the economy and class from the perspective of the non-poor, the study of gender from the perspective of the dominant male is done not strictly from the outside but from the other side. We need to understand not only what oppression along gender and class lines does to women and impoverished people but also what it does to men and the non-poor. Participating in the lives of my twin daughters, Helen and Annika, and my wife, Rosemarie Henkel-Rieger, reminds me daily of the subtle and often barely visible persistence of patriarchal structures that distort my own life and work. Likewise, my experiences in West Dallas and other places of economic and racial oppression continually remind me of the equally barely visible persistence of exploitation and prejudice. In all these settings theology becomes truly a matter of life and death.

This book aims at developing a new constructive theological vision. Readers interested in this vision might start with the introduction and then read chapter 6. Chapter 5, which lays the theoretical foundations and takes a closer look at the blind spots of contemporary theology, is a must-read for anyone looking for a deeper grasp of the new ways of theological thinking introduced here, but less theoretically inclined readers might save it for last. The structure of the book displays certain parallels to the four elements combined in the so-called quadrilateral of Bible, tradition, experience, and reason, developed out of the Methodist tradition but now also used in other contexts. In various parts of this book I deal with French and German authors. I have used their texts in English translation where possible. Where I refer to the French and German originals, translations are mine.

Let me add a word of thanks to those colleagues and friends who have been important dialogue partners at various stages in the process of writing: Teresa Berger, Rebecca S. Chopp, Danna Nolan Fewell, Mary McClintock Fulkerson, Kristin Herzog, M. Douglas Meeks, Charles M. Wood, and Michael West of Fortress Press. Conversations with many students at Perkins, with Gabriel Castilleja and his family, with other residents of West Dallas, and with my wife, Rosemarie, have also contributed to keeping me grounded. This project has been supported by a sabbatical and two grants: a Junior Scholar of the Year Award of the Southwest Commission on Religious Studies of the American Academy of Religion, and an Academic Outreach Award of Perkins School of Theology, Southern Methodist University.

Introduction

Theology, or What's Left of It

What's left of theological reflection at the beginning of the twenty-first century? In this book I do not side with the doomsday prophets who, idealizing the status quo of yesterday, revel in announcing the end, or at least the decline, of a long list of things, from personal family values to academic standards to Western civilization as a whole. Neither do I argue that the beliefs and doctrines of the church are vanishing. What is often perceived as a doctrinal crisis is perhaps not so much that doctrine as such is evaporating but that the operative doctrines are changing. People still hold many beliefs about God and the world. The polls have remained fairly consistent over the years: More than 80 percent of all Americans claim to believe in God. It can hardly be argued, then, that our current crisis has to do with a lack of belief in God per se.

The more pressing question is, How can we assess and engage the changing beliefs and doctrines of the church in ways that are both constructive and self-critical, thus developing new receptivity and openness to God's power? More specifically, how can we do this in ways that integrate accounts of those aspects of our current dilemma which usually go unnoticed in mainline theological reflection and the churches? In this book I will focus on the (still mostly unconscious) mechanisms of exclusion by which the majority of humanity, particularly those who do not have a share in the structures of privilege and power, are prevented access not only to the centers of theological reflection but also to the benefits of society. A growing number of theologians around the globe have, often independently of each other, come to suspect that the major problem today is the exclusion of more and more people tied to shifting structures of power and changes in the global economy.[1]

Sorting through the major challenges to theological reflection today, I will reassess the traditional guideposts of theological thought, such as questions of authority, critical reflection, and matters of doctrine. Two insights are at the heart of this study. First, we need to develop new sensitivity to the fact that theology is never done in a vacuum. Theological thought is often shaped by what its practitioners barely notice, including political and economic structures.[2] If theology is to have any future, it is no longer sufficient simply to follow the ideas of the great theological minds and one's own theological and ideological preferences. Second, if this is clear, the question becomes how to develop not only resistance to those pressures but also theological alternatives.

It is a sign of hope that many theologians are becoming increasingly aware of the fact that theology is connected to everyday life. More and more of us are no longer content with getting the doctrines right or developing ever more elaborate theological systems. Looking beyond the tranquil halls of academia, however tentatively, theology is starting to claim broader horizons. Yet even where theology begins to hook up with life, our horizons often either remain fairly narrow, determined by a self-centeredness, or they become so broad that we are unable to discern the cracks and fissures of everyday life. As will become clear in the argument of this book, a closer look at the tensions of everyday life and an encounter with people who live on the underside of history are necessary.

In this book I will explore how the traditional guideposts of theological thought relate to the mechanisms of exclusion established in modern and postmodern times. I develop my argument in relation to four prominent modes of theological reflection, constructed during the past two centuries, which represent the major options available today: liberal, neoorthodox, postliberal, and liberation approaches. These options manifest in their own ways some of the competing ideological pulls on theology and the churches today. How do they mirror and perpetuate the mechanisms of exclusion? What is their potential for providing theological guidelines that are able to develop resistance to exclusion and, in the process, promote new forms of inclusiveness in both church and world? Exploring the impact of exclusionary social structures on theological thinking, I will specifically investigate the web of connections between the exclusion of other people and the theological displacement of the divine Other. This connection, which is at the heart of this book and much of my theological work, will further our understanding of how the problem of exclusion has become one of the most pressing theological problems today.[3]

In sum, exclusion is not just a social problem; it is also a theological problem that threatens the future of theology as a whole. Theology appears to be affected by the structures of exclusion, for instance, where it shows signs of becoming a self-serving monologue—a discourse of like-minded individuals talking primarily to each other (the danger of the liberal modes of theology), a discourse about the divine Other that never really connects to God's and other people's otherness (the danger of the neoorthodox modes), a turn to the language and the texts of the church that shuts out differing readings (the danger of the postliberal modes), or a turn to others that ends up in identity politics or special-interest deals (the danger of liberation modes). Without going against the grain of exclusion, without cutting through those structures that unconsciously impact theological reflection, no progress can be made. Theology that develops resistance to the powers of exclusion may help to develop new models that prove useful in restructuring not only the process of theological reflection but also the church and, ultimately, even society at large.

Crisis of Interpretation

At first sight the growing uncertainty of theological reflection at present appears to be related primarily to a broader crisis of postmodern interpretation that has received considerable attention. Its main characteristics are the loss of the modern self's confidence in its own power and autonomy, the end of various types of foundationalisms and the related dreams of finding new Archimedean points, and the destabilization of the major referents and narratives of modern discourse. In short, we are confronted with the loss of most of those things that used to guarantee meaning, stability, and unity in the modern world. Various postmodern thinkers, including many theologians, have picked up on those problems. Nevertheless, while this crisis of interpretation has received much attention in academic circles, such crisis-talk increasingly fails to attract the interest of anybody else. Why should people care that at the end of modernity the projects of theologians and other intellectuals are falling apart, if those projects never included the majority of humanity in the first place?[4] The crisis itself needs to be reassessed from a broader and less exclusive point of view.

The urgency of the matter becomes clearer when we understand that there is a broader framework for the contemporary crisis of theological reflection. The current crisis of interpretation is itself part of a much larger dilemma that has now reached global dimensions. Its extent ranges from ecological disasters to issues of increasing poverty and hunger to tensions along the lines of race and gender. Without needing to claim a systematic correlation, we must keep in mind that theological reflection does not remain untouched by these larger issues. Where this is overlooked, theological reflection is often simply pulled into the competing structures of power. Conversely, where those larger structures are taken into account, theological reflection might better contribute its own forms of resistance and develop specific sets of alternatives.

Questions raised by human suffering and by the exploitation of all of creation can, in the long run, not be shut out where Christians reflect on the teachings of the church and on God's relationship with humanity and creation. The crisis of theology is not primarily an intellectual crisis, as many theologians still think, but the fact that we have separated ourselves from most of humanity. Theology need be reminded of these broader connections, especially at a time when, as one contemporary theologian has pointedly observed, "much theology has dissolved into a narcissistic examination of its own methodology."[5] This does not necessarily mean that thinking about theological method is irrelevant or that our project of searching for theological guidelines itself needs to be sacrificed to an all-inclusive analysis of the present. We simply need to remind ourselves that theology is not an end in itself. If that is clear, theology might be able to make its own contribution to dealing with the contemporary dilemma. In the following chapters I will presuppose the broader view of the contemporary situation that I develop here.

A Global Crisis

At first sight things may not look so bad from a North American perspective. At the turn of the millennium the alleged victory of capitalism seems to have taken care of most other rivals for power and the authority to interpret the state of humanity, the world, and even God. This situation has inspired numerous theologians to announce the end of liberation and other theologies that used to listen to people at the margins. Once again, the position of the mainline appears to be secure. The so-called culture wars between liberals and conservatives, representing the two sides of mainline thought, seem to remain strangely untouched by anything outside their purview.

But it is not quite that simple. In many ways things have gotten worse at the dawn of the new millennium, posing new challenges. Theology is increasingly being pulled into matters of life and death. The victory of capitalism and the related euphoria in certain circles need to be seen in relation to the lives of billions who live in poverty, including children. In the United States child poverty has been dramatically on the rise. In fact, it remains the highest among Western industrialized nations.[6] A new study on homeless children in the United States reports that more young children are without homes today than since the Great Depression. More than 1 million children are homeless at present. In 1988 women with children constituted 66 percent of the U.S. homeless population.[7] One in ten U.S. households, including 12 million children and 19 million adults, cannot afford to buy the food they need. Worldwide, more than 35,000 children die of hunger and other preventable causes every day.[8]

Yet these problems often remain invisible. We manage to compartmentalize and hide the worst of situations. In the United States, for example, we make certain that most of us never have to encounter the problems of poverty by building highways around low-income housing and by maintaining strict boundaries between rich and poor neighborhoods. Unfortunately, when it comes to theological discourse, the invisibility factor seems only to increase.

But can we afford to ignore much longer the ever widening gap between rich and poor? The victory of capitalism has benefited a comparatively small group of people. Wage inequality in the United States today is higher than at any time since World War II. While the compensation awarded to top executives of the largest U.S. corporations was never completely out of proportion to that of their workers, in the global economy this has changed. Links between the top executives and their workers, often employed in different parts of the world, are vanishing. By the end of the 1980s, top executives earned seventy times the after-tax wage of their workers, compared to twelve times in 1960. In 1999 that ratio had risen to 419 times. Income disparities are even greater. The top 1 percent of U.S. citizens receive 13 percent of the nation's after-tax income, but they hold almost 40 percent of its wealth.[9] Economic decision making in the United States is now in the hands of the top 5 percent of wealth holders.[10] Despite these alarming developments, even the powers that be seem less visible than ever before and are easily overlooked in analyses of our current crisis.[11]

Robert B. Reich, professor of economics and former secretary of labor, develops the following scenario for the near future if things continue the way they are now: "Distinguished from the rest of the population by their global linkages, good schools, comfortable lifestyles, excellent health care, and abundance of security guards," a new class of citizens who dominate areas as diverse as science, education, business, and law "will complete their secession from the union."[12] Other reports confirm the trend. Gated communities are popping up quickly all around the country.[13] Education tells a similar story. American schoolchildren are behind those of other industrialized nations: 17 percent of American seventeen-year-olds are functionally illiterate, while 15 to 20 percent of American children are receiving a first-rate education and preparation for leadership.[14] We will find that theology is also pulled into these structures, often without being aware of it: the most obvious example is that the emergence of this new social class, safely gathering on one side of the gap, provides an unexpected boost for the autonomy and power of the individual, values of modernity which were supposed to have been settled in postmodern times. In this context modern liberal theology gains relevance once again.

The globalizing economy presents new structures of exclusion, including a new slavery. This new exclusion goes beyond the economic exploitation of people in Third World countries to produce new forms of total control over people's lives. According to conservative estimates, 27 million people, and perhaps as many as 200 million, live in such slavelike conditions all over the globe, and the numbers are growing. The author of a new study on the subject points out that this new slavery "focuses on big profits and cheap lives. It is not about owning people in the traditional sense of the old slavery, but about controlling them completely. People become disposable tools for making money."[15] This reflects once more the problem of the invisibility of the structures of exclusion. There are more slaves today than all the people taken from Africa in the days of the slave trade, yet the problem is not even on the map. In addition, this new slavery begets yet another form of exclusion. Slave and slaveholder were once closely bound together, but now that relationship is growing ever more distant. Today's slaveholders, who are often respectable businesspeople, may never even meet their slaves.[16]

The gap between the richest and the poorest is more drastic than ever before. The wealth of Microsoft cofounder and chairman Bill Gates nearly doubles every year, rising from $51 billion to $90 billion between 1998 and 1999. Gates, now the wealthiest person in the world, has as much money today as the combined assets of the top nine billionaires ten years ago.[17] The combined wealth of the world's 225 richest people is equal to the annual income of the poorest 3 billion of the world's population. What is more, a mere 4 percent annually of the combined wealth of those

225 would make up the deficit needed to guarantee education, basic health, adequate food, clean water, and sanitation for all.[18]

At the same time, we do not yet understand that the victory of capitalism changes even the situation of the victors, reinforcing rather than alleviating structures of exclusion within the First World. The global market no longer benefits even the workforce of the First World automatically.[19] In a situation where the lives of citizens are ever more determined by market forces, not even more intimate relationships such as that of the family provide safe havens in the battle against exclusion.[20] The same is true for the church. Noting that economics can no longer be reduced to finance, critical theorists Donna Landry and Gerald MacLean remind us of "the pervasive power of the economic when the market is 'in' everything and nothing is incapable of being commodified."[21] Theology does not remain untouched by all of this. Although we need not devise a complete grasp of the matter, we have to pay more attention to the interdependencies of theology and economics.

While it is often assumed that Christian theology simply would need to reassert itself against those developments, things are more complicated. Economists are the first to remind us that in this situation the market itself has become God. Its view of God and the world, its "theology," is promoted not only on Wall Street but also in everyday relations.[22] In this context Christian theology, too, is pulled into the flow of the dominant streams. Liberal theology and even some of its mainline alternatives are easily co-opted. Although our critical theological tools may be more finely tuned than ever before, there is no critical apparatus in place that allows for much resistance to the powers of exclusion in the global market, or that would be able to deal with the suffering of people who are excluded. Thus theology itself is, by default, drawn into exclusivist relationships and the widening gap between those who are "in" and those who are "out."

To be sure, what is at work here is not ill will. One of the major problems is that all this happens primarily on an unconscious level and thus can hardly be resisted. The medical world had to face the hard truth in early 1999. A study making front-page news across the country showed that black people, particularly black women, were less likely than whites to get the proper testing for serious heart disease. One reporter notes the challenge: "The problem is unconscious bias rather than easily identified intentional bigotry. . . . And that makes the ethical challenge particularly difficult, because doctors who are prejudiced probably think they aren't."[23]

The structures of exclusion not only are mirrored in our deepest sensitivities, but extend to macro levels as well, all the way to the environment.

Recent insights into what is now called environmental racism, for instance, are beginning to reshape our concern for the environment—a concern that in its First World manifestations often disregards the survival of the poor and marginalized who are in fact most affected by environmental problems.[24] The transformation of dominant environmental discourses in relation to people who are excluded exemplifies theology's challenge.

Postmodernity

One of the major cultural streams related to this global crisis is postmodernity. Closely tied to shifts in a social fabric shaped by political and economic structures, the postmodern phenomenon needs to be seen in light of the overall challenge we presently face. Celebrations or rejections of the postmodern, still typical in the contemporary intellectual and theological scene, make little sense. On a global scale, developments in the United States have led the way into postmodernity. Recently a group of North American theologians and social scientists put it even more strongly, claiming that "postmodernity is America," naming Disneyland as its first symptom.[25] Three of the four modes of theology addressed in the following chapters, beginning with neoorthodoxy, are related to the postmodern camp in one way or another.

French poststructuralists, the most famous among the contemporary postmodern thinkers, have drawn out the implications of the postmodern situation for the intellectual task. Their wide reception in the United States and the fact that many of them pay close attention to the cultural situation in the United States as paradigm for their work underscore the relevance of this material. The thought of Jacques Derrida, one of the most well-known examples, is not just another abstract philosophical discourse (as is often falsely assumed); it needs to be seen as holding up a mirror. By reflecting the end of the modern feeling of control and security, it helps us in mapping where we are.[26]

Derrida calls into question what he terms the "metaphysics of presence," promoted by philosophical systems that guarantee firm foundations for thought and reflection. According to his analysis, all of the different foundations in use throughout history have fallen apart at the end of modernity, whether they are called "*eidos, arche, telos, energeia, ousia* (essence, existence, substance, subject), *aletheia*, transcendentality, consciousness, God, man, and so forth."[27] Modern thought, though it admits the reality of human finitude, has assured itself of its access to the infinite.

Postmodernity, on the other hand, first reminds us of a "rupture"that disrupts the false security of modern thought.

This rupture pushes us one step further into understanding that the foundations on which modern thought (and much of modern theology) are built are shakier than we care to admit. There is no absolute point of reference that grounds our intellectual efforts once and for all. One of the traditional foundations that Derrida's list rules out is God. No doubt some would blame this loss for the dilemma of contemporary theological reflection. But perhaps it is the other way around. What if the misuse of God as a foundation for human reflection, acting as if God were available as warrant of human thought, has led theology in the wrong direction to begin with? At least one of the theologians introduced in this book, Karl Barth, has suspected this. Recent developments in feminist theological thought also share in this awareness. Going beyond Barth's initial concern, we are beginning to understand that here may be one of the reasons for the growth of structures of exclusion: Mainline modern theology frequently started theological reflection with the assumption that God is accessible to the modern self. One of the most basic lessons for contemporary North American theology is that as the modern confidence in the self's immediate relation to God's presence is being questioned, doors open up into a new and exciting theological future which—building up resistance to the powers of exclusion—allows for new relations not only to the divine Other but also to human others.

At the same time, however, we need to keep in mind that the postmodern phenomenon in itself does not automatically produce greater inclusivity. Jean Baudrillard, another of the French postmodern theorist stars, has analyzed the cultural ramifications of the conditions of postmodernity in the United States. One of the characteristics he finds is a certain historical amnesia in which the struggles and fault lines of American history are simply forgotten. As a result, he argues, tensions and fault lines in the present become unimportant as well. Rather than produce greater inclusivity, this constellation perpetuates exclusivity. Baudrillard concludes: "If utopia has already been achieved, then unhappiness does not exist, the poor are no longer credible. If America is resuscitated, then the massacre of the Indians did not happen, Vietnam did not happen."[28] Baudrillard discerns a state of "enchantment" of postmodern American society that has slowly eroded not only the awareness of those who suffer but also the awareness of any limits or boundaries of those in charge. While the gap between rich and poor continues to grow, postmodernity tends to erode a sense for those who fall into the cracks.

Fredric Jameson, noted North American theorist and literary critic, helps us to analyze the problem further when he relates the symptoms of the postmodern situation to the cultural makeup of late capitalist society. Tying together observations on architectural styles, political art, cultural studies, literary criticism, and philosophy, he describes the postmodern as promoting a "new depthlessness"[29] resulting from the erosion of the hub of the modern world, the modern self. In this situation, we might infer, the tunnel vision introduced by the modern self and its exclusivist and elitist tendencies may perhaps be reconstructed. Yet Jameson is also aware of the dangers of this situation when he observes, not unlike Baudrillard, a new perception of history that allows for "the random cannibalization of the past."[30] This move appears to be related to what we might call the "cannibalization" or "commodification" of large groups of people and the environment in the global market. Everything is now integrated into the market as commodity. While we are faced with the breakdown of unified worldviews and the pluralistic fragmentation of all of life, pluralism itself, where things take place in parallel universes as it were, does not automatically guarantee a more inclusive perspective.

The economic connotations of postmodernity have been analyzed by David Harvey, pointing out a relation between the rise of postmodernist cultural forms and the emergence of more flexible modes of capital accumulation. Harvey also notes a fictitious quality of relationships in postmodernity that is mirrored in the economic realm. Yet these fictions are far from harmless: "Fictitious capital is even more hegemonic than before in its influence. It creates its own fantastic world of booming paper wealth and assets."[31] Like Baudrillard, Harvey is concerned that in such a world the voices of people at the margins go unheard.

Theological Resistance

It should be clear by now that resistance to the powers of exclusion and the call for more inclusive structures has nothing to do with common sentiments to provide handouts, be nicer, or be more welcoming to excluded others, attitudes that pervade in much of North American church and societal culture. Simply trying to alleviate the results of exclusion without facing our own complicity will no longer do. Without awareness of our blind spots and what shapes us unconsciously, we will not be able to overcome the current impasse of theological reflection.

Cutting through the maze of the contemporary theological market with an eye to the structures of exclusion, a curious reversal suggests itself.

Even theologies that had always understood themselves as pursuing the common interest of humanity are beginning to show some of the traits of special-interest arrangements, not unrelated to an inclination to join the theological enterprise wherever the market permits. Early contextual theologies of liberal provenience, for example, initially intended to integrate theology more closely with the concerns of humanity as a whole, are now easily adapted to diverse trends, be they related to waves of postmodernity, pop psychology, or avant-garde art. Theologies that have so far often been classified as special interest, on the other hand, those theologies that take seriously specific settings of marginalization and oppression along the lines of gender, race, and class, for instance, may in fact be closer to the common interests of all of humanity where they capture the roots of our common pain. Attention to specific structures of exclusion seems to be a necessary step in promoting greater inclusivity. This paradoxical reversal invites new theological construction and opens up new vistas that include places that so far have not appeared on our theological maps.[32]

This reversal of special interest and common interest allows for an important glance into the dilemma of contemporary theology and, by extension, into the current troubles of the mainline churches as well. Much of what is considered mainline theology seems to be pursuing special interests: the presuppositions of our theological reflections appear to be suspect (or simply irrelevant) to more and more people. Reflections of this problem can also be found in the churches. It should give us pause that even at the beginning of a new millennium the churches are still among the most segregated places in society. Mainline church membership is in decline, especially in highly diversified areas such as inner cities. Many churches and theologies that are flourishing at present do so because they represent more or less homogeneous groups, frequently composed of members of the dominant races and classes, as represented, for example, by the still fairly homogeneous populations of U.S. suburbs. Other mainline enterprises that are more intentional about inclusivity often assume that it can be achieved by "welcoming anybody who walks through our doors," as one pastor put it recently. No doubt those who are willing to join us and to share our ecclesial and theological positions are always welcome.

We need to understand that even between the lines of our announcements of inclusivity, structures of exclusion are at work. The problem is best exemplified in a comment about racism by Woody White, an African American United Methodist bishop in the Indiana area: Racism in the northern United States—in areas proud of their racial openness—is "more pervasive, subtle, silent, and sinister; sometimes ugly."[33]

The tension between inclusion and exclusion is now one of the major problem areas for theology. Until recently theology in general, and even those theologians who understood their work as contextual, rarely worried about the universal relevance of their work and matters of inclusivity,[34] but now it appears that no position can claim universal validity anymore. Even mainline theology can no longer afford to disregard the limits of its reach and the vast differences between contexts that were once taken for granted. Hanging on to older claims of universality will only make the problem worse. Whether we realize it or not, both the differences between contexts and the mechanisms of exclusion are deeply embedded in the structures of contemporary life. But does theology, in the wake of growing pluralism, necessarily have to wither away into special-interest ventures and post-modern indifference?

In this book I will assess alternatives and develop new perspectives. We are slowly beginning to understand that more inclusive theological positions cannot successfully be built from the top down. Contrary to conventional wisdom, the view from the top is often narrower than the view from the bottom. Positions at the top are often handicapped by an odd shortsightedness, marked by an inability to take seriously the contributions of others who are different and less powerful. What would happen if we would move in the other direction, from the bottom up? Searching for a more comprehensive set of theological guidelines, what can we learn from positions at the bottom that, out of necessity, integrate their own perspectives with the perspectives of those in power?[35] Theologies that take into account perspectives unaccounted for by the mainstream might help all of us to resist the hidden temptation of exclusionary structures and develop those more inclusive theological markers and guidelines that are needed in the multicultural contexts of the twenty-first century, including a greater awareness of global horizons. Relativism can be resisted not by universal claims but by embracing relativity. Fragmentation may not be inevitable if we recall the common roots of our pain.

Theology will not make much of a difference without facing the actual conflicts and crises of the present. Otherwise what is left of it will remain the domain of a few professional theologians and the special-interest groups that fund them. In the following chapters I will argue that those theologies taking particular settings of exclusion and marginalization seriously might offer solutions to the contemporary theological impasse, ultimately recharging and reconstructing the best insights of other theological models that have lost not only steam but also credibility, even within the churches themselves.

The Material of the Book

In our search for valid theological guidelines that resist hidden structures of exclusion and incorporate renewed openness for both the human others and the divine Other, we need to understand what currently motivates theology. This analysis includes an assessment of the location of authority, the construction of critical self-awareness, the understanding of doctrine and truth, as well as consideration of usually neglected factors such as the social location of theological reflection, how theology shapes what is happening in the churches—this may be a good starting point for more practically inclined people—and assumptions hidden between the lines. Yet the extent of the crisis in theological reflection cannot be fully understood if it is seen as an isolated problem that has emerged only recently. To come to grips with this theological crisis we will need to pay close attention to some of the major trends in theological reflection in the modern and postmodern worlds, starting with the Enlightenment. Here a major reconstruction of theology begins that still impacts theological reflection today, not unrelated to a major reordering of political and economic structures in modern market societies which, having been born in Europe, have now spread around the globe.

In response to broad social and intellectual changes in the modern world beginning with the dawn of modernity and extending to subsequent postmodern shifts, theology has followed various turns in the road, starting with the modern turn to the self in liberal theology. This is the subject of chapter 1. Turning to the self allows theology to tap into the new energy source of the modern world, the modern self's entrepreneurial spirit. One of the results of this turn is an approach to theology that is potentially more democratic. Yet what, exactly, is the role of the self in theological reflection, and who are those people gaining access? Assuming that theological reflection finds its mirror image in the church, how do the churches that have assimilated the ethos of modernity shape up when it comes to structures of exclusion?

Chapter 2 enters into a dialogue with the early critics of modern theology in the first half of the twentieth century, often identified as neoorthodox in the English-speaking world. In the collapse of the foundations of liberal theology and the premises of the modern world in light of the Holocaust and the World Wars, theology uncovered a new source of power, turning to God as the Wholly Other and challenging the modern self's position of control. The greater concern for God's Otherness and a better sense of the difference between God and humanity found here may open up new space for people who have not yet been part of theological reflection. But what are the consequences of the confession of God's Otherness? Holding up the ecclesial mirror once more, are those churches that are concerned about the holiness and majesty of God better able to break through the contemporary barriers of exclusion?

Chapter 3 deals with postmodern forms of theology that address the question of theological reflection in new ways. Postliberal theology, the example chosen due to its prominence in the church, has shifted attention to the language and the texts of the church, further exposing the limitations of the modern reliance on the experiences of the self. While the problem of the exclusion of other people is left open in this theological turn, the postliberal ways of challenging the power and self-centeredness of the modern self may be helpful in curbing structures of exclusion tied to excessive special interests. But how are the free spaces that are produced here related to the structures of exclusion? Do confessionally oriented churches deal better with issues of inclusivity?

In a context where social and ecclesial structures are deeply shaped by the powers of exclusion, some of the most interesting alternative modes of theological reflection have been developed by theologians who have been in touch with those excluded, or who have themselves been excluded, from the mainstream of theology. Chapter 4 demonstrates how in these approaches we encounter new voices. Turning to others, the theological horizon is broadened to include those who have so far been excluded from the theological enterprise. The search for that which has been repressed—a fresh theological move—leads to a constructive reinterpretation of the overall task of theological reflection. But how does this position contribute to greater inclusivity? How do churches that are shaped by this model differ from the other models introduced in this book in terms of inclusivity? Examples for this approach might be drawn from a global context.[36] In this book, however, I will limit myself to a North American perspective. Feminist theology, in dialogue with issues of class and race, will serve as an example for a growing awareness of others and its impact on theological reflection.

Chapter 5 lays the theoretical foundations for a new theological paradigm, making use of the work of French psychoanalyst Jacques Lacan. In this chapter, which less theoretically inclined readers might want to read last, I expand the traditional set of theological tools and the overall theological grid of interpretation, and develop impulses for a new constructive approach to theology. My reading of Lacan matches the material of this book in two ways. First, Lacan's analytical model of the four discourses parallels the four modes of theology and emphasizes their interrelatedness. Each discourse is closely related to all the others, and no discourse is complete in and of itself. Second, Lacan develops tools that allow the search for what is repressed and excluded by each discourse, something that has not yet been done from a theological point of view, thus further extending theological horizons into unfamiliar territory. Looking at the four modes of theological reflection in this way makes possible a new account of their advantages as well as their strengths. In the process the potential for resistance to the powers of exclusion will become clearer.

The relevance of Lacan's four discourses to contemporary theology does not primarily depend on certain parallels in the realm of ideas and concepts. More important is the fact that both share in a common predicament. Lacan writes in what he calls the "ego's era," that moment in history when the modern self has finally won most of its battles for autonomy and power and is confronted with the transitions of postmodernity. This model is of particular interest because it takes up important aspects of the contemporary postmodernist discussion while also offering a critical analysis of some of its limitations. There is no need to forge a correlation between Lacan and theology after the mode of classic systematic theology. We need not first establish a common essence or play down the difference between the two; neither do I consider the Lacanian perspective as normative for theological decisions. This model relates to theological reflection, not through a common essence, but through a common praxis: What we are searching for is unconscious truth, that truth which we have repressed so far in modern capitalism all the way to its postmodern globalizing forms. Chapter 5 will entail two things: a new perspective on Lacan through the eyes of a theologian, and a new way of making use of his insights for theology.

Toward a New Theological Paradigm

Drawing together the insights of the four modes of theology in light of the challenges of the present, several crucial impulses for a new constructive theological proposal emerge in chapter 6. Theology is reconfigured in light of the challenges of the global market and a postmodern world in which difference and the loss of foundations are not only celebrated ideas but manifest in structures of exclusion and everyday marginalization, suffering, and oppression. We need a new paradigm that takes shape between God and the excluded, rethinking the traditional texts of the church and the human self in that context.

No doubt one of the greatest weaknesses of present Christian theology is, as Alister McGrath has pointed out, a "reluctance to recognize that models are complementary, rather than mutually exclusive."[37] Yet a simple adding up of different approaches, as McGrath seems to imply, will not do. The relationships of different theologies need to be seen in greater relief, including a better understanding of their repressions and blind spots and more specific understandings of how different modes of theology relate and reconstruct each other. In the search for connections one of the most difficult things to acknowledge is that other modes of theological reflection may perhaps have the key to understanding the truth about one's own mode.

In the process it will become clear in which ways those different modes might work together in resisting the powers of exclusion and in serving the interest not only of one group of people or another, but of all. Encountering the four modes of theology in the midst of a new global context, the question for theology is this: How can these approaches help to overcome both the notorious exclusion of other people, which has become so characteristic of contemporary life, and the related but little-noticed displacement of the Other, so that we can follow once again the movement of the Spirit?

1

Theology of Identity: The Turn to the Self

In response to broad social and intellectual shifts beginning with the dawn of modernity, theology has followed various turns in the road, starting with the modern turn to the self. In the classic liberal modes, theology—understanding more clearly than ever before that God can only be known in relation to us—turns to the self. Theology now grows out of specific relationships between God and the human person. Here the development of relevant theological guidelines relies in large part on the religious powers of the modern self, be they rational or emotional. This move allows the theologian to tap into a new energy source of the modern world, the self's entrepreneurial spirit.

One of the results of this turn is an approach to theology that is potentially more democratic. Human involvement in theological reflection is now not only tolerated but valued. More people gain more access to theological reflection and have more impact on theological processes. Yet who are the people gaining access? How is the theological turn to the self related to, and even shaped by, modern structures of exclusion, and what is its potential for resistance? Envisioning the human self in terms of basic identities, how does modern theology deal with the growing awareness of human diversity? Can we still work with the assumption of much of modern theology that one's own self is the safest point of contact with God? Assuming that theological reflection finds its mirror image in the church, how do the churches that have assimilated the ethos of modernity shape up when it comes to structures of exclusion along the lines of class, race, and gender?

Many theologies that follow this approach are still related to the work of Friedrich Schleiermacher (1768–1834) who, responding not only to a dominant premodern orthodoxy but also to the excesses of modern theology of his day (and best known as the "father of liberal theology"), set the stage for constructive reflections about God which take seriously the achievements and qualities of modern humanity.

The importance of Schleiermacher's work for the argument of this book lies in the fact that his influence extends far beyond the nineteenth century and the German context. Early on in the United States, the work of Horace Bushnell (1802–1876) and others paid tribute to his thought. More recently Paul Tillich (1886–1965) helped to keep Schleiermacher's influence alive by reconstructing some of the central elements of his method in ontological terms. Like Schleiermacher, Tillich begins theology with the concerns of the modern self.[1] Although Tillich's neoorthodox contemporaries introduced a more critical look at liberal theology, its influence was never really in danger in the United States. Already in the 1970s John Macquarrie announced yet another rise of interest in Schleiermacher's thought, and *Time* magazine called Schleiermacher the "most significant Protestant theologian since Luther and Calvin." Now, at the beginning of a new millennium, Schleiermacher studies have again picked up steam,[2] while the so-called revisionist theologies—dominating the theological market together with postliberal approaches (see chapter 3)—have carried on the project.[3]

There are various reasons for the deep impact of the liberal mode of theology in North America. Although modern liberal thought was born with the Enlightenment in Europe, the United States provided the only free space for its development.[4] While in Europe modern thought was held in check by older structures and traditions, the modern liberal framework could unfold relatively freely on this side of the Atlantic and, from the time of the Founding Fathers on, gradually became the North American way of life. It is no accident that thinkers in the United States never produced critiques of Enlightenment thought as radical as their European counterparts. The so-called masters of suspicion—Sigmund Freud, Karl Marx, and Friedrich Nietzsche—were all European. Even the events of the twentieth century that left much of European liberal theology in shambles, especially the two World Wars and the Holocaust, had less impact in the United States. Generally speaking, modern North Americans do not feel the same need for self-critique as modern Europeans.

The much celebrated victory of capitalism has given yet another boost to the powers of modernity supposedly overcome in postmodern times, insofar as the entrepreneurial spirit of the modern self, particularly the belief in personal autonomy and power and the confidence that anyone can make it, has once again been justified in principle (at least by those at the very top of the ladder). These economic developments are tied back to theology. The modern self's ascent to power and autonomy in the last 250 years did not happen on the level of ideas alone. Theological trends have always been related to matters of economic status as well. The modern entrepreneurial self's gain in theological authority cannot easily be separated from its support by economic forces and the expansion of its power across the globe. No wonder the modern turn to the self is still a major theological option, despite much talk about postmodernity and the death of the self.

In light of these developments, which define much of the theological market, the question is, what keeps theology going? How can theology continue in ways that the modern structures of exclusion are not automatically reproduced and in such a way that more and more of humanity is represented, and included, and finds a place in theological reflection?

Here and in the following three chapters I deal with this question in five parts. The first three pick up the most crucial questions of theological reflection that have crystallized over the last two centuries: the strategic starting points of theological reflection and what authorizes theology, the critical self-awareness of theology, and the understanding of notions of doctrine and truth. Parts four and five add reflections on the (often unconscious) interests underlying each of the theological positions, including social location and the function of the church, perspectives that can no longer be neglected at a time when theology is becoming aware of its place in matters of life and death. The horizon of each chapter broadens as I move along, testing complicity with and potential resistance to the structures of exclusion in relation to the development of theological guidelines.

Feeling Absolutely Dependent: Authority

The modern theological turn to the self responds to a crisis. Modern thought in general begins to call into question humanity's grasp of God and the world and, in fact, the grasp of all objects outside the human self. René Descartes formulates the problem this way: "Seeing that our senses sometimes deceive us, I was willing to suppose that there existed nothing really such as they presented to us."[5] As a result, the impact of outside authorities on humanity is also called into question. If one's perception of God or the world can be wrong, it cannot really serve as a strong basis for authority. Later, Immanuel Kant drafts the motto of the Enlightenment and of modernity as a whole:

"Enlightenment is man's leaving his self-caused immaturity. Immaturity is the incapacity to use one's intelligence without the guidance of another." The motto of the Enlightenment: "*Sapere Aude!* Have the courage to use your own intelligence!"[6] Political and other structures, not least of all the churches, Kant suspects, have played a major role in promoting humanity's immaturity. Enlightenment thinkers were also painfully aware of the fact that in the history of Europe, this perceived immaturity had disastrous consequences, for religious tensions had produced decades of devastating wars and other forms of disagreement.[7] The Enlightenment, therefore, promotes the opportunity to make use of the power of one's own reasoning abilities and promises a fresh start.

In response to the critique of traditional authorities, which found one of its early and most radical expressions in the French Revolution, modern thought rebuilds itself in different ways, but always with reference to the self. Descartes, for instance, finds a way for reason to affirm itself in relation to the self of the thinker, independently of the influences of the outside world.[8] Kant, even though more aware of the limits of human reason than Descartes, nevertheless affirms the capacity of human reason to guide life without much help from outside authorities. The common message: Have the courage to use your own reason! Aware that external authority has often misled people—whether epistemologically (Descartes's point), morally (one of Kant's concerns), or politically (as in the Wars of Religion of the seventeenth century)—humanity gradually becomes aware of its own powers.

Schleiermacher zeros in on this fundamental challenge from a theological perspective. He searches for a way to take the achievements of modern humanity seriously without moving modern humanity to the center of the universe and removing everything else, as the Enlightenment's most radical promoters did. Schleiermacher seeks ways to keep God and humanity, God and the modern self, together and to reconcile the tensions that this gap has caused within both the church and society. But one thing is clear now, as never before in the history of theology: Theology cannot begin with a description of God in Godself. Traditional metaphysical speculation about God cannot give us access to God's mystery. Like Kant, Schleiermacher understands that there is no metaphysical proof for the reality of God. The premodern foundations of the theological enterprise have crumbled. God can no longer be grasped and controlled metaphysically. How, then, can modern theology come to terms with the gap between humanity and God, a gap that is related to a broader chasm between subject and object, the self and the world?

Accepting the fact that God as the object of theological reflection cannot be reached in and of itself, theology develops various attempts at mediation, including a deeper understanding of the role of the modern self in theological reflection. Attention is now refocused on the evolving modern self, gradually convincing itself of its religious genius—this after the French Revolution and Adam Smith's reflections on the nature of early capitalism had proven the self's political and economic genius.

Schleiermacher realizes that if theological reflection cannot offer a description of God in Godself, it needs to take place in the relation of God and humanity.[9] He accepts our inability to know the infinite in itself as part of human limitation: "Any proclamation of God which is to be operative upon and within us can only express God in His relation to us; and this is not an infra-human ignorance concerning God, but the essence of human limitedness in relation to Him."[10] Yet Schleiermacher is confident that the modern self (moving up socially and learning to assert its powers) plays a major role in making theological reflection possible. Unlike postmodernity, the death of God (as an entity that can be grasped metaphysically) in modernity does not imply the death of the self. Modern theology thus is able to rebuild itself on the grounds of this self; theology now grows directly out of the self's encounters with God's reality.

But how is the relationship of God and humanity developed theologically? Which elements of this relationship are most important? Which can be considered authoritative? The essence of religion, according to Schleiermacher, rests on a point of contact between humanity and God, a point that establishes a relation between the finite and the infinite, the two poles separated by a growing gap in the modern world. Philosophers in both the fields of metaphysics and ethics have failed in their own ways to establish this contact. Neither "knowing" nor "doing" can support theological reflection. Faced with this impasse, only the human capacity for feeling and intuition can offer a way out.[11]

In the lengthy introduction to his magnum opus, *The Christian Faith*, Schleiermacher outlines his method by way of "propositions borrowed" from non-theological disciplines. He defines the essence of human nature as the "feeling of absolute dependence," as both an awareness of humanity's relation to God and an immediate awareness of self.[12] While humanity is dependent on many things, the only relationship of absolute dependence is the human relation to God. Here Schleiermacher finds the element that provides for the possibility of theology even after the Enlightenment announced, explicitly or implicitly, the end of classical metaphysics and thus the "death of God."

The origin of the self's feeling of absolute dependence, the "*whence*" of it, as Schleiermacher says, is "to be designated by the word God."[13] This assumption, made at the outset of the theological enterprise, summarizes the main point of his theology. Based on the fact that there is a guiding light within human existence, it is still possible to do theology. Schleiermacher is fully aware that language and culture, too, have a function in shaping experience,[14] but the experience of God in the feeling of absolute dependence is unconditioned.[15] He distinguishes between the "sensuous self-consciousness," made up of sensual impressions that are affected by influences other than God, and the "immediate self-consciousness," also called "God-consciousness," which stands for the self's immediate, unmediated relation to God. Thus theological reflection becomes possible once again on the grounds of the religious genius of the self, its intuitive awareness of God.

Here a basic identity between God and humanity is established and the ground is laid for future attempts of constructing what might be called a "theology of identity."[16] While Schleiermacher does not stop here (those who did not read any further were always bound to misinterpret him as a religious individualist, a crude foundationalist, or simply an ultraliberal), this is the cornerstone upon which everything else rests. Only on this ground does it make sense to go on and discuss the way in which human self-consciousness is then shaped through participation in religious practices and in culture in general.

For Schleiermacher, feeling God and our absolute dependence on God is the true light from God which shines directly into the human heart. Schleiermacher describes this feeling as the "first contact of the universal life with the individual." This relationship is the basis of all religion and of all knowledge of God and the world. Yet theology must be very careful. There is a fragile quality to this feeling: "it is fleeting and transparent as the vapour which the dew breathes on blossom and fruit."[17]

While the turn to the self participates in this fleeting quality of religious intuition, it is nevertheless a stabilizing move. The principle of identity guarantees not only a fundamental relation between humanity and God but also a certain degree of self-identity. This is true in principle for all of humanity. Schleiermacher describes humanity at this point in universal terms. All human beings are basically alike in their connection to God in the feeling of absolute dependence, to the point that this notion of feeling tends to assume the status of an a priori anthropological constant. In other words, everybody has access to it. Nobody is excluded in principle from the relation to God.

Here, however, our postmodern awareness of differences between human beings, be it in terms of race, class, culture, or gender, raises questions. What if the idea of universal human nature cannot be sustained? Setting up theology based on the self becomes a dangerous enterprise once the unity of the self is called into question. In postmodern times the turn to the self easily disintegrates into the turn to a plurality of independent selves. There is a constant danger that the turn to the self leads to a breakdown of theology into special-interest ventures. In order to keep modern theology afloat other universals have been suggested. Where Schleiermacher found the feeling of absolute dependence to be a given, that is, self-evident, the anthropological common ground for all of theology and religion, a contemporary Roman Catholic theologian has argued for its opposite, the "feeling of freedom,"[18] still couched in universal terms. In the age of the global market there may be common feelings of absolute affluence or of absolute scarcity, internalized so strongly that they may have indeed become part of what Schleiermacher called our "immediate self-consciousness." But it is becoming clearer every day that those feelings are no longer universals, independent of our social location.

At this point, the turn to the self, while designed as an inclusive move by Schleiermacher and the fathers of liberalism, empowering people who had never been taken seriously in the order of things, tends to join the structures of exclusion. If universal humanity does not exist, each group will have no choice but to promote its own principle of identity with God. Thus God is drawn into more and more exclusive relationships. In this way the structures of exclusion affect not only relationships between human beings but also their relation to God. This observation throws new light on liberal theology. If the universal nature of the relation to God cannot be sustained, it may not be an accident that Schleiermacher's interests ended up being mainly with people of a certain social class, people whom he addresses in his speeches as the "educated among the despisers of religion," the upwardly mobile middle class that starts asserting itself in modernity. Here the limits of a theology of identity and the turn to the self begin to become visible.

Schleiermacher's interests in hermeneutics further illustrate what is at stake. In fact, with Schleiermacher theology becomes a hermeneutical enterprise. Shifting its attention away from metaphysical phenomena, theology no longer reflects directly on God but on the meaning of the Christian faith and experience. Even though theology and hermeneutics are not identical for Schleiermacher (theology having to do with the relation of humanity and God, hermeneutics having to do with the relation of interpreter and author), they share the same foundation. Both proceed from the inside out, starting with the self.[19]

In his hermeneutics Schleiermacher distinguishes between what he calls a psychological and a grammatical interpretation. While the latter deals with the structure of the text in more traditional fashion, the psychological interpretation is his original contribution to hermeneutics. Psychological (also called "technical") interpretation seeks to go behind the words of a text or speech to connect directly with the author.

Schleiermacher finds a new and exciting level of meaning between the lines of the text. He wonders, "Who could move in the company of exceptionally gifted persons without endeavoring to hear 'between' their words, just as we read between the lines of original and tightly written books?"[20] Psychological interpretation involves two related methods, a divinatory one and a comparative one. The divinatory method depends on the personal connection between interpreter and author: "By leading the interpreter to transform himself, so to speak, into the author, the divinatory method seeks to gain an immediate comprehension of the author as an individual." The comparative method, on the other hand, subsumes the author under a general type; the divinatory element assumes "that each person contains a minimum of everyone else."[21]

Hermeneutics and theology are closely connected at this point, since both are founded on a basic identity between humanity and God in theology and between author and interpreter in hermeneutics. The common identity that interpreter and author share is ultimately rooted in God as well. Hermeneutics is based on the fact that humanity shares in a prelinguistic consciousness, "the immediate consciousness of the universal existence of all finite things in and through the Infinite."[22] All of humanity shares in this nonlinguistic awareness that enables the search for truth and, in the end, holds everything together.

Since the relationships assumed by Schleiermacher include not only a relationship of self and God but a relationship of the self and other persons as well, this bears great promise for a more inclusive theological position. A basic connectedness exists among human beings. Schleiermacher is convinced that these similarities in human nature lead "necessarily . . . to fellowship or communion." He assumes that "fellowship . . . is demanded by the *consciousness of kind* which dwells in every man, and which finds its satisfaction only when he steps forth beyond the limits of his own personality and takes up the facts of other personalities into his own."[23] The inclusiveness of community is based on fundamental identities and similarities: the greater the similarities, the closer the community. Schleiermacher is confident that this will keep humanity together.[24]

But how does theology of identity deal with people who are different? Does Schleiermacher's emphasis on identities leave room for difference? His account of other religious perspectives may offer a first clue. One of the great merits of his work is that he opens the door for conversation with other religions. Other religions, too, share in the relation of God and humanity. But those relationships are not all the same; in different religions there are different degrees of identity between humanity and God. Different religions represent different stages, and Christianity happens to be the highest stage.

While fundamental identities on the religious level create common ground, they also offer a basis for comparison that leads to a hierarchical structure. The criterion is the quality of the self's consciousness. Idol worship, for instance, is "based upon a confused state of the self-consciousness which marks the lowest condition of man."[25] The three highest stages of religion are Judaism, Islam, and Christianity. Yet neither Judaism nor Islam represents as pure a state of the feeling of absolute dependence, since—in Schleiermacher's opinion—too many references to other objects (idols) and other emotions are sprinkled in.[26]

Ultimately Schleiermacher strives for a wholistic perspective. In his reflections on Christology, for example, he comments on the fact that human beings "are originally different from each other," some are "more and less gifted." In this situation, he summarizes, "we only arrive at the truth of life when we . . . correlate those who differ from each other."[27] In other words, just as there is no use playing down the difference between Christ and humanity after the fall, there is no use playing down the difference between human beings. But, once again, this vital relationship is structured from the top down: difference implies stages, and those on the higher stages are supposed to assimilate those on the lower ones.

No doubt liberal theology following Schleiermacher has potential for resisting the most drastic forms of exclusion—the individualistic denial of any form of connection between self and others. Nevertheless, the relation of self and others is fairly unidirectional, moving from the higher to the lower, from the self (self-assured about its relation to God) to others. Others, especially those who are different, are not at the core of the theological enterprise as such. Is it possible that the lack of respect for the otherness of the neighbor also affects the respect for the divine Other?

The Self as Foundation: Critique

As we have seen, in liberal theology religious feelings provide a solid and unquestionable foundation for what is most real. Those feelings are a given, available to a certain degree even in other religions. But how can these feelings be rightly used? Schleiermacher understands that the crisis of theology in the modern world is not to be overcome simply by developing a new starting point. The critical task is equally important: theology must find ways to keep itself honest. Schleiermacher is concerned not only with the sheer possibility of theology in modernity (a factor frequently overlooked in post-Barthian interpretations of his work) but also with avoiding theological misunderstanding as a result of the two opposing theological camps of his day.[28] The orthodox position (represented by theologians such as Johannes Franz Buddeus and Christoph Matthias Pfaff in the eighteenth century, for example) employed rational thought merely to shore up traditional church doctrine. Radical liberal positions such as "neology," on the other hand, represented by Schleiermacher's contemporary Johann Joachim Spalding, argued that Christian doctrines should give way to increased concern for the moral needs of society. While traditional orthodoxy often fails to do justice to the human components of the Christian faith, Schleiermacher understands that a crude theological liberalism that reduces the mystery of faith "altogether to the level of ordinary daily experience"[29] is equally problematic. Most of Schleiermacher's critics in recent times did not get it quite right when they accused him of simply replacing theology with anthropology, as did the Enlightenment liberalism of his day.[30]

Schleiermacher does not set out to pit God and the human being against each other (or the doctrines of the church and the self of the theologian). When it comes to the critical task of theology, however, he once again attributes a prime place to the human self. Of the three elements that come together in the construction of Christian dogmatics—the descriptions of the human state, the divine attributes and modes of action, and the constitution of the world—the first element is at the center. Schleiermacher points out "that descriptions of human states of mind . . . can only be taken from the realm of inner experience, and that therefore in this form nothing alien can creep into the system of Christian doctrine; whereas, of course, utterances regarding the constitution of the world may belong to natural science, and conceptions of divine modes of action may be purely metaphysical."[31]

Theological misunderstandings can be avoided, Schleiermacher argues, only on the basis of humanity's innermost experience: "We must declare the description of human states of mind to be the fundamental dogmatic form."[32] In other words, ideological tendencies, where "alien" elements "creep into" theology, can be filtered out only if descriptions of the attributes of God and the constitution of the world are developed out of propositions related to the inner experience of the self. Unlike other human senses, feeling, particularly the type that is unmediated and part of the "immediate self-consciousness," is "raised above all error and misunderstanding."[33]

The image of the self on which Schleiermacher bases his observations is a unified image. Except for those with the "lowest or animal grade of consciousness," there are two main forms of consciousness, elsewhere called the "sensuous self-consciousness" and the "immediate self-consciousness" (the latter being the place where the feeling of absolute dependence is located). Normally these two forms, tying together the awareness of self and the awareness of God, coexist peacefully "unless the Ego is to be split up," which for Schleiermacher seems to be quite inconceivable at this point.[34] We must keep in mind, of course, that Schleiermacher writes long before Sigmund Freud's research into the divisions of the self. But even though the unity of the self continues to be challenged in postmodern times, many still trust that it can be restored. The basic unity of the self is still assumed, for instance, in pop psychology and manifest in a plethora of self-help books, and even in many respected modern psychological schools. For Schleiermacher and much of liberal theology ever since, the self is the foundation of the theological enterprise, the safest place for theological reflection, and the place where everything comes together.

The unity of the self sets the standards. Theology shares in this unity and thus shares a common concern and interest. It does not seem to occur to Schleiermacher, however, that the self may be deeply divided. In his theology, for example, he does not account for the fact that humanity is divided into classes that promote exclusive structures, from the top down. The ideological distortions subject to critical theological reflection are therefore not so much self-critical in nature (reflecting on the blind spots of the self and its inherent divisions) but related to other theological statements—those dealing with the divine attributes and the constitution of the world which have not yet taken seriously the "death of God" and the end of metaphysics.

The distortions Schleiermacher worries about can be understood along the lines of what Schubert Ogden has called the "justification of positions already taken."[35] The self, by giving a critical account of metaphysical, scientific, and other presuppositions, is in a privileged position to recognize and screen out what is ideological at that level. Preconceived images of God and the world, for example, need to be assessed and critically examined for their soundness. But we must not overlook another form of ideology that is even more dangerous: justification of positions one is not aware of. Ideology can also affect theology in the form of "false consciousness" (the famous term suggested by Karl Marx), at work below the surface. What about those positions one is not aware of, the self's blind spots? How does liberal theology deal with matters of ideology located at the unconscious level, as the most powerful structures of exclusion usually are? The overt racist, for example, is easily recognized and identified. Most people, however, believe that they are not racist, unaware of their own hidden sentiments or of the fact that they still benefit from racist structures. The liberal model of critical reflection needs to be augmented by a self-critical move.

Today, more than ever, we must wonder whether even the innermost feelings of the self are as immediate as Schleiermacher assumed. Yorick Spiegel has shown that Schleiermacher's theological thinking is closely connected to the logic of the emerging middle class, for instance, where he incorporates its democratic ideals into his vision of how God rules.[36] No doubt Schleiermacher's approach is thoroughly shaped by societal influences. We are beginning to understand more clearly than ever before that the human self, even if it locks itself into a Cartesian closet, can never escape being shaped by its context. In our own situation, in the global market economies at the beginning of the twenty-first century, even the "immediate self-consciousness" is pulled into new force fields. The advertising industry, for example, represents the power of the economy to reshape our deepest desires: its goal is to reach below the levels of consciousness to reconfigure feelings of dependence. What guarantees that the absolute feeling of dependence remains unaffected?

Once more, a look at Schleiermacher's hermeneutics is instructive. Like the theologian, the interpreter establishes an immediate form of understanding that will help to overcome the split between subject and object, author and interpreter, and ultimately also between humanity and God. An interpretation of a text is successful not simply when it understands that which the author understood but when it understands authors better than they understood themselves.[37] Truth is found by reading between the lines. This insight becomes one of the fundamental premises of modern hermeneutics. The interpreter completes the work of the author, uncovering the fundamental intuitions that were hidden even to the authors themselves. Hans-Georg Gadamer rightly suspects that the interpreter thus finds himself—and his failure to use inclusive language is not inappropriate in this case—in a certain position of superiority.[38]

For Schleiermacher, the self keeps things together. Not only do matters of the interpretation of texts become manageable in this way, theological matters become more accessible as well. On the flip side, of course, this means that the subject matters both of hermeneutics and of theology are only available as filtered through the self.[39] This is also true for those who do not fit the implicit description of the modern self: others, those who are different, people at the margins, are also filtered through this lens. They are included, but only on the terms of the self. As we sometimes tell our children, "They [meaning, for example, people of different races or cultures] are just like us." No wonder the modern self, educated and middle class, feels as if it understands others better than they do themselves. Charles M. Wood shows how this plays itself out in another modern thinker who promoted a turn to the self, Joachim Wach. Like Schleiermacher, Wach assumed that self-knowledge is the basis for all understanding. For this reason he assumed that people who are different can be understood by adjusting, that is, lowering, ourselves to their level: "Remembering our childhood mentality, our games and associations, may give us insight . . . into the 'primitive mind,' for the patterns of thought which dominate our childhood are 'immersions into archaic modes of consciousness.'"[40] The integration of others becomes a one-way street: the self remains in control.

In late capitalism, when even our deepest desires and concerns are determined more and more by the lurings of the marketing powers of the economy, the tendency to start theology with one's own experiences and feelings is still widespread. But it is becoming ever more doubtful whether the self remains the safest starting point for theology or how much it is capable of filtering our ideological distortions. And while others are not necessarily excluded, they may find themselves in a subordinated position.

Feeling Put Forth in Speech: Doctrine and Truth

Schleiermacher's reconstruction of theological reflection has achieved two things. First, he provides a new foundation for the theological enterprise by introducing a link between God and humanity with the concept of the feeling of absolute dependence. Second, this feeling serves to steer us clear of the dangers of ideological distortion.

Schleiermacher's understanding of Christian doctrine clarifies what is at stake. Doctrines are not metaphysical or propositional truth claims, as many traditionalist theologians would argue, nor are they scientific data demanded by modern empiricists. Doctrines are "accounts of the Christian religious affections set forth in speech."[41] The doctrines of the church are now seen as grounded in, and to be purified and reconstructed by, the Christian self's awareness of God. Doctrines are not metaphysical statements that define their divine point of reference conceptually (thus enabling them to claim ownership of the divine), nor are they empirical data available to our senses. The doctrines of the church are circling around the presence of God in the religious feelings of the self. In this process Schleiermacher reconfigures the criteria for determining the truth. Doctrinal truth is not primarily verified by any external authority but by the internal authority of the self's experience, its feeling of absolute dependence.

While the self takes on the central role, Schleiermacher reminds us that this self is not an individualistic monad, as much of modern ideology would have it. Although the experiences of the self are deeply personal, the self is also part of a community. In the encounter with Christ, he believes, a "corporate feeling of blessedness" arises, and "a self-enclosed life of feeling within a sensuous vital unity" is transformed into a "sympathetic feeling for others and the whole."[42]

Schleiermacher's theological turn to the self, therefore, does not drift off into sheer individualistic subjectivism. He rejects pious individualism when he insists that "the statement and support of a body of propositions which are preponderantly deviant and which express merely the conviction of an individual we would not term a 'Dogmatics.' "[43] As John Thiel has pointed out, the validity of dogmatics is determined "not by its style, structure, or the reputation of its author but by the faithfulness with which it articulates the faith experience of the church the theologian serves."[44] The communal context of doctrine is important since the structures of religious feeling are shared by all the members of the church. For this reason the shape of the current doctrines of the church must be taken seriously. But personal feeling, "religious affection," nevertheless remains the foundation for their validity.

This dialectic of self and community is important when thinking about the impact of structures of exclusion on modern theological thought. The self is always seen as part of a larger structure. At the same time, the church that Schleiermacher has in mind seems to be a fairly homogeneous group. What matters is the *unity* of experience. There is room for diversity only insofar as it ties back into this unity. Those at the margins may not necessarily be aggressively excluded, but they have no choice other than to adjust to those at the center. Without necessarily being aware of it, the modern self—a member of the class that feels closest to God—sets the norm. There is no other authority that can be appealed to. As a result, not only are the human others assimilated to the self and its exclusive aura, the divine Other is also in danger of being sucked into the structures of exclusion in the modern world.

Schleiermacher's reflections on hermeneutics illustrate once more the central position of the self. He is not only interested in what lies behind a text, but also in the text itself.[45] Applied to his understanding of doctrine, this suggests that he may be more concerned about the actual text of the doctrines than has commonly been realized. For example, he talks about the importance of language in a little-known review of a children's book. Defining language as "the common element of the formation of humanity," he argues that history is only the result of language.[46] It must come as a surprise to many that Schleiermacher in his own way shares in what today has hit the theological markets as the postmodern turn to language. But this concern for language is immediately qualified. Young bees, Schleiermacher illustrates, should be taught about flowers "from which they have to extract the substance for their life's work and their works of art" rather than about previous histories of their species.[47] While Schleiermacher equates language with the flowers in his example, the focus of his argument clearly is not on language itself but on the substance or essence behind it. Language is primarily a medium, and the interpreter needs to get at the underlying substance, guided by personal intuition.

Here the story of modern hermeneutics begins.[48] The theologian can make use of hermeneutics by "reading between the lines" of church doctrine to find out the "substance," that which really matters. In this case the interest of theological reflection shifts from the text of church doctrine to an examination of what lies deeper. Doctrines are no longer metaphysical truth claims about the way things really are; rather, they are pointers to a truth that needs to be uncovered via a hermeneutical process, a process which depends primarily on the capacity of the self. Gadamer summarizes what is at stake: "The ultimate ground of all understanding must always be a divinatory act of corresponding genius."[49] What holds this model of theological reflection together is, once again, the genius of the self based on the assurance of a certain degree of identity with God.

Ultimately both hermeneutics and systematic theology are impossible without the intuition and the feeling of the self. Even the systematic aspect is more solid when it is related to feeling. In the first of a number of aphorisms from the years 1800 to 1803, Schleiermacher puts it this way: "I am still able not only to think all systems but to feel them as well. This is perhaps the surest test of a healthy intellectual sensitivity."[50]

The strength of this model is that the position of the self before God is taken seriously. In his sermons, for instance, Schleiermacher does not motivate people by humanistic moralizing or by pointing to the demands of an orthodox catalogue of doctrine. The center of his sermons is the living relationship of self and Christ, creating awareness for the divine Spirit at work in human life. Binding together God and humanity, "the way to God and the gospel is not alongside the daily human life but leads through it and into it."[51] No doubt this theological enterprise shows certain democratic tendencies since its authority is shared with the people.

Unlike other modern ideologies, Schleiermacher's does not intend to make the self absolute. His emphasis is on the relation of God and self. This concern is mirrored in his sentiment toward the Prussian nation. Despite supporting nationalist tendencies, Schleiermacher does not absolutize people and state. In his *Christian Ethics* he points out that "where the unity of the people is the final point of reference, there one finds nothing but self-love and the absence of morality."[52]

Although he limits the role of the self to a certain degree, Schleiermacher nevertheless proceeds from the inside out in reconstructing the process of theological reflection. Before anything else can be done, theology must establish that underlying reality which both authorizes the theological enterprise and keeps it honest. Schleiermacher is convinced that "the time is not far off when . . . some later thinker occupying the same standpoint will be able to write a much shorter Dogmatic."[53] In other words, theology in its search for truth, grounded in the self's feeling of absolute dependence, does not need the full records of the tradition or the thirteen volumes of *Church Dogmatics* which Karl Barth will start writing roughly one hundred years later. Too much diversity can be harmful not only for society but also for theology.

While Schleiermacher's turn to the self does not want to render the self absolute, there is a very real danger that theology becomes a function of its own starting point. Everything comes together ultimately in the self of the theologian and the Christian within the community of the church. The genius of the modern middle-class self, its identity with itself and with God, comes first. Difference and otherness are to be measured in terms of it.

Middle-Class Interests in Theology and the Church

A look at the historical setting of Schleiermacher's turn to the self will help us to pull things together and draw out more specific parallels into the present. No doubt the focus on the self has the potential of opening theology more fully to all of humanity. In the relation of God and humanity, humanity learns to assert its own role. All of humanity is included since, at least in principle, everybody has access to some form of religious consciousness. Here are the roots for the turn to the self's potential resistance to the powers of exclusion, which at the beginning of the twenty-first century threaten not only the future of theology but human community as a whole.

The self-perception of the modern self is shaped in no small part by encounters with people who are completely different. In Schleiermacher's times the expansion of the modern self into other parts of the world is in full swing. The nineteenth century is the heyday of global travel-writing and new forms of exploration.[54] Like everybody else, Schleiermacher is deeply interested in these events and, for several years, even worked on a major historical assessment of the settlement of New South Wales on the east coast of Australia by the English.

Discussing the encounters of Europeans and natives, Schleiermacher acknowledges in general the equality of all human beings. He praises the peaceful strategies of the English explorers and settlers who, he assumes, are rooted in their rational superiority. In this way, Schleiermacher feels, the modern self's actions in the colonies are on a much higher moral level than those of previous generations. The European self of the nineteenth century is no longer the same as the European self of the Latin American conquest which, starting three centuries earlier, controlled its others by sheer force and the sword. It is easier for the modern self to be generous, of course, because in Schleiermacher's own judgment, the English have nothing to gain from the natives who are entirely primitive, arrested at the lowest stage of life. They seem to lack all social organization, even religion or superstition. "What use would there have been for these people?" he wonders.[55] They were not even suitable as slaves.

The modern self does not need to defend its position in the modern world since it can rely on its inherent superiority. The same is true for the relation of the middle and the lower classes. Schleiermacher is deeply convinced that any improvements made in the modern world have to start with the middle class, gathered in the cities. In rural areas improvements can only happen much slower and less directly.[56]

At the same time, believing that nothing is completely excluded from an overarching nexus of interdependency,[57] liberal theology fights against radical exclusion. Representing the sentiments of the newly emerging middle classes, Schleiermacher opposes aristocratic governments where the ruling class separates itself completely from the lower classes. Despite this emphasis on unity and community, however, there remains a hierarchy in his own thought, apparent when he places the clergy over the laity and male over female, an order never to be reversed.[58] Where differences are perceived, they are often naturalized, as Schleiermacher's reflections on the nation-state show. The differences of language and lifestyle of people, for instance, are seen as God-given. By the same token, where differences are imagined and not rooted in nature, they will end automatically at some point. Revolutions that seek to overthrow those differences are thus of little importance.[59]

We must not forget that the modern self, which comes to the rescue of theology and assumes central authority, does not emerge in a vacuum. The purest and most advanced forms of the feeling of absolute dependence are shared not by all of humanity but by a specific group of people, all part of the educated middle class. This is no coincidence. Schleiermacher's work has deep roots in the rise of the European middle class in the eighteenth and nineteenth century. His work has refocused theology on the interests of the educated middle class occupying the leading positions in the church and the world of the nineteenth century, a focus that has remained in place in much of liberal theology in the twentieth century (Rudolf Bultmann and Paul Tillich are among the examples) and is alive and well at the beginning of the twenty-first century.[60]

At the heart of the modern world and modern theology, therefore, is not humanity in general, as the liberals tend to assume, but the middle class. This class is the engine of much of the intellectual and cultural production from the nineteenth century onward. What is more, this class also managed to shape the modern world in its own image through economic and political expansion. Unlike in France, the middle class in Schleiermacher's Germany did not openly revolt against the aristocracy, but advanced to positions of power and wealth mainly through education that guaranteed a secure position in the royal bureaucracy. Those who were left out were seen as excluding themselves: those who lack education, for instance, exclude themselves from the community of the educated.[61]

On the intellectual level, the modern middle-class self established itself by claiming access to the universal meaning of the universe and the right to reshape the key concepts and master signifiers of the modern world.

This claim established itself only gradually, supported by political and economic shifts. After the French Revolution had succeeded, the middle-class claim of universality became more and more the awareness of the reality of the universal in all areas of life.[62] Schleiermacher provides an example of this process when he takes the success of modern society as proof for the power of the Christian faith. His view on miracles is telling: "Even if it cannot be strictly proved that the Church's power of working miracles has died out . . . in view of the great advantage in power and civilization which the Christian peoples possess over the non-Christian . . . the preachers of to-day do not need such signs."[63] Even philosophy begins to reintroduce a reflection on God as the ultimate universal. While Schleiermacher does not buy into this development without reservations, his project could still be described in part as reconciling Christianity with the emerging middle-class claim to universality.[64] The position of the modern self becomes normative for humanity in general and, in the process, also normative for matters related to God.

Here the turn to the self shows once again some potential for resistance against the powers of exclusion. Struggling against the hierarchical structures of the premodern world, manifest not only in the political structures of feudalism but also in the medieval church and its control of doctrine, the world of the middle class appropriates the ideals of equality and rationality. These ideals are manifest and still upheld today in political programs and structures, most prominently in the U.S. Declaration of Independence, grounded in the essential qualities and rights of the modern self: "We hold these Truths to be self-evident, that all Men are created equal, that they are endowed by their Creator with certain unalienable Rights, that among these are Life, Liberty and the Pursuit of Happiness."[65] The positive aspects are obvious. Categories based on this view of the self, such as interdependency, connectedness, and wholeness, set limits for the powers of exclusion. Everything works together for the greater good.

But there is also another side. In the early history of the United States, only the equality of white men with a certain amount of property was in fact guaranteed by the Declaration of Independence. In the further development of modern societies, social bonds are often used as means for the advancement of the self. While the modern self depends on others to secure its own success, those others often remain strangers. In this sense both individualism and mutual dependency are tied together, but their relationship is negotiated and weighed by the needs of the self.[66] The modern self, in the process of emancipating itself from premodern spiritual and material bonds, likes to think of itself as in control. Society as a whole is now shaped by the modern self's struggle for self-realization, its individual pursuit of happiness. This attitude most likely affects not only the way we relate to human others, especially to people in less powerful positions, but also the way we relate to the divine Other, God.

More specifically, one of the basic difficulties of the turn to the modern self is that the self in control has trouble developing a self-critical stance, resulting in a number of fundamental blind spots. The ideal of equality, for example, is severely limited. Here is a tension in the worldview of the middle class. Despite great emphasis on equality, community, and democracy, modern society is still composed of two major classes. Even in liberal democracies a gap between the middle class and the proletariat is carefully maintained.[67] German idealism reflects this gap in a distinction of the spiritual and the sensual (*geistiges* and *sinnliches Bewusstsein*), marking a split between the educated middle class and the lower classes. Despite the fact that Schleiermacher generally values the contributions of women, a similar split is also assumed between male and female.[68] Schleiermacher's distinction between the immediate and the sensuous self-consciousness reflects a similar concept. These positions are maintained in relation to something that does not even appear on the theological map: the economy and the means of production.

Not surprisingly, Schleiermacher does not account for this gap in his theological reflections. The ideals developed by the middle class, such as its claim to universality and the idea of the wholeness of the self, seem to be unaffected by this tension.[69] In its eagerness to shape the world for the better, the middle class does not realize that it is perpetuating structures of exclusion which leave out large parts of humanity. The middle class does not realize that its freedom depends on the unfreedom of others.[70] The self is idealized. No wonder that in Schleiermacher's patriotic sermons there is a strong emphasis on the self's domination of the world without reference to repentance.[71] Ultimately this failure to truly connect with others who are members of a different class affects the relation of the self and the divine Other as well.

At the beginning of the twenty-first century, equality has become a generally accepted principle for those shaped by the modern mind-set. Throughout the nineteenth and twentieth centuries the modern self has been reminded of its commitment to equality. The Civil War and the Civil Rights struggle are among the most prominent examples. Yet the ongoing tension between the races shows that the relation of the modern self to those who are different is far from settled. The white middle-class self has found new ways of maintaining its position of superiority, and liberal theology has followed. In the United States the middle class continues to expand its control. The new class of leaders emerging in late capitalist society gives an unexpected boost to the self's autonomy, supposed to have been called into question in postmodernity. As in Schleiermacher's day, not all is individualism. Robert B. Reich shows that among this class there is plenty of collaboration; in fact, collaboration is a basic value, but applies only to those within the same class.[72] Despite commitments to equality, the turn to the modern self is not able to overcome the powers of exclusion completely. Mainline liberal theology thus easily becomes special-interest theology.

The Liberal Church

The way the theological turn to the self shapes up in the contemporary church illustrates what is at stake. One of the most powerful impulses of turning to the self is the appreciation of humanity's role in the theological enterprise. In relation to God, the self sets free a new burst of creativity. Older structures and traditions, while not necessarily abandoned, are filled with new life and developed in new directions.

Even when immersed in the ocean of modern individualism, liberal theology can still make use of the sense of community that Schleiermacher develops—a sense that is also preserved in the networking efforts of those in charge in the global economy. At present this sense of community may well be one of the principal reasons for church attendance. Broadly speaking, liberal theology grows out of the community. Older structures of hierarchy are exploded, aristocratic forms of exclusion are resisted, and modern liberal churches develop more inclusive styles.

Yet the ideal of community that takes shape here often generates trouble when dealing with tensions. Inclusivity is seen as a matter of conforming to the community, particularly to those who are in charge and set the pace. In addition, the widespread assumption prevails that tensions can be resolved by greater love, and that love outweighs justice. Given this kind of climate, those in need of justice easily fall through the cracks; in fact, if they speak up, they are seen as the ones who are unable to generate the necessary love for the others. They are the troublemakers who do not quite fit in, unwilling to conform, and thus are perceived as excluding themselves. The recent statement by the pastor of a liberal inner-city congregation sums it up: "We are a radically inclusive church: everyone who walks through this door is welcome." Indeed, those who submit to the community (symbolized by walking through a very specific door) and thus promise not to create trouble are always welcome.

Churches shaped by liberal theology often try to help others. They attempt to be compassionate. Many of those efforts, however, end in one-way streets. One large, affluent liberal church in Dallas recently donated twenty computers to an inner-city project. A worship service of celebration to which children from the poor neighborhood were invited focused on the hope that these computers would help them to get ahead, giving *them* a chance to become more like *us*. Another recent report praises church members who serve food at a homeless shelter on Sunday mornings.[73] Afterward, the report continues, they go home, take a shower, and go to church. The homeless are subject to outreach programs, but do not appear as a part of what really goes on in the church. The symbolic process of showering *after* the contact with the others and *before* the worship service is telling.

Nevertheless, not everything ends in a one-way street. Modern liberal churches often have some understanding that in bridging the gaps of exclusion, those who serve are also also at the receiving end. This is an important improvement over churches that stress only the moral or theological imperative to serve. Receiving from others in the liberal context, however, often simply means feeling good about oneself rather than letting oneself be challenged by those others who are served.

The problems compound each other: The repression of actual conflict (including conflict along the lines of oppression, such as class, gender, and race) prevents any real understanding of the plight of others. Moreover, it is often taken for granted that the suffering of others can be alleviated without challenges to oneself. Here the emergence of special-interest groups can hardly be avoided. The interests of those who are excluded appear to be different from those in power, and there is little understanding of what the common interest might be.

In sum, in modern theology humanity takes on a more important role. This closer theological attention to humanity and the self has often been seen as liberating. Humanity no longer is merely the passive object of superhuman powers, but moves into a position where it is able to pose its own questions and concerns more clearly. Using a theological image, the creature advances to the status of cocreator, without necessarily doing away with the Creator altogether. Theology "from below" now becomes a real option, if the designation "from below" refers to theology that starts with the concerns of humanity.

Modern theology, whether shaped more directly by the social and intellectual shifts produced by the Enlightenment or developed in response to those challenges (such as the romantic influences that can be traced in

Schleiermacher), follows Kant's encouragement to make use of one's own reasoning capacities. While there are different opinions about the exact nature of those reasoning capacities (Schleiermacher locates them mainly in feeling and intuition), modern theology in general encourages a certain amount of freedom from guidance by others, including certain doctrinal statements and the hierarchical structures of the church.

Yet what if theology "from below" turns into another theology "from above"? What if the humanity that informs Schleiermacher's approach is in fact not humanity in general but a certain group of people, all part of an elite social class? Would not the structures that exclude other people also affect the modern self's openness to the divine Other? Keep in mind that the "turn to the self" is not a turn to abstract humanity or the absolute individual; it is a turn to the members of that group which is in charge in modern times: the middle class.

If God's presence in Jesus Christ is utterly inclusive, however, gathering those on the "streets and lanes of the town . . . the poor, the crippled, the blind, and the lame" (Luke 14:21), does not Godself reverse the "from below" and "from above" dichotomy? Godself ends up "below," inviting everybody, and thus doing away with the dichotomy and creating space for the development of common interest. While Schleiermacher does not promote a dichotomy between "from below" and "from above," in his model God is pulled closer to the position of the middle class and both seem to share in the "from above," thus not only picking up but also reinforcing and perpetuating the structures of exclusion.

Conclusion

One of the great merits of Schleiermacher's approach is that he does not succumb to the Enlightenment while, at the same time, taking its questions seriously. He does not solve the crisis of theological reflection in his day by selling out to the dominant trends. Schleiermacher wants to preserve God's role. He searches for a way to deal with the loss of metaphysical foundations and the split of subject and object, and to keep God and humanity, God and the modern self, together. Theological critics sometimes overlook that both of Schleiermacher's famous contemporaries, Kant and Hegel, tried to do the same thing in their own ways. Yet more than both Kant and Hegel, Schleiermacher continues to emphasize God's role. Since contemporary theology does not always give him credit for that, we need to remind ourselves that the history of liberal theology must not be presented as the loss of God, or as God simply being pushed aside.

The basic problem of liberal theology is that the theological turn to the self is easily pulled into modern political and economic structures of exclusion, where the modern self is the norm that determines who is in and who is out. No wonder that modern theology is never quite able to resist a tilt toward special-interest solutions. Developing the relationship to God on the grounds of basic identities between God and self leaves out other people. Loving God and loving the neighbor, while not necessarily divorced in this model, drift apart and both are subordinated to the self. In liberal circles it has often been pointed out that to love one's neighbor, one would first have to love oneself. Here, the self remains firmly in control. Yet the controlling nature of the self's relationship to others might also affect the relationship to the divine Other. Would one not also, to stay with the above logic, first have to love oneself in order to love God?

Still, there are definite advantages to liberal theology's position. Both Schleiermacher's hermeneutics and his theology invite a process of listening to things that are often overlooked in theology and the church. The concern for "reading between the lines" opens new dimensions of reality. Theology and hermeneutics are based no longer on absolutes but on relationship. Hermeneutics is built on a relationship of interpreter and author: "In interpretation it is essential that one be able to step out of one's own frame of mind into that of the author."[74] The same is true for theological reflection.

At the same time, Schleiermacher is also aware of some limits. Even though he understands the growing importance of the role of the self, he does not attempt to repair completely the gap between humanity and God and between subject and object. He follows neither Johann Gottlieb Fichte, who dissolves the object into the subject, nor Friedrich Schelling, who argues for the absolute identity of subject and object.[75] Yet in the end identity wins out. In hermeneutics there remains little room for difference: "In reality, each word, even a particle, has only one meaning, and the various meanings of words must be understood by tracing them back to their original unity."[76] Jacques Derrida's suspicion, therefore, appears correct: Even though modern hermeneutics is moving away from metaphysical structures of control, it has not completely gotten rid of the modern dream of mastery.

While Schleiermacher's concern for relationships between the self and others and between the self and God is important, it has often been idealized. Anthony Thiselton, for example, goes too far when he praises Schleiermacher's "ability to listen, before rushing in" without qualification.[77] Manfred Frank commends romantic hermeneutics and

Schleiermacher for relying on intuition and the ability to put oneself into the mind-set of the other.[78]

As we have seen, Schleiermacher's work is at times in danger of overemphasizing the role of the self. Even in its relationship to others the self never gives up control, assuming that it has access to the truth within the reach of its own intuition, thus not having to spend too much time with others. In this way it involuntarily mirrors the larger structures of exclusion in modern society. Since there is little opportunity for the self to double-check its efforts in self-critical fashion, this type of theology is in trouble, especially if the self happens to be the self of the privileged—that is, if the self is one that can afford to circle around itself in narcissistic fashion and shape its own reality. Given that the self to which theology turns in its modern form is often also the self in power in the modern world, a stronger self-critique than the one offered by modern theology is called for and will be provided by the three remaining modes of theology.

2

Theology of Difference: The Turn to the Wholly Other

The early critics of modern theology in the first half of the twentieth century, often identified as neoorthodox in the English-speaking world, proclaimed the end of the modern search for identity. The collapse of the foundations of liberal theology and the premises of the modern world in light of the World Wars and the Holocaust, as well as shift in the international economic situation and the tectonics of power, led to a greater awareness of the overstated promises of theology based on the identity of the modern self and a new appreciation of the value of difference. Turning to God as the Wholly Other, theology now uncovered a new source of power, challenging the modern self's position of control. Pointing to God's Otherness, these thinkers demonstrated the courage to face the open-endedness of the theological enterprise. In contrast to modern claims of foundational identities between humanity and God, here theological guidelines are developed that promote a better understanding of the limitations of the driving force of modernity. The starting point of theological reflection now lies with the Wholly Other and thus can never be completely secured by theological reflection. Prefiguring more recent postmodern sentiments, theology can no longer define its own center.

The greater concern for God's Otherness and a better sense for the difference between God and humanity might help to create new space for people who have not yet been part of theological reflection. But how is the confession of God's Otherness related to, and also still shaped by, the powers of exclusion? How does the encounter with God's Otherness help to appreciate better the otherness of the neighbor and thus to move to the next step in the breakup of the narcissistic tendencies of the modern self? And, holding up the ecclesial mirror once more, are those churches that are concerned about the holiness and majesty of God better able to break through the contemporary barriers of exclusion?

The theology of Karl Barth may serve as an example. Barth's early critiques of liberal theology were highly influential and established an alternative approach to theological reflection. Even though the Barthian paradigm was never quite able to displace its theological competitors in the United States, Barth is still the most-read systematic theologian in this country and, at the end of modernity, his popularity is on the rise.[1] In fact, there is hardly any place in the world today, including Europe, where his ideas are as influential as in the United States. Recently Barth's name could be found on a list of seventeen Christian leaders thought to have most influenced U.S. culture in the twentieth century.[2] In contemporary theology, concerns for divine Otherness have gained momentum and are being pursued also by other schools, as different as the classical apophatic tradition of Eastern Orthodox theology that is receiving increased attention, and the postmodern Roman Catholic setting of Jean-Luc Marion, now supported even by a revisionist theologian such as David Tracy.[3] Certain postmodern agendas are also linked with the Barthian turn to the Other, and in these and other connections some of the aspects of the critical impulse of Barth's work are being recovered.[4]

Like Schleiermacher, Barth is aware of a fundamental dilemma of theological reflection. Unlike Schleiermacher, Barth comes to accept the gap between God and humanity, created by the questions of modernity. Trying to bridge this gap can be a dangerous enterprise, since the modern self—used to being in control and to being able to shape its world—may not find much more at the other end than its own mirror image. With Barth, theology starts facing a dilemma that is today becoming even more pressing as we try to navigate the beginning of the twenty-first century. The crisis of theological reflection is no longer just related to the fact that we cannot know God in Godself. Barth notes another problem: We can no longer rely on the religious powers of the modern self for guidance either. The modern critique of absolute images of God is now expanded in the critique of absolute images of the self.

Barth does not think about the theological crisis in abstract terms but develops an initial understanding of the broader framework of the crisis of modernity. From the eighteenth century onward, he identifies the social location of the modern self in relation to a "grandiose self-confidence" that treated "everything given and handed down in nature and in history as the property of man, to be assimilated to him."[5] He worries about the domestication of the gospel—not by humanity in general but by those who can afford it, the middle class. And unlike the majority of his neoorthodox students, even the later Barth could never quite do away with the sense that God takes sides not only with the oppressed but also against the oppressors.[6] Unfortunately, such analyses are often missing from the reflections of those who have echoed Barth's sentiments. In many cases analysis is replaced by a simplistic idealization of the premodern or a rejection of the self on moralistic grounds. As a result, the potential for resistance to the powers of exclusion is diminished.

Barth writes at a time when the foundations of a theology that had just become comfortable with the modern world start to crumble again. The end of certainty in matters of God that had shaken traditional theology at the beginning of modernity is now, at the dawn of postmodernity, followed by the end of another certainty in matters of the human being. Modern theology's trust in the religious, moral, and political qualities of the modern self is unsettled most dramatically, however, not by new ideas but in the face of the atrocities of the twentieth century. Modern humanity has failed to live up to its own standards. One of Barth's later books, *Dogmatics in Outline*, involuntarily illustrates the problem: it is literally produced out of the ruins. The ruins of Bonn University at the end of World War II speak for themselves, signifying the ruins of modern liberal theology and its trust in the powers of the modern self.[7] What breaks down is not only what we now recognize as evil, such as the Third Reich, the Nazi Party, or anti-Semitism. Already at the time of World War I Barth had realized that what we think is good does not necessarily provide a firm foundation either, including the traditional institutions of society such as the state, international relations, art and science, the economic order, and—perhaps most surprisingly—even the family.[8]

On the North American shores of the Atlantic these perspectives may be harder to grasp. We do not have to deal with ruins at home—at least not the ruins of what those of us in charge have built. Neither do those who join in the now common critique of institutions (such as the government) have to deal with a complete breakdown; they usually cling to other institutions like the family or the economy. In the history of the United States, things economic picked up fairly quickly after the Great Depression and have continued into the present. And, except for a glitch in Vietnam that temporarily set back national self-confidence, the United States has won most of its wars. Nevertheless, at the beginning of the new millennium we are faced with a new set of crises. While those in power celebrate the so-called victory of capitalism, others increasingly doubt whether the modern self will be able to get its act together in light of the towering economic and environmental crises—crises that most strongly affect people at the margins. What if the modern self is no longer a reliable guide through the maze? The general loss of respect for politics and politicians, for example, that continued through the 1990s is not primarily about the qualifications of political leaders. Instead, it seems as if political endeavors as such, related to the power of the modern self to shape its world freely and autonomously, are increasingly losing control and other powers, primarily economic, are taking over. At the same time, however, these economic powers continue to protect the privileged position of the elite, the modern self. The rich get richer and the poor get poorer.

The emerging postmodern sentiment in the last quarter of the twentieth century has created a situation where Barth's critique of liberal theology is receiving more sustained attention than ever before. But how does the theological critique of liberal theology relate to deeper crises? Is this position able to go beyond questioning the integrity of the modern self—the main point of the postmodern sentiment—helping to resist the structures of exclusion of late capitalism and the lurings of the marketing powers of the economy? Does it create alternatives?

Discerning Difference and Facing Conflict: Critique

While Schleiermacher starts theological reflection by searching for the authorizing ground of theology, Barth starts with a critique. The task of theology—or dogmatics, as Barth prefers to call it—is not the "exhibition of a point of contact for the divine message to man but wholly and utterly in the divine message itself as it has gone out and been received."[9] Theologians, therefore, need to become aware of the limits of their work. At the beginning of theology there must be, according to Barth, not the search for identity of God and humanity, for common ground, or for what authorizes theology, but the awareness of the difference of God and humanity. Theology needs to wake up to the fact that what we might have thought was God is really not God at all. God is neither the "Supreme Being that determines and dominates all that exists," according to the classic metaphysical model, nor the root of the search for meaning or human hope, according to the liberal approaches to theology. Neither can God be found in human piety and religiosity.[10] The main target of Barth's critique is the central position of the modern self, its "feelings of absolute dependence" (Schleiermacher) or "ultimate concerns" (Tillich), in founding the theological enterprise. Barth engages the work of Schleiermacher for good reason. Schleiermacher's influence, he writes, is so overbearing that "nobody can say today whether we have really overcome his influence, or whether we are still at heart children of his age, for all the protest against him."[11]

Barth's project is to disentangle theology from what might be called its "Babylonian captivity" to the modern self. Aware of the ambiguity of the central position of the modern self in both church and world, Barth argues that the primary task of theological reflection is not to defend the possibility of theology in the modern world to those who have trouble acknowledging any authority besides themselves, but to provide a critique of the ideological distortions in the church's reception of the divine message. The subject of this critique is not the divine message itself, nor even primarily the biblical or traditional ecclesial texts, but the ways in which this message is received and proclaimed by the church today. Theology is therefore defined as the self-examination of the church on the grounds of its ongoing talk about God in light of Jesus as its "basis, goal and content."[12]

Moreover, the main task of theology is not the debate between faith and faithlessness (or faith and philosophy) which, in trying to address faithlessness on its own grounds, assumes that the matter of dogmatics is already settled, or at least not too difficult to resolve. The theologian is not called to establish possible lines of identity between faith and faithlessness but to become aware of a conflict that is going on all along in the church—a "conflict of faith with itself," the struggle of "faith and heresy."[13]

Barth rejects any attempts to resolve the crisis of theological reflection in the modern world through the search for underlying essences, a "point of contact,"[14] or methods of correlation that establish a certain identity between humanity and God. Theology first needs to come to terms with the fact that human beings are not even able to ask the right questions. Humanity in the state of sin cannot rely on its own capacities as guide to God. There is a good chance that our intuition and feelings mislead us and we ask all the wrong questions. When theologians pose their own questions and determine their own starting points, theology is in trouble. Extending the line of Barth's argument, we might suspect that the more powerful and influential theologians are, and the more they are convinced of the truth and accuracy of their own understanding, the more troublesome this problem becomes. The tendency to put one's own concerns first and to make them universal results in two related problems: the tendency to assimilate others to the self, and the tendency to assimilate the Other, Godself.

The basic problem that theology at the end of modernity needs to address, therefore, is the temptation of those in control to establish false identities. Barth understands the basic problem as what we might call the "misrecognition" (to borrow a term from the postmodern debate) of the difference between ourselves and God and, we might add, between ourselves and other people. Theological critique must therefore begin with a recognition of difference. In one sense Barth's radical critique of liberal theology is not unlike that of more recent critiques by postmodern thinkers. Resisting the temptation to reduce everything to the reach of the modern self, these voices demand the recognition of "difference," marking the difference between self and others, and thus leaving room for diversity and providing resistance to the structures of exclusion.[15]

In his book on Romans, Barth begins with the difference of humanity and God. *The Epistle to the Romans* is all about the shattering of false peace promoted by the middle class and its theological representatives, according to which God and humanity are brought into a "peaceful, mediating relationship" where humanity takes over control in the end.[16] This peace leads to a vicious circle since God and humanity, the two poles of the equation, "draw relentlessly closer to one another."[17] In this process the self-critical potential of theology is severely diminished. There is a constant tendency to remake God in the human image. The same is true for the relation of the modern self and other people. Others are remade in the image of the self and, by the same token, excluded from participation in the structures of power.[18] What looks at first sight like an inclusive move, the inclusion of human others and the divine Other into the structures of the self, takes on exclusive shapes if the self remains in control.

It is often forgotten that this concern for difference does not fade out in Barth's work. The popular distinction between the early Barth as a dialectical thinker and the later Barth as neoorthodox theologian does not hold. Barth's insights into the limits of humanity and his concern for God's power do not change throughout his theology.[19] Even the greater appreciation of humanity at the end of Barth's work only makes sense if seen in this context.[20] And we will see shortly what impact Barth's emphasis on respect for the difference of the divine Other might have on the development of greater respect for the difference of human others and resistance to the powers of exclusion.

In his book on Anselm of Canterbury, which Barth himself continued to see as a "vital key, if not the key" for understanding his subsequent theological thought, he puts it like this: "Every theological statement is an inadequate expression of its object." In other words: "God shatters every syllogism."[21] Barth thereby redefines the theological crisis and what is left of theology. The problem is not that there is a gap between humanity and

God but that theology has become obsessed with the idea of bridging this gap. Theology, according to Barth, must acknowledge that it faces a constant crisis and that it is the nature of theology that it cannot make ends meet. Only with this recognition can theology promote a new respect for the truth.[22]

The trouble with Protestant liberalism is therefore its critical potential (or lack thereof). While Schleiermacher may be more genuinely concerned about the conflict between faith and heresy than Barth credits him, his critique turns out to be a one-way street. According to Schleiermacher, the modern self shapes dogmatics but does not itself need to undergo critique. In other words, there is always the danger that the self is drawn into narcissistic preoccupation with its own special interests. Barth's approach reshapes the way theological critique functions. Instead of the critical, the *self*-critical element of theology is now of the utmost concern. Barth's theology adds an important element of critique, providing new resistance to ideological structures, especially where ideology has to do with false consciousness, those positions we do not even know we are holding. Theology thus also gains new insights into those powers of exclusion of which we are not even aware.

Barth's sharp critique of modern theology is one of the reasons his theology has been misunderstood as a return to older orthodox modes of theology, a cliché that is now thoroughly questioned on both sides of the Atlantic.[23] It is often overlooked that Barth responds to *two* opposing camps in the church, which have in common only the fact that they impose restrictions on God. With this critique Barth's own work explodes the common liberal-conservative distinction that still haunts much of mainline theology and its popular derivatives, and offers an alternative.[24] While, according to Barth, the problem of mainline Protestant theology from Schleiermacher on is that it is in danger of simply relying on the reflection of the (faith-) experiences of the people gathered in the church, the problem of mainline Roman Catholic theology, especially before the Second Vatican Council, is understanding theology as a collection of, and commentary on, the revelatory truths or dogmas located in the church. In the first case, the problem is that "the action of God immediately disappears and is taken up into the action of the recipient of grace," and, in the second, "that which is *beyond* all human possibilities changes at once into that which is enclosed *within* the reality of the Church."[25] In both cases the problem is that what is "beyond" is confused with what is "within," leading to the establishment of improper identities between humanity and God.

In other words, while Barth develops the critical tools to deal with the modern approach to theology, he does not fall into the other extreme of uncritical orthodoxy, one of the major concerns of Schleiermacher, or into an uncritical acceptance of the doctrines of the church.[26] At the heart of Barth's theology is a double critique which he formulates thus: "The place from which the way of dogmatic knowledge is to be seen and understood can be neither a prior anthropological possibility nor a subsequent ecclesiastical reality, but only the present moment of the speaking and hearing of Jesus Christ Himself, the divine creation of light in our hearts." There can be no identity, no "there is" [*es gibt*]. We cannot say, as certain Roman Catholic or orthodox approaches do, that "there is revelation." But neither can we say with liberal Protestant theology that "there is faith."[27] Theological reflection needs to face its ultimate limit: we do not own God. Barth never quite understood why even a sympathetic theologian like Dietrich Bonhoeffer would charge him with holding to a positivism of revelation.[28] Here the special-interest deals of liberal theology, unconsciously promoting the powers of exclusion, are overturned. Theology does not start with human interest but with God's interest.

The critical potential of Barth's approach can also be seen in his hermeneutical presuppositions. How does Barth fit into the process, beginning with Schleiermacher, of theology moving out of its metaphysical shelters and becoming a hermeneutical enterprise? No doubt Barth is even more deeply aware than Schleiermacher of the end of metaphysics. In an early lecture he puts it like this: "Dead are all 'things in themselves.' . . . Dead are all mere facts. Dead is all metaphysics. Dead were God himself if he moved his world only from the outside, if he were a 'thing in himself.' " This announcement goes hand in hand with Barth's rejection of "authority for its own sake." Barth agrees with the radical youth movements of the early decades of the twentieth century (prefiguring the 1960s) that things such as the family, art, and work can easily become idols. Going one step further, Barth applies this critique also to "religion for its own sake."[29] Rejecting authority for its own sake—this is the basic thrust of the protest—is no doubt an important step in limiting the impact of the powers of exclusion on theological reflection.

While Schleiermacher found new Archimedean points after theology had moved out of its metaphysical shelters, Barth, not unlike poststructuralism and deconstruction, makes us aware of the limits of hermeneutics in a world whose struggles, disorderliness, and discontinuity we need to face. All warrants for the theological enterprise, even the position of the modern self, must be rejected. This insight opens up theology for new encounters with God. Theological reflection thus sets out to encounter God anew, a search that is often understood as yet another hermeneutical move. Especially Barth's interest in the texts of the church and the church itself have led interpreters to assume that he is simply recasting the hermeneutical endeavor in different terms.[30] Yet Barth does not continue with business as usual.

Not unlike Derrida, Barth calls hermeneutics into question. Universal hermeneutics breaks down at the point where "it thinks it has a basic knowledge of what is generally possible, of what can have happened, and from this point of view it assesses the statement of the text." Universal hermeneutics introduces an "alien factor."[31] No universal point of reference can save the hermeneutical or theological enterprise, not even the modern confidence in the self. Already in the 1920s Barth, borrowing Søren Kierkegaard's terminology, begins to understand that the fundamental problem is "not only the sickness of man" but a "sickness unto death." He knows that this lesson, reinforced by the period after World War I, points to a truth that people often tend to forget.[32] In the later volumes of *Church Dogmatics* Barth is even clearer when he talks about "the disastrous influence of what is regarded as the normative [worldview] and its related hermeneutics."[33]

Exposing the normative worldview, Barth develops new theological tools that might be useful for resisting modernity's structures of exclusion. The normative worldview, it turns out, is not universal. The perspective of the modern self is limited and, by failing to recognize these limits, ends up promoting its special interests as universals. While Schleiermacher had encouraged the participation of the modern self in theological reflection, thus liberating theology from the metaphysically legitimated powers of exclusion which often produced hierarchical chains of being that could not be questioned, Barth's sense of the limits of the self also has a liberating aspect. Questioning the (often unconscious) elitism of this self that takes its normative position for granted creates a potential opening for those who are excluded. The special interests of modern theology are broadened where the limited horizons of the modern self are broken open and theological reflection is reminded of the Otherness of God, a reminder that might have the potential to open the doors further for human others.

It must be kept in mind, of course, that Barth never understands God's Otherness primarily in terms of God's remoteness or transcendence. God's Otherness has to do with the fact that God is different from what we expect. The highness of God is understood relative to God's descent into the "utter depths of the existence of his creature."[34] But do Barth's efforts go far enough in a world where the gap between the rich and the poor, those in power and those without power, is growing? Does the turn to the Other ultimately escape the current theological crisis? While Barth's theology provides an initial critique of the modern self, how effective is it in light of the self supported by the new powers in the global economy that exclude no longer just people in the poorer nations but even large parts of the First World? How closely is the Barthian concern for the exclusion of the Other related to an awareness of others?

Decentering Theology: Authority

While the search for authorization was an important concern for Schleiermacher, it may look at first glance as if Barth is not at all interested in this question. The fundamental premise, and this goes against any theology of identity, is that theology "cannot think of itself as a link in an ordered cosmos, but only as a *stop-gap* in a disordered cosmos."[35] But where is theology going once the modern self and its theological intuitions have been deconstructed? Can Barth give any account at all of the way in which God and humanity work together?

Barth solves this problem in a way that is diametrically opposed to identity theology. Theology, unable to establish its own possibility, has to face a void. According to Barth, the importance of an apostle, or a theologian for that matter, "is negative rather than positive. In him a void becomes visible. And for this reason he is something to others. . . . The Spirit gives grace through him. Possessing nothing, he has nothing of his own to offer, and so, the more he imparts, the more he receives; and the more he receives, the more he imparts."[36] Here we have the basic credo of Barthian theology. God is radically different from humanity: any search for common ground can only throw us off. Almost three decades later Barth still pushes the same point: "When we Christians speak of 'God,' we may and must be clear that this word signifies *a priori* the fundamentally Other, the fundamental deliverance from that whole world of man's seeking, conjecturing, illusion, imagining and speculating." In God humanity encounters a reality that it has never sought. Theology is possible only because God assimilates humanity to Godself,[37] which, of course, turns the theology of identity on its head.

The theology of the autonomous self of modernity, taking charge of its world and owning it, is superseded by a new theology that promotes humility and openness. Barth understands theology as a form of asking for the Holy Spirit. Like John the Baptist, theologians point away from themselves to Christ. Theology, structured in three circles (biblical, practical, and dogmatic), cannot control the center. The three circles "intersect in such a way that the centre of each is also within the circumference of the other two, so that in view of that which alone can be the centre it is as well neither to affirm nor to construct a systematic centre, i.e., the centre of a circle embracing the other three."[38] Even though theology is called to distinguish critically between truth and untruth, it has no immediate access to or control over the center.

Barth's concern for the biblical texts is a case in point. It is well known that it was what he calls his "biblicism" which sparked his critical encounter with modern theology.[39] His initial critique grows out of the circle of biblical theology, but this does not mean that the biblical text becomes the basic warrant for theology, its authorizing factor. While the Bible functions both as source and norm in Barth's theology, it does not contain the center.[40] The same is true for Barth's account of the Christian tradition, which also plays a significant role in his work.[41] Barth does not naively confuse either the words of the Bible or tradition and the word of God.

As a result, theology can no longer narrowly restrict God's word or God's work. Both are encountered not in a theological synthesis but in God's own life. Barth reminds us that while God's word and work "are a *unity,*" we must keep in mind "that his is no monolithic work and no monotonous word. Rather, this unity is the work of the living God—a *unity* of rich and diverse forms, all of which are evident in the witness of Scriptures." In the German original Barth puts the emphasis not only on unity but also on diversity: God's work is *one* precisely in the *diversity* of its forms.[42] If the theological starting point lies with the Wholly Other, it can never be completely secured by the human self's religious ambitions and its search for identity with God. Early on, Barth used the image of the "bird in flight" when referring to the movement that theology follows: "Our concern is God, the movement originating in God, the motion which he lends us—and it is not religion."[43]

The theologian's dilemma, according to Barth, is that "our thinking can be realistic or idealistic but it cannot be Christian." The realistic position knows God's word in its worldly form, including human feeling and existence, and the idealistic position discerns its divine content. A mere synthesis of the two "would be the least Christian of all, for it would mean no more and no less than trying to do God's miraculous act ourselves."[44] The authorizing moment of the theological enterprise can only come from God. Theology must wait for this to happen. Its main task is to create the necessary openness, resisting the establishment of any fundamental identities between humanity and God. If Barthian theology follows any principle at all, it is that God can only be known through God, keeping in mind that this knowledge remains "relative" and "imprisoned within the creaturely."[45]

This turn to the Other is the most characteristic trait of Barth's theology and implies a radical deconstruction. The Other, as he had observed early on, "does not permit of being applied, stuck on, and fitted in. . . . It does not passively permit itself to be used: it overthrows and builds up as it wills."[46] The object of deconstruction is the modern self—self-assured not only in its social position but also in its religious ability to make contact with the divine. By decentering the modern self, theology is now ready to transcend the special interests that have invaded its liberal forms. Barth advocates radical openness for God. No mediation or point of contact is required, so that even the faith or unfaith of the theologian is no longer all that important.[47]

The major thrust of Barth's theological alternative is introduced in his book on Anselm. Barth's appropriation of Anselm's theology goes against the grain of both modern systematic theology and general hermeneutics, let alone metaphysics. This approach, he claims, is not "even remotely affected" by Kant's critique of the metaphysical proofs of the existence of God. In his inquiries into the existence of God, Anselm "'assumed' neither the Church's Credo nor his own *credere* ['faith'], but he prayed and the Church's Credo and his own *credere* were assumed. God gave himself to him to know."[48] Theology, as Barth describes it here, does not start with the doctrines of the church or with the self's religious powers, but is first of all an encounter with God in which both doctrines and personal faith are reconstructed. He explains it this way: "Anselm is distinguished from the 'liberal' theologians of his time in that his *intelligere* ['understanding'] is really intended to be no more than a deepened form of *legere* ['reading,' 'reflecting']." But Anselm also differs from the traditionalists since he intends a "deepened *legere*, an *intus legere*, a reflecting upon." Against liberal theology Barth points out that the hermeneutical enterprise is not based on the modern self's rational capabilities. Theology is simply a deepened form of reading the texts of the church and equally important of being read by them. Against traditionalist theology Barth points out that reading is not primarily accepting a text at face value, but is a reading that searches for the truth. Thus, while Barth searches for a deeper truth or an "inner text," he is aware that "this inner text can be found only within the outward text." At the same time, this inner text "cannot simply be heard or read along with the outward text, for it can be sought and found in the outward text only by virtue of a distinct intention and act and also—and this is decisive—only by virtue of special grace."[49] Barth's hermeneutics shatters both the confidence of the modern self that it has access to the truth and the confidence of traditionalist dogmatics that the inner text and the outward text are always the same.

But how can we make certain that the center does indeed stay open for God? How can we make certain that the promising turn to the Other does not disintegrate? Barth's theology relies not on the good will of the theologian but on the texts of the church. In this sense the texts function as an important double check for narcissistic theological tendencies where the self ends up turning around itself and its own questions, perpetuating modernity's structures of exclusion. This is one of the important focal points of Barthian theology. While Schleiermacher's hermeneutics also displayed a certain interest in the outward text, Barth goes one step further. He allows the outward text to set the pace: "Because it is truth that disposes of all *rationes* and not *vice versa*, the revelation must ensue first and foremost in the form of authority, in the form of the outward text: above all the *ratio veritatis* can be nothing more than something dictated."[50]

But there needs to be at least one more step. In liberal theology, as I have shown, the unintended exclusion of the sovereignty of the divine Other is related to an equally unintended and, for the most part, unrecognized exclusion of other people. If Barth is right about the central position of the self in modernity and its inability to admit difference, can theological encounters with the divine Other be sustained without new encounters with human others? In a situation where the self has trouble opening up, even if it is so inclined, could not the encounter with others teach a few valuable lessons in the encounter with the Other? Respecting the position of the Other is never completely unrelated to respecting the position of others. No doubt the theological turn to the Other may help to stir up resistance to the structures of exclusion. By the same token, resisting the powers of exclusion might benefit the theological turn to the Other, while accommodation to the powers of exclusion may sabotage it. To make use of the promise of the turn to the Other in the midst of the pressures of a global economy we need to recognize to a greater extent than Barth those who are excluded and reassess the modern self from this angle as well, beginning with the use of inclusive language and listening more closely to the lessons of others.

Encountering God's Presence: Doctrine and Truth

Paul Tillich, siding with Schleiermacher in principle, argues that the latter's failure to construct a coherent synthesis between the finite and the infinite has led orthodox and neoorthodox theologians to conclude that this is not possible.[51] For this reason he proposes, even after Barth's fundamental critique, to take up Schleiermacher's project once again. Yet it was not so much Schleiermacher's failure but his success that sparked Barth's criticism. The problem is that Schleiermacher's synthesis worked so well that the modern self could take over theology without having to give an account of its blind spots, unaware of its perpetuation of special-interest deals and, as is now clear, of the often hidden powers of exclusion.

In this context doctrines can no longer be understood as the self's feelings put forth in speech or as texts from the church's tradition. Doctrinal formulations that have the status of dogma—authoritative teachings of the church—must grow out of theology's self-critical task. Barth understands the "self-examination of the . . . Church in respect of the content of its distinctive talk about God," as dogma or "the true content which is sought."[52] Dogma is that part of the teaching of the church which has been verified by theological reflection. The church must therefore constantly examine "to what extent that which takes place in Church proclamation corresponds to dogma."[53]

Theology is responsible for checking the truth of dogmatic statements against God's truth. For Barth, truth is a dynamic concept, tied to the encounter with God's presence that can never be owned. As something that cannot be pinned down once and for all, God's presence is diametrically opposed to the "metaphysics of presence," called into question by Jacques Derrida and others. In other words, God's presence is not available as a blueprint or an Archimedean point that would guarantee the accuracy of our theological and doctrinal reflections. In this model neither God's presence nor the authoritative doctrines of the church can somehow become the private property of the church. Like God's presence, truth can never be owned—a fact that provides a major step forward in the struggle against the powers of exclusion. There is no "in-group" that has preferred access to the truth, not even academics or those gathered in the church. Truth, the validity of doctrinal statements, is tied not to a particular theological system or method but to God's presence. "Where God is present as active Subject," Barth writes, life is "light, truth, Word and glory." Here is the source of truth—the problem is simply that theology fails to pay attention: "The true and living God is eloquent and radiant. If He is in large measure mute and obscure to us, this is another matter."[54]

In the absence of any conceptual center for theology, Barth is interested in a theology that can be understood "only with reference to its origin and goal in practice."[55] His notion of truth is not stuck in the realm of ideas. This is an important move because, in dealing with structures of exclusion, we are beginning to realize that ideas are never independent of practical affairs. A notion of truth that overlooks that all ideas are shaped by life is a dangerous illusion. But whose praxis are we talking about? Liberal theology is, often merely by default, determined by the praxis of those who are in a position to act and to determine their own destiny. Praxis in Barth's theology, on the other hand, is not the praxis of the autonomous self that is always tempted to create its own truth and its own gods. He, in fact, rejects any confusion of our praxis and God's praxis. The validity of theology "depends on the avoidance of this confusion, or this comparison and contrast, between His life and ours."[56] Praxis is, first of all, God's own praxis in Jesus Christ, theo-praxis, christopraxis, and Spirit-praxis, to use Frederick Herzog's terms.[57]

Barth's theological emphasis on God as Wholly Other does not mean that God is distant or static. His comments on God's Otherness are mindful of God's involvement in the struggles of the real world. God's highness consists in God's descending. One of Barth's sons, Markus, expressed it like this: "What kept Karl Barth's theology together was neither a principle, nor definitions, nor a position but the *way* which he had to follow. In his thought and conduct Karl Barth did nothing else than follow the way of God toward man."[58] For Barth, God's praxis breaks open the closed circuits of the powerful, descending to those who are excluded. God is the one who "materially changes all things and everything in all things."[59] God's being is a "being in praxis." Against the metaphysicians and idealists Barth claims that "there is no going back behind this praxis . . . there is only the grasp of his liveliness."[60] This is why, elsewhere, he talks about the Bible as a "history book" rather than a philosophy book. "Knowledge of God in the sense of Holy Scripture and the Confession is knowledge of His existence, His life, His action, His revelation in His work."[61] The doctrines of the church are not primarily related to concepts and ideas but to praxis. Barth turns the metaphysical equation around: it is not that praxis follows being but that being follows praxis. Yet unlike Schleiermacher, he does not rely on the human self as mediator and agent, for the notion of praxis refers first of all to the work of God.[62]

Truth is therefore only known in the encounter with the living God. Truth is dynamic. Where it is static, as in the encounter with ontological structures like "being" or "the way things are," Barth finds only the "very 'natural' capacity to persuade [one]self and others of a higher and divine being," adding that "all idols spring from this capacity."[63] Moreover, the dynamic nature of truth cannot be pressed into a system. Barth explains that "systematization is . . . opposed by the great variety of the forms and aspects of the single object of theology."[64] Theology always breaks out of established systems (including the systems of systematic theology) and worldviews, even if those worldviews would be classified as Christian.[65]

In this dynamic vision the reach of the powers of exclusion is reduced by tearing down not only the classical metaphysical chain of being that mirrors the hierarchies of the status quo but also the control of the modern system builders such as Schleiermacher or Tillich. Seen in this light it is no wonder that, while Schleiermacher believes in the possibility of a shorter dogmatics, structured tightly around a systematic principle, Barth produces a longer one. The task of dogmatics is never quite finished. Theology is called to constant self-analysis. The wisdom of the older Barth, knowing that he will not finish the *Church Dogmatics*, is instructive: "There is a certain merit to an unfinished dogmatics . . . it points to the eschatological character of theology!"[66] Even Barth's language demonstrates this dynamic quality, constantly circling around its objects yet never quite naming them directly as if it would own them, thus resisting the structures of a rigid otherness. Barth resists precise definitions of his terms, thus critiquing reality—the status quo and its terminology—which is always subject to change in light of God's own reality and work.[67]

Barth's reflections on hermeneutics illustrate the form that his theological enterprise takes. In many ways hermeneutics remains the "supreme question." Although the enterprise of a general hermeneutics is questionable at best, Barth suggests a theological or biblical hermeneutics, which promotes a more radical listening to the biblical text. The power of the text, the "force of a picture meeting us in a text," must be allowed to challenge the readers and their world.[68] Hermeneutics needs to be reconstructed in light of the Christian interpretation of the Bible, not the other way around.

No wonder hermeneuticians have had trouble dealing with Barth's suggestions. To some this simply looks like an incomplete hermeneutics. Werner Jeanrond makes the commonly accepted point that Barth's hermeneutics fails because he does not take into account the "double need of theological hermeneutics" to develop both an adequate text interpretation and an adequate world interpretation.[69] But is it true that Barth is unaware of the context of theological reflection? No doubt theology turning to the Other approaches matters of context differently than theology turning to the self. Barth's theology takes context seriously (he is constantly responding to the problems of his day), but it does not allow contextual matters to dominate theology in any way. Unlike the liberal theologians, Barth emphasizes the challenge that context poses to theological reflection: "The difference between the times and situations in which the theological act of knowledge is carried out opposes any thoroughgoing and consistent systematization."[70] Like text interpretation, world interpretation does not aim at developing more control; interpretation in general aims at opening up. Barth's hermeneutics seeks to promote openness for that which transcends both the grasp of the context and the grasp of the texts and doctrines of the church: "When we read the Bible we are not to think that we are dealing with an ultimate authority which has to put itself at our disposal." Barth argues that in reading the Bible "we must see that we keep the doors and windows open. We must not keep to a room which is 'after the flesh,' even if this 'flesh' seems pious and rational flesh. No, we are in this room, but: 'Open the window!,' 'Open the door!' so the wind can come in."[71] This is Barth—not the early Barth but the old Barth of the 1960s!

Is Barth's theology able to create an openness that is capable of resisting the temptations of the postmodern world and the structures of exclusion of late capitalism? His reflections on God's praxis are promising. Differing radically from the implicit assumption of liberal theology that God is always on our side—implicit in the synthesis between finite and infinite—any "preferential option" that theology conceives of only makes sense if it is God's own option. An example is the way Latin American liberation theologians such as Gustavo Gutiérrez have promoted the preferential option for the poor, an option grounded not in the goodness of the poor but in the goodness of God.[72]

But is Barth's reliance on the tradition of the church and its theological language sufficient to create more openness for God? Despite his declared focus on God's praxis, the reader can at times have the impression that Barth often does not get much beyond the framework of the texts of the church.[73] The exclusive use of the male pronoun for God, for instance, is a striking indication of this problem: Here Barth simply takes over mainline linguistic conventions without critical theological reflection. A focus on God's praxis, however, would necessarily have to explode masculine images. The classification of his work as neoorthodox points indeed to a potential problem. Thus while Barth develops ways of keeping the modern self in check—the resemblance to post-structuralist concern for language is remarkable[74]—the question remains whether the theological turn to the Other is in itself able to develop resistance against the structures put in place by the modern self which exclude those in lower classes, women, and other ethnicities. While promoting a new openness, how does the turn to the Other get through to those at the underside, those who are most excluded? Is it possible that, in focusing on the divine Other rather than on human others, structures of exclusion enter through the back door and ultimately paralyze the good intentions of the theological turn to the Other?

Nonconformist Interests in Theology and the Church

In order to understand the turn to the Other more fully, a look at how the crisis of theological reflection displayed itself in Barth's context will help to draw things together and identify additional parallels to the present. Barth develops his theology against the backdrop of the theology of an entire period. While Schleiermacher pioneered a fresh approach to theological thought in a new era, the modern world, Barth stands at the end of that era, pointing ahead.

Barth talks about the world and history as something "which we can finally interpret only in biological categories" and "which we can finally interpret only from the point of view of economic materialism."[75] In comments like these Barth implicitly questions the modern liberal assumption that history is shaped by the Spirit alone. According to Dieter Schellong, a German theologian, Schleiermacher's trust in the reign of the Spirit in the world has led theology to put too much trust into anonymous powers and principalities.[76] Moreover, this emphasis on the reign of the Spirit leads to an approach from the top down: from the educated to the common people, from those in power to those without power, and from the rich to the poor.

In contrast, Barth's new approach is closely tied to his awareness of the "underside" of this Spirit. As pastor of blue-collar workers in Safenwil, Switzerland, and by observing the events that led to World War I (most of his liberal teachers of theology signed a petition in support of the war and a surprise attack on neutral Belgium), he learns to see different aspects of the world that are invisible to those at the top. At this point, theology is about to be reshaped in relation to resistance to the modern structures of exclusion that created the proletarian plight and in relation to the imperialism leading to World War I. This perspective puts Barth in a position to uncover the strange dialectic of the modern self, growing out of the eighteenth and nineteenth centuries: "two things were actually being done simultaneously by absolute man: piety was practiced at home, reason was criticized, truth made into poetry and poetry into truth, while abroad slaves were being hunted and sold. The absolute man can really do both."[77] Yet, taking another look at the problem in light of our own awareness of the omnipresence of the structures of exclusion at the present, there appears to be a closer connection between the two than meets the eye: enslaving others does not leave the modern formation of piety, reason, and poetry untouched.

Barth himself glimpses the problem where he begins to question the middle-class values in which most modern theologians, including Schleiermacher, were rooted. He realizes that those values are not just located in the ideal realm. From the eighteenth century onward he notes that "grandiose self-confidence" treated "everything given and handed down in nature and in history as the property of man, to be assimilated to him and thus to be humanized." No wonder "this attempt extended not least to the subject-matter of theology, to Christianity."[78] The modern self, confident in its own powers and abilities, has a long history of appropriating anything in its reach, including the realm of ideas and the Spirit. Already the conquest of the Americas had contributed to the increasing expansion of the reach of the modern world.[79] The spirit of the much-celebrated victory of capitalism of the 1990s continues this tradition with a twist: everything, even the political realm, is now pulled into the force field of the economy.

The fundamental problem of modern liberal theology is related to the growing power of the self, a power that includes also the realm of ideas. Even the gospel is made "respectable" here. In the German original Barth says that making the gospel respectable is not a general problem but the specific problem of making it respectable to a particular group of people, the modern middle class. He talks about the "*Verbürgerlichung des Evangeliums*": the gospel is domesticated not by humanity in general but by the middle class.[80] Thus the gospel now fits into the world that the modern self creates for itself, and in this process the modern self ends up assimilating even God for its own purposes.

Barth takes these reflections one step further and arrives at a surprising conclusion which is deeply rooted in a historical shift that can best be seen in his own life as a pastor. Early in his career, as one of the few pastors of that time who came to understand the plight of the workers, Barth began to side with those under pressure, taking a stand not only for the workers but also against the interests of the industrialists. If remembered at all today, this move is often attributed to the youthful fervor of Barth. Nevertheless, many years later Barth still put it this way: "God always takes His stand unconditionally and passionately on this side and on this side alone: against the lofty and on behalf of the lowly; against those who already enjoy right and privilege and on behalf of those who are denied it and deprived of it." Salvation is "a saving divine intervention for man directed only to the poor, the wretched and the helpless as such, while with the rich and the full and the secure as such, according to His very nature He can have nothing to do."[81] Here is another point at which Barth radically turns Schleiermacher's approach on its head. The powers of exclusion are also turned on their head: those who exclude others from participation in their privilege and power exclude themselves from God's presence.

Barth's awareness of the plight of those who do not share in the powers of the modern world makes a difference in his theological thinking. Even though never reflecting on it systematically, he somehow brings together the encounter with the otherness of the neighbor and respect for the Otherness of God. In a controversial book the German theologian Friedrich-Wilhelm Marquardt has argued that Barth's emphasis on the Wholly Other was not a metaphysical but a historical category. What Barth had in mind was nothing less than the revolution of modern society. Likewise, according to Marquardt, Barth's emphasis on God's transcendence was not a philosophical issue but a matter of critiquing the ideology of religious systems based on the powers of the modern self.[82]

Marquardt represents the opposite extreme of the standard North American interpretation of Barth as neoorthodox theologian. There is no need, however, to reduce Barth's theological thought to its contextual setting and thus play down his extraordinarily strong concern for reconstructing the realm of ideas and the formation of doctrine. Marquardt, nevertheless, helps us to keep in mind the historical implications of Barth's position. Barth's solidarity with the workers and his lifelong empathy with the concerns of socialism cannot be overlooked, shaping up to be important factors in our own concern for the formation of theological resistance to the powers of exclusion as well. The critique of the elites of modern society opens the doors of theology to a broader group of people; the working class appears on Barth's horizon at a time when in

Europe it had become thoroughly alienated from the church. The parallels between the respect for human others and the divine Other in Barth's work are significant. Nevertheless—and this is the reason why the reception of Barth's work usually makes no mention of this—these sentiments do not yet serve as theological guidelines, nor does Barth reflect on them explicitly.

Barth's initial connections with the working class may have helped him to raise the right questions. At the end of the synthesis of the middle class and Christianity in Europe—a synthesis that is still alive and well in North America today[83]—Barth is not at all interested in yet another synthesis. For good reasons he allows no other historical subject to step into the place of the modern self; not even the blue-collar workers are given permission to take over the modern self's theological position. And Barth clearly rejects the efforts of his contemporaries Hermann Kutter and Leonhard Ragaz who proclaimed the proletariat as the theological successor of the modern self.

As we have seen, Barth describes apostles as nothing in and of themselves. They are not self-made revolutionaries, nor the ones who take up the place of those who went before. Barth knows that much of revolutionary discourse is still based on the discourse of the self, that this discourse merely produces new masters and new claims of divine-human identity, and that it is never able to listen to those voices that are different. He expects not a revolution but a new human being, already present in Christ. In *The Epistle to the Romans* he points out that God sends God's son "not to change this world of ours, not for the inauguration of a moral reformation of the flesh, not to transform it by art, or to rationalize it by science, or to transcend it by the Fata Morgana of religion, but to announce the resurrection of the flesh; to proclaim the new man who recognizes himself in God."[84] Such an announcement flies in the face of the last two hundred years of the rise of the middle class, tied to a strong sense of its own moral, artistic, scientific, and religious progress.

At this point, we need to remind ourselves that Barth is not leveling his critiques against the middle class from the outside. As a university professor in Germany and Switzerland he belongs to an elite group that is regarded as providing the primary leadership of the middle class. In other words, Barth's critique is not looking backwards. Barth's resistance is not primarily directed against Schleiermacher and the nineteenth century but against his own class in his own time. He struggles with his own vocation, sensing that there are only two options for a professor of theology: either to give up all sensitivity to real life or to "explode" one day.[85] His attacks on general hermeneutics, one of the most popular fields in the academy of his day, are a case in point. As a result, the established theological world had a difficult time seeing Barth as anything other than a maverick.[86]

In essence Barth never gave up his critical stance. During the early days of the Cold War, when the public's critique was directed against the East, Barth criticized the West. To many this looked as if he was sympathizing with the East. Even the old Barth remained a dialectical theologian, pursuing difference rather than identity—the radical difference of God and humanity rather than the liberal trust in a smooth identity between the finite and the infinite. His *Evangelical Theology*, written as an introduction for students of theology, sums it up: "To become and be a theologian . . . is an impossibility (*etwas das es nicht gibt*), it is grace in its most concrete form. As recipient of grace one is no longer able to recognize oneself."[87]

Barth makes an invaluable contribution to theological reflection, insisting that it must first face the void that is left in exorcising the modern self. Theological reflection is only possible because the theologian "is the one whom God makes an 'I' by addressing him as a 'Thou.' "[88] Theology turning to the Other is marked by awe before the power of God. The encounter with the word of God transforms not only the tradition of the church but also the desires and dreams of the theologian. What is not yet accomplished at this point, however, is a self-critical stance which reconstructs the modern self in positive ways. Barth's critiques never quite escape the temptation simply to do away with and repress the self. Ultimately the courage to identify the new self (shaped according to Jesus Christ) in the world, a move that does not necessarily have to end up with another identification of a specific group or class of people with God, is lacking.

If the modern self is not "it," where else might we look? Are there other selves that might help to maintain the concern for God's own power? What is the theological role of those who, unlike the modern self, are not in a position to rely on their own power? A closer look at the relation of those in control and those at the margins might have helped Barth to reshape the image of the self. What might those who understand that they cannot help themselves and that they are part of a larger web of relationships teach us about the human self's role in theology? Without a closer look at the alternatives, it seems as if the modern self, repressed but not reconstructed, keeps on haunting the theological turn to the Other. The vacuum of the position of the self cannot be maintained. Jesus' own story points to the fact that no new self can emerge without sustained attention to others. While Barth is right that people on the underside of history must not pick up where the modern self has left off, what might be their contribution to the theological enterprise?

Even the radical passages in *Church Dogmatics* about the difference between the rich and the poor, the powerful and the powerless, indicate that the later Barth may no longer take this issue quite as seriously as the earlier Barth. He concludes that "when we encounter divine righteousness we are all like the people of Israel. . . . We are all widows and orphans who cannot procure right for themselves."[89] In response Helmut Gollwitzer, a student of Barth, observes that the "antibourgeois elan of the Safenwil pastor lost its force, when upon his entering the academic milieu, the previous praxis could no longer be continued."[90]

The Confessing Church

How does the theological turn to the Other shape the church? Barth's own efforts need to be seen in relation to the Confessing Church in Germany during the Third Reich. The Barmen Declaration, a statement of the first synod of the German Confessing Church in 1934, was an important part of the resistance against the Third Reich and the so-called German Christians who were about to take over the power in the church.[91] While the German Christians saw a godsend in Adolf Hitler and the Third Reich, the Barmen Declaration raised important questions about these developments.

In this situation the church went back to its roots, taking Scripture and tradition more seriously. The opening confession of the Barmen Declaration, affirming the importance of scripture, reads: "Jesus Christ, as he is attested for us in Holy Scripture, is the one Word of God which we have to hear and which we have to trust and obey in life and in death." But even Hitler's Reichsbischof, Ludwig Müller, proudly proclaimed that he believed in all of the church's doctrines. Each confession is therefore coupled with a rejection. "We reject the false doctrine, as though the Church could and would have to acknowledge as a source of its proclamation, apart from and besides this one Word of God, still other events and powers, figures and truths, as God's revelation." The turn to the authority of the divine Other, in this case to Jesus Christ, levels all other claims to authority and power. Turns to other authorities, especially to the Nazi government and its leader, Adolf Hitler, are therefore mistaken. No other authority, whether based on the power of Hitler or on the power of the modern self, must influence theological decisions. The final rejection emphasizes this point once more: "We reject the false doctrine, as though the Church in human arrogance could place the word and work of the Lord in the service of any arbitrarily chosen desires, purposes, and plans."

No doubt the turn to the Other can play a subversive role in the church. Theology in touch with God's Otherness is able to point out the difference between the word of God and human desires, purposes and plans, no matter how successful or how well intentioned they are. Theology must not accommodate anything but the word of God. Following the Otherness of God establishes theology as a critical enterprise, challenging both church and world. Even the Confessing Church was not free from mistakes and, in retrospective, Barth comments that while there was "plenty of serious, profound and living Christianity and confession" in those days, the confession "did not translate what was being excellently said in the language of the Church into the political attitude demanded at the time."[92] Theology turning to the Other, always in resistance to the status quo, does not pretend to be unpolitical.

While Barth seems to suggest that the church could have easily translated its theology into political action, however, there may be a deeper problem. The turn to the divine Other in and of itself does not seem to go far enough in countering the powers of exclusion, especially if it is not closely connected to an awareness of others, of those who are excluded. This suspicion is supported by historical assessment. While the Confessing Church spoke out against the Nazi regime, there remained a certain blindness to the plight of others, especially the Jews. As the pastor and theologian Martin Niemöller, one of the church people involved, put it later: "They first came for the Communists, but I was not a Communist—so I said nothing. Then they came for the Social Democrats, but I was not a Social Democrat—so I did nothing. Then they came for the trade unionists, but I was not a trade unionist. And then they came for the Jews, but I was not a Jew—so I did little. Then when they came for me, there was no one left who could stand up for me."[93] While the church understood the basic theological challenge, the fact that it had difficulty with a closer understanding of the plight of others points to a theological problem.

The actions of the Confessing Church in Germany were serious business, often even a matter of life and death, but the turn to the Other lacked the support that a more conscious turn to others could have given it. This problem continues in the church today. Turns to the Other, to God's holiness and majesty, often fail to develop into a concern for others which would prevent the unconscious perpetuation of the structures of exclusion. Thus they remain in an ecclesial-spiritual realm, promoting "spiritual retreats" that are just that: withdrawals from real life issues which fail to reconstruct the powers that be so that important aspects of the structures of exclusion go unchallenged.

At a time that is characterized by exclusion, the failure to develop respect for others also limits the ability to develop respect for the divine Other. Despite the proclamation of the Otherness of God, if the self is not reconstructed in the encounter with others, God may still be unconsciously reshaped in our own image. Notions of God's transcendence that locate God outside of this world, for example, often leave the structures of exclusion unchallenged. The impression, not untypical for many churches, that in approaching the holy God in the church's worship we need to leave our everyday worries and struggles behind, points to a similar problem.

At first sight, the so-called confessing movements that have arisen in various churches today seem to be related to the Barthian project. Many even claim the connection to the Barmen Declaration. Yet here we are faced with a slightly different phenomenon, for the main emphasis is not the focus on God's power, the turn to the Other, but the focus on the texts and traditions of the church. The Confessing Church is not the same as what in the next chapter I will call the "confessional church."

In sum, reconstructing theological guidelines in light of the Otherness of God does not in itself guarantee that this Otherness is really acknowledged. In a world where the powers of the global economy increasingly tend to determine our sense of what is possible and what is not, the confession of God's Otherness is too easily co-opted, if not complemented, by respect for the otherness of those who are different from us. While the awareness of God's Otherness helps to develop greater respect for people who are excluded by modernity because they do not fit into the identity of the modern self and God, lack of relationships with others who are different introduces new problems. The practical consequences of a detached confession of God's Otherness can be seen, for example, in the well-meaning attempt to become color-blind. While becoming color-blind is the well-meaning refusal to judge people on basis of their race, this move also often implies an inability to develop adequate respect for the specific humanity of the neighbor and his or her difference—a position often translated into failure to develop adequate respect for God as well: the wholly Other is thus reduced to a theological catchphrase.

Conclusion

The great merit of Barth's position is that it offers an alternative to the self-centeredness of modern theology. Turning to the Other both offers a critique of modern theology and provides new constructive possibilities. Resisting the narcissism of the self, the turn to the Other is an important move in overcoming the structures of exclusion at work in the modern world. The modern self is deconstructed and no longer the primary theological agent. In many ways Barth must be seen as an influential forerunner of the postmodern critique of modernity, breaking open the modern focus on the self, challenging false security, and offering theological alternatives. Like few other theologians, Barth has had the courage to confront the ruins of modernity, culminating in World War II and the Holocaust, head on.

Nevertheless, the power of the modern self is not completely overcome. Taking seriously the lessons of the previous chapter on modern liberal theology helps to uncover the hidden elements of Barth's approach. Even when theology turns to the Other, the modern entrepreneurial self does not totally disappear. The self may be easily repressed here, but it continues its influence on theology even in its repression, at work between the lines, always coming back to haunt the Other who is thought to be in charge. Theology turning to the Other, no matter how pristine and well intentioned, needs to be aware of these hidden hazards and develop new forms of resistance. In turning to the Other the biggest challenge is to develop constructive relationships between the modern self and others, those in power in the modern world and those who are excluded. How does the divine Other reshape our selves and our relationships to others? Barth's strong resistance to Schleiermacher sets the stage with a critique of the self, but more work is needed. The same is true for Barth's relation to people at the margins. Aware of our own complicity, the predicament of theology in the modern world needs to be assessed more self-critically. If this does not happen, simply pointing to the Other becomes an escape from reality.

Barth is clear, nevertheless, that the negative cannot stand for itself. He does not join "the eternally skeptical theologian who is ever and again suspiciously questioning . . . fundamentally always legalistic and there in the main morosely gloomy." This is a common response to the German situation after the war. Barth is obviously not interested in yet another culture-protestantism, another adaptation of theology to cultural trends, this time of the negative sort. Already in the Old Testament, Barth observes, "the bitterest indictments and the most somber threats of judgment of the Old Testament prophets are uttered only in the context of the history of the covenant founded by Yahweh and faithfully preserved despite all the unfaithfulness of Israel."[94] The turn to the Other, while providing serious critique, is ultimately about good news. In order to flesh out the good news, however, the turn to the Other, as I will show, needs to be reconnected with the self and others.

3

Theology and Postmodernity: The Turn to Language and the Text

At the end of the twentieth century, postmodern theologies have addressed the question of theological reflection in new ways. Postliberal theology, one of the most prominent representatives of the postmodern approaches in the church, has shifted attention to the textual reality of religion, further exposing the limitations of the modern reliance on the experiences of the self. In this mode the focus turns to language, especially the language of the texts of the church, informing another set of theological guidelines. Here "the subject is spoken rather than speaking" (to borrow an expression from Lacan), and the self is integrated into the transpersonal world of language.

This approach addresses a dilemma that is often found not only in the academy or within the safe walls of our churches but also in the lives of middle-class people who are able to maintain a certain control of their lives: the tendency to become self-absorbed. The proverbial ivory towers of modern academia and the gated communities of our suburbs may have more in common than meets the eye. While the problem of the exclusion of other people is left open in this theological turn, the postliberal ways of challenging self-centeredness may be helpful in curbing structures of exclusion tied to excessive special interests. But how are the free spaces that are produced here related to the structures of exclusion? Are they able to resist the dominant models of society, particularly the hidden challenges of exclusivity? Is the postliberal theological mode able to overcome the gated-community model? Do confessionally oriented churches deal better with issues of inclusivity?

The approach of George Lindbeck will serve as an example. Lindbeck and Hans Frei, colleagues at Yale Divinity School, give each other the credit for having laid the foundation for what has become known as postliberal theology. While postliberalism is not the only postmodern mode of theology today (in many ways the Barthian turn to the Other is closer to the more radical questions raised by postmodern thinkers), it seems to be the most influential one. Postliberalism is widely regarded as one of the most important developments of Western theology since 1980, registering increasing popularity at the beginning of the new millennium. Most recently, concerns similar to postliberalism have been expressed in an approach called "radical orthodoxy."[1]

In theological circles there is broad agreement that Lindbeck's approach is one of the few alternatives left in a postmodern world. A remark by Richard John Neuhaus reflects the tacit agreements among diverse theological approaches that "for those who have abandoned the certitudes of preliberalism and have recognized the dismal dead-endedness of liberalism, there is no choice but to move on to something like postliberalism."[2] Lindbeck's influential book *The Nature of Doctrine* sparked interest in this approach far beyond the confines of Yale circles.[3] Highly influential in North America and Britain, Lindbeck's book has commanded attention in other theological contexts as well. Ten years after its original publication it has even penetrated one of the more monolithic theological markets when it appeared in a German translation.

In North America, where the Barthian critique of liberal theology was muffled by its adaptation into the neoorthodox camp, soon to be superseded by yet another rise of liberal theology, the postliberals see themselves as the true heirs of Barth's critique of modern theology.[4] Yet their solution differs more strongly from Barth's work than is commonly realized. Like both Schleiermacher and Barth, Lindbeck develops his own understanding of the crisis of theological reflection. Lindbeck sees modern theology and Schleiermacher as part of the problem, as did Barth. Unlike Barth, however, Lindbeck is not concerned about Schleiermacher's attempt to bridge the gap between God and humanity. The fundamental dilemma of modern theological reflection, according to Lindbeck, is not that it has maintained identity between humanity and God but that it has made a mistake in identifying the basis of this identity in religious experience. Instead, Lindbeck argues that religious experience is not the foundation but the result of the Christian life. What is primary, what guarantees our relation to God and therefore matters most for theological reflection, is the way in which a given religion expresses itself in language, grounded in its sacred texts.

Lindbeck shares Schleiermacher's and Barth's awareness that we can no longer talk about God in Godself. Together with both Schleiermacher and Barth he shows little interest in a doctrinal propositionalism which claims that doctrines correspond directly to reality. At the same time, like Barth, he is also aware of the fact that theology can no longer rely on the human being's relation to God in religious experience. A new understanding of religion in terms of its canonical texts enables Lindbeck to transcend the impasse of theology in both the modern and the postmodern world.

This approach is self-consciously postmodern. Lindbeck senses that the intellectual climate as a whole is changing. The mark of the postmodern situation is that with the loss of Enlightenment confidence in reason "the worlds within which human beings live are increasingly thought of as socially, linguistically, and even textually constructed."[5] Religion is no different, and not even the natural sciences are exempt. He believes that the "crumbling of modernity" brings Christians closer to the situation of the first centuries of the church since Constantine, and closer to premodernity since the Enlightenment.[6] In other words, the theological crisis is self-made. Lindbeck seems to agree with Schleiermacher that, despite the critiques of the Enlightenment, the basic connection of God and humanity has never been in question. The perceived gap between God and humanity must be attributed to the fact that the Enlightenment looked for God in all the wrong places.

Like the theological approaches of Schleiermacher and Barth, postliberal theology is closely connected to broader social and economic phenomena. At the end of the twentieth century the globalization of the economy is sending shock waves through inherited structures and traditions. Market structures such as the job market or the economic amenities offered by the suburbs (lower insurance, taxes, "safety" issues, and so on) draw people out of their traditional environments. Even conservatives subordinate values to the market; issues such as background checks for gun purchases, minimum wage, and welfare are often debated more in terms of concern for the freedom of the market than in terms of traditional values. Acutely aware of the breakdown of traditional structures and values, postliberal theology identifies a need for reweaving or preserving social patterns. In a world where economic relationships determine most of our lives, a certain vacuum is created in which new visions of community and proposals for preserving the church's doctrinal fabric have a strong attraction. No wonder the postliberal model is in high demand in the churches. Lindbeck, arguing that "fewer and fewer contemporary people are deeply embedded in particular religious traditions," has his own ideas about the demand for the postliberal model. He identifies the market for the theological turn to language and the text as "most educated people" not embedded in religious traditions.[7]

What potential does this model have for creating alternatives to the powers of exclusion? Are the new relational webs that are being built on the grounds of religious texts able to include not only the educated but also those who are now excluded, particularly those excluded by the structures of the global economy? The potential openness for excluded others may give us, once again, a clue as to this theological mode's potential openness for the divine Other as well.

A Coherent Semiotic System: Authority

Like the turn to the self and the turn to the Other, the turn to language and the texts of the church responds to a crisis. This latest theological turn takes seriously the postmodern suspicion that anything built on the experience of the modern self, often called "foundationalism" in theological circles, is easily corrupted and fails. Postmodern critics of all shades agree on this one issue: contrary to what modernity believed, the human self is not the Archimedean point of the universe. Human experiences, even our innermost feelings and intuitions, are only by-products of larger cultural structures. Instead of humanity shaping culture and the world, as modernity assumed, postmodern thinkers realize that humanity is deeply shaped by these factors. The modern displacement of God is followed by a postmodern displacement of the self. Theology can now no longer start with experience, as in modern theology since Schleiermacher. Theology—and this is the new insight of the postliberal camp—starts with cultural and linguistic structures. Language, Lindbeck argues, is "primary for all aspects of life—theoretical, practical, and experiential."[8] Postliberal theology emphasizes that "human experience is shaped, molded, and in a sense constituted by cultural and linguistic forms."[9]

In this model the self is no longer at the center, but neither is the encounter with the divine Other. Theology now turns to language. According to Lindbeck, initiation into any religion, into the Christian faith in particular, and even into theology can be compared to the learning of a language. This move has the added benefit that linguistic structures work, regardless of whether or not they are believed at a deeper level. "Once they penetrate deeply into the psyche, especially the collective psyche, they cease to be primarily objects of study and rather come to supply the conceptual and imaginative vocabularies, as well as the grammar and syntax, with which we construe and construct reality." This was the case, according to Lindbeck, until the early twentieth century, when the Bible "permeated the culture from top to bottom."[10]

At the end of modernity theological guidelines need to be regrounded in the texts of the church. Postliberal theology is so directly rooted in the texts that any textual interpretation, as long as it focuses on the texts of the church, is a theological enterprise. In Lindbeck's words: "Even profane close readings of the canonical sources, such as are now becoming popular in a few English literature departments such as the one at Yale, are to be preferred to theology, however liberating, edifying, or orthodox, which turns attention away from scripture."[11]

This move to the canonical texts of the church and away from experience shows some potential for resisting the powers of exclusion. The stage for theological reflection is no longer set primarily by certain influential individuals and their circles but set by a reality that transcends the special-interest configurations of the modern self. Dealing with the texts of the church means that the main emphasis of the theological task is no longer primarily on the theologian reading the Bible but on the Bible reading the theologian. The texts are now allowed to shape theological guidelines and concerns. Theology moves from self-interest to the interests of the texts. Yet how effectively are the interests of the text able to resist structures of exclusion and to integrate the interests of those who are excluded? Are the interests of the text always identical with the interests of the divine Other?

Unlike Barth's attempt to break open established theological structures, a move that coincides with more radical postmodern sentiments, the turn to language is more interested in tying things together again. Like modern theology since Schleiermacher, Lindbeck operates with a universal notion of religion and determines how religious language functions "always and everywhere." On these grounds he proceeds to determine, once again parallel to classic liberal theological method, the essence of religion. Religions, like cultures, are determined as "the *lenses* through which human beings see and respond to their changing world, or the media in which they formulate their descriptions."[12] In other words, religions—based on language and texts—are the most comprehensive frameworks of human life. Religion, shaping personal experience, enables the individual to make sense of the world as a whole. Doctrines, in turn, are rules that shape, and to a certain extent control, the lives of believers. Conforming to those doctrines may well lead the individual beyond narrow special interest. But how do religions hold themselves accountable in light of the powers of exclusion? How can religions make certain that the socially constructed worlds which they legitimate, even though they may be countercultural to a certain degree, are not still reflections of the structures of exclusion that have now become global?

The often-neglected difference between the turn to language and the turn to the Other illustrates what is at stake. Lindbeck finds Barth's work in line with the postliberal approach and with "some literary critics" who argue for the priority of the written word over the spoken word, since the biblical text as a whole controls the readings of the church. In this way "scripture can speak for itself and become the self-interpreting guide for believing communities amid the ever-changing vicissitudes of history."[13] This is an important concern for Barth, but Barth does not go on to equate the word and the Word. For Barth, the Bible is only one part of the word of God, while for Lindbeck, interpreting Psalm 119:105, it is *the Bible* that is "indeed a guide to the feet and a light to the path, sweeter than honey and the droppings of the honeycomb."[14,15] While for Barth it is Godself who is at work in church and world, Lindbeck puts more emphasis on the text as actor: "That Scripture upholds the community is not something Christians can fabricate by their own . . . but is something that Scripture achieves of itself."[16]

This close relation of God and the word of Scripture elevates the biblical texts into a strong position of authority. This authority can indeed challenge certain contemporary structures of exclusion. But how does it deal with structures of exclusion in which the biblical authors and their communities participated and which are reflected in the texts? Do those structures become normative for us? What if old structures of exclusion provide protective cover and justification for new structures that are even worse, as, for example, the acceptance of slavery in antiquity and the progressively worsening patterns of the modern/postmodern slave trade? The biblical texts themselves demonstrate a constant struggle to keep the doors open for others and the Other, a struggle that is not always successful.[17]

The turn to language that we find in Lindbeck's work is not completely new in itself but is foreshadowed in the development of hermeneutics from Schleiermacher on. The modern emphasis on hermeneutics has led us to take language more seriously than Lindbeck realizes and to rethink its relation to experience. Here, then, is a potential connection between liberal and postliberal theology. In the preface to another important postmodern approach to theology by Jean-Luc Marion, David Tracy challenges liberals to become a little more postmodern, paying more attention to language, while not giving up the focus on reason and experience.[18]

Lindbeck, however, is not interested in the hermeneutical dialectic between text and experience. For him, hermeneutics is no longer primarily referential hermeneutics, not even in the modified ways that Tracy suggests. To use Schleiermacher's image of the flowers and the bees, language is no longer the flower from which something is extracted but the essence itself that the bee extracts. The language of the church needs to be taken seriously in and of itself. Unlike Schleiermacher and most of modern theology, Lindbeck does not worry too much about checking its "references."

Postliberal hermeneutics shares with other postmodern modes of thought the emphasis on the importance of language as constituting the world. Lindbeck even agrees with Derrida about the priority of writing over speaking and the priority of polysemy (multiple meanings of a text) over univocity. Derrida, he argues, fails to understand that Christians have not always understood the word in terms of ontotheology. Christ's "present meaning—what he says to believers through Scripture, worship, etc.—continues to be 'new every morning.'" Yet while Lindbeck agrees with the emphasis on multiple meanings and even a critique of a metaphysical referent, he does not go along with Derrida's emphasis on the endless and undecidable play of signification. Lindbeck wants to give privileged status to a "given text and a given hermeneutic."[19] He argues that this is where theology is anchored.

God on the Side of the Text: Critique

The advantage of postliberal theology over modern theology is that theological and doctrinal statements no longer have to be understood as functions of the feelings, intuitions, and ultimate concerns of the modern self. Not unlike Barth, Lindbeck overcomes Schleiermacher's dependence on the inner experiences of the self (Lindbeck calls this "experiential expressivism") and an older-but-still-prevalent "propositionalism" or traditionalism, which claims the immediate correspondence of doctrinal concepts to ultimate reality. Postliberal theological critique addresses these two distortions of theology.

Lindbeck's main critique regarding Schleiermacher's "experiential-expressive" error has to do with the fact that Schleiermacher and other theologians in the liberal camp had it backwards, since they "regarded the public or outer features of religion as expressive and evocative objectifications . . . of internal experience."[20] One of the problems with Schleiermacher's approach is that it takes up the modern turn to the subject, shared by romantic, idealist, and later existentialist thinkers alike where doctrines appear as an afterthought, subordinated to "individual freedom, autonomy, and authenticity."[21] While Schleiermacher defined doctrine as religious feelings (not necessarily individualistic, to correct Lindbeck's account) put into speech, Lindbeck argues that doctrines, as an already existing framework and part of a social reality, produce religious experience. Schleiermacher proceeds from the inside out; Lindbeck proceeds from the outside in. For Schleiermacher, the inside, the deepest level of the self, was the place most likely to be free of ideology; for Lindbeck, it is the outside, the religious doctrines and texts of the church.

In contrast to his critique of modern experiential-expressive theology, Lindbeck seems to be less concerned about the "propositionalist" error of the traditionalists. Propositionalist approaches to theology emphasize the fact that doctrines refer directly to objective reality.[22] Lindbeck's concern is that this view of doctrine makes ecumenical dialogue more difficult since doctrinal reconciliation would then entail the capitulation of one side. Furthermore, propositionalism makes it difficult to understand the phenomenon of doctrinal development. But the most significant problem with this position, which he finds best embodied by "popular attitudes," is that it confuses the letter and the spirit, thus becoming too rigid.[23] Still, Lindbeck does not find an ideological distortion in this position comparable to the modern one; he appreciates the fact that the texts of the church assume an important place.

Lindbeck develops an alternative to the two camps, arguing that doctrinal concepts constitute neither first-order propositions of metaphysical status, immediately capturing God, nor mere reflections of personal experience, immediately capturing the truth about human nature; rather, doctrinal concepts constitute second-order propositions. He emphasizes religion as that which shapes the community of believers through "the story" that is told and through "the grammar that informs the way the story is told and used." This grammar, in which theology is to be rooted, is extracted from the actual use of language. Such grammatical rules direct the theologian's attention away from an endless process of speculative interpretation and focus instead "on the concrete life and language of the community."[24]

The critical thrust of Lindbeck's approach is aimed at the modern self's position of authority. The emphasis on the texts of the church creates a framework that limits the self's autonomy. Liberal theology's tendency to assume that God is always on our side is reconstructed in postliberal theology: God is first of all on the side of the text. In the postliberal approach self-critique becomes a real option. Providing a critique of the autonomous modern self, postliberal theology creates a certain potential for resistance to those who, in sync with the logic of the free market, profit the most from the structures of exclusion. At the same time, however, the Christian self, insofar as it claims to be shaped by the texts of the church, is no longer subject to critique. Lindbeck is so confident about this new self and about the beneficial nature of the influence of the texts of the church that no other double check is necessary. The basic idea is that God's word as embodied in text-shaped selves and in text-shaped communities is the most reliable source for theology, and while it may not be above all distortions, a safety net against which the text could be double-checked in regard to its referent does not seem necessary. There is no plan for examining the texts' relation to the divine Other or the texts' relation to other people.

At first glance the critical elements that Lindbeck's approach introduces resemble Barth's earlier critique. Formal identity claims, whether between doctrinal concept and underlying reality (as in propositionalism), or between the finite human self and the infinite reality of the divine (as in modern experiential expressivism) are unnecessary for Lindbeck. Postliberal theology can do without foundationalism and the modern search for a secure referent that haunts both liberals and conservatives in their own ways.[25] Despite postliberal claims to Barth's heritage, however, there are also significant differences. Most importantly, Lindbeck does not have much sympathy for Barth's concern for the encounter with God as the Wholly Other. He rejects Barth's prolegomena in the first volume of *Church Dogmatics* as "baptizing bad epistemology," aiming particularly at Barth's confidence in "the rationality and self-evidence of the event of the knowledge of God."[26]

Postliberal theology takes a different turn. While Lindbeck seems to agree with Barth's critique of experience as a fundamental category in liberal Protestant theology, he does not deal with the more general problem: the (liberal and conservative) search for identity that bridges the gap between God and humanity. Neither does his critique of propositionalism address a similar problem in various Roman Catholic, orthodox, or fundamentalist theologies. Orthodox doctrines, for example, that are thought to reach their referent, also establish a basic identity between God and humanity which can lead to humanity controlling God. Lindbeck does not appear to see much of a problem in the claim of identity as such. The Barthian hermeneutics of reading biblical texts, he assumes, "is logically independent of the apparent starting point."[27]

Thus the identity between God and humanity is preserved in Lindbeck's position, although at a different level: he no longer presupposes the correlation of God and humanity in general, or the direct correlation of God and individual doctrine, but the correlation of God and religious systems. If a religion, particularly the Christian one, maintains its conformity to its sacred texts, then the identity between God and humanity is not in question. The danger, as we have already seen in regard to the turn to the self, is that the assumption of basic identities with God can easily lead to the legitimation of structures which are not ultimate. In so doing there is always the risk that, without even being aware of it, structures of exclusion are legitimated as well.

While for Schleiermacher the inside was the place most likely to be free from ideology, for Lindbeck it is the outside, the canonic doctrines and texts of the church. But what guarantees that the texts themselves are not taken over (if they have not already been shaped to a certain degree) by the special interests of those in power? In historical perspective this takeover of doctrine by the powerful appears to be one of the continuing problems with the texts of the church. The Crusades of the Middle Ages are among the better-known examples of Christian doctrine being pulled into the force fields of the powerful. Even the sixteenth-century conquest of Latin America was sanctioned by the doctrines of the church. The institution of the Inquisition shows how serious a crime resistance to doctrinal conformity could be, providing a direct challenge to the status quo. In a setting where the texts of the church supported the existing powers, the Inquisition understood that doctrinal deviations, resistance to the worldview of the church, could be far more dangerous than moral deviations. For Barth, on the other hand, there is no place at all that is free from ideological distortion. And while our critique identified one of the dangers of Schleiermacher's theology as simply becoming a function of the modern self or at least of the pious community, we have reason to suspect that for Lindbeck theology becomes a function of the (doctrinal) text and its embodiment in the Christian community.

The new framework itself, whether it be called "intratextual" or "cultural-linguistic," is not subjected to any substantial theological critique. The assumption seems to be that this is a framework that is unlikely to be ideological, just as Schleiermacher assumed that the position of the self was the one least distorted. Postliberal theology is built on a set of presuppositions that shelter an important part of the Christian faith from critique. In such a model the potential for resistance against structures of exclusion is at least diminished since possible distortions not only of the ecclesial texts but also of their interpretation are hard to filter out. In the postliberal resistance to the modern self neither the positions of the divine Other nor that of other people make much of a difference.

Like Barth, Lindbeck is aware of certain limits of modern hermeneutics. Yet unlike more radical postmodern thinkers, he does not want to do away with the hermeneutical enterprise as such. He is convinced that nothing less than "the church's future depends on its postcritical reappropriation of precritical hermeneutical strategies."[28] Even though Lindbeck wants to recover the premodern point of view, he is not going back to the metaphysical enterprise that Schleiermacher had already wanted to leave behind. In light of the demise of modern hermeneutics, Lindbeck wants to retrieve what he variously calls a "premodern hermeneutics," a "classical hermeneutics," an "intratextual hermeneutics" or a "hermeneutics of social or ecclesial embodiment."[29] In recovering premodern hermeneutics, three things are decisive for Lindbeck. The term *premodern* refers to a time before modern foundationalism, before the inerrancy and inspiration theories, and before modern individualism[30] or, in other words, to a time before the split of theology into propositionalist and experiential-expressivist camps.

Postliberal hermeneutics is descriptive rather than prescriptive. Rather than imposing limits on the biblical text, hermeneutics is the interpretation of the way the Bible is actually put to use in the church. Like the ethnographer or the post-structuralist, the theologian seeks to describe the church's language.[31] Yet rather than read for the breaks and the fissures in the text like a post-structuralist, a postliberal theologian looks for the coherence and consistency of the language of the church. In this effort there are few disruptions since, just as there are no immediate outside referents that would interfere with the language of the church, Lindbeck rejects the idea that other nontextual elements such as economic, psychological, or power factors, and even authorial intentions would interfere with the meaning of the text. Doing away not only with metaphysical (as do Barth and Schleiermacher) but also with "historically reconstructed referents," Lindbeck rejects all possible external influences on the text.[32] The texts of the church provide a safe haven in the midst of the turmoil of the postmodern world, a place where even the structures of exclusion seem unable to reach.[33]

The search for coherence is made easier, furthermore, through the definition of a center. In the Christian faith the center is in the "story of Jesus." Lindbeck develops three hermeneutical criteria, starting with "textual faithfulness" and "christological coherence." The third criterion is pragmatic, preferring "the interpretation that seems most likely . . . to serve the upbuilding of the community of faith."[34] These criteria do not demand absolute identity, as in modern theology, but allow for a certain margin of conflict and diversity. Yet while the postliberal search for coherence includes a certain openness, postliberal hermeneutics nevertheless demands strong confidence in the discourse of the mainline church. It is taken for granted that this discourse is a safer haven than anything the world can offer. Lindbeck finds that "the burden of proof rests on those who deny that the Christian mainstream has on the whole and in the long run rightly discerned God's word in Scripture."[35] The ongoing guidance of the Holy Spirit is generally on the side of the mainstream.

Although this does not mean that the mainstream is infallible, Lindbeck's fundamental hermeneutical premise is clear: the task of theology and hermeneutics is "corrective" rather than "constitutive." This is what, he argues, has been mostly ignored in recent centuries, by conservatives and liberals alike. By describing and correcting, theology "seeks to identify and correct errors by first-order interpretation's own implicit standards."[36] Distortions in the church's discourse are mainly due to "unthinking acquiescence" to the way things are. The existence of structures of exclusion such as sexism and master-slave attitudes in the church may serve as an example. The problem, according to Lindbeck, is that texts such as Gal. 3:28 have been deprived of much of their meaning. Yet he does not fully account for what went wrong, except to assume that somehow Christianity unintentionally adapted to its environment. Lindbeck's use of the term *acquiescence*, of course, seems to admit that larger structures of exclusion indeed have an impact on the texts and the way in which they are read.

The solution seems fairly simple. One mark of the truth of the church's tradition is continued reflection. Lindbeck concludes that, along these lines, the doctrine of the Trinity and Christology are part of the Christian tradition but not patriarchy, since the first two have been argued but not the latter.[37] Sustained and continued reflection on both the superiority of men and the inferiority of women and slaves have, however, more often been part of the Christian mainstream than Lindbeck seems to notice. One need only consider early remarks about the nature of women by the church fathers and contemporary debates about the ontological fitness of women for the priesthood in the Roman Catholic Church and the (better hidden but also rationalized) Protestant praxis of promoting men to higher positions in the church.

Finally, how do we assess whether even the readings of the texts of the church that are considered faithful have been pulled into the current capitalist system? How can we be sure that the church is more or less exempt from the system? Is it possible that, despite the attempt to root out the special interests of the powerful by turning to the texts of the church, special-interest deals sneak in the back door? Is the acquiescence that Lindbeck mentions only the product of a lack of theological attention, or does it point to a deeper problem?

Living within the Text: Doctrine and Truth

Lindbeck's understanding of doctrine clarifies the whole of what is at stake. Christian doctrines are neither propositional nor experiential truth claims. The doctrines of the church are "communally authoritative teachings regarding beliefs and practices that are considered essential to the identity or welfare of the group in question."[38] What counts is their use by the community of the church and how they shape the Christian life. Doctrines function like the grammar of a religion; they grow out of actual languages, summarize them, and, while providing stability, maintain a dynamic character.

The truth of doctrines is not determined primarily by an external authority but by their intrasystematic coherence. Lindbeck's understanding of the truth of doctrines has drawn broad attention. What has been noted across the board is the fact that he is not primarily interested in an external referent. This has led both liberals and conservatives to worry that his notion of truth remains purely self-referential. At no point, however, does Lindbeck explicitly reject referential notions of truth in general. In *The Nature of Doctrine* he wants to keep together two different understandings of truth, one "intrasystematic" and the other "ontological." Intrasystematic truth claims focus on coherence within a linguistic system. Does a statement cohere with all others? Is it consistent with the whole? Ontological truth claims, by contrast, focus on a statement's reference to and correspondence with a reality beyond itself.

From this dialectic Lindbeck develops what he calls a "modest propositionalism." "Religious sentences," he points out, "acquire enough referential specificity to have first-order or ontological truth or falsity only in determinate settings," yet this is not the biggest theological problem since "this rarely if ever happens on the pages of theological treatises or in the course of theological discussions."[39] Lindbeck reverses the propositionalist point of view, which claims that what corresponds best with reality are official doctrinal statements. Instead, he argues that what manifests correspondence (or noncorrespondence) with God's reality is "ordinary religious language when it is used to model lives through prayer, praise, preaching, and exhortation."[40] At this point, ontological and performative notions of truth come together.

Often overlooked is that the postliberal mode of theology grounds dogmatic truth at the grassroots level. Not unlike Schleiermacher, Lindbeck grounds dogmatics in its performance in and by the church. Dogmatic truth cannot be evaluated abstractly in and of itself, but needs to be seen as inextricably connected to the actual use of the texts of the church. Yet while Schleiermacher finds this performance rooted in the self, Lindbeck roots it in the text. The modern search for other foundations, Lindbeck argues, can only weaken the authority of Scripture and doctrine.[41] Without rejecting referential notions of truth, Lindbeck thus opens a new door for theology in a postmodern world.

The main point of theology is to give a "thick description" of the texts of the church: "The theologian, like the ethnographer, should approach 'such broader interpretations and abstract analyses from the direction of exceedingly extended acquaintances with extremely small matters.' "[42] Theology does not primarily deal with abstract ideas but with lived texts. This concern for small details, thick descriptions, and attention to the use of the texts at the grassroots level could provide helpful tools in the struggle against structures of exclusion. An understanding of religion as historically shaped helps to keep things open-ended and in flux. One of the important contributions of the turn to language and the text is that it forces us to keep our ears to the ground. Here theology is finally in a position where it could learn how to listen to the faith expression not only of the elites but of all of God's people.

But how are the postliberal analyses of doctrine and truth related to issues of oppression? Attention to popular culture may lead theology beyond a more elitist focus on the educated self. Popular culture, however, can be read in various ways, from perspectives that mainly admire its traditional flavor and fidelity to dominant traditions, to perspectives that pick up the symptoms of repression. Merely giving a thick description of the texts of the church may not be enough. We need to learn how to read between the lines of the text to discern where structures of exclusion distort even the use of highly respected traditions.

Lindbeck relocates the core of reality once more. While Schleiermacher found what is most real in the depths of human feeling, Lindbeck finds what is most real in the texts of the church. Regarding the canonical writings of religious communities, he says that "no world is more real than the ones they create. A scriptural world is thus able to absorb the universe."[43] Schleiermacher assumed that the gap that the Enlightenment found between God and humanity was overcome in the immediate self-consciousness. Postliberal theology, however, overcomes this gap in the text. In the words of Roger E. Olson, talking about Hans Frei, the other major player in postliberal theology: "In contrast to both liberal and conservative hermeneutics, Frei asserted that the true meaning of Scripture is what it says. There is no 'gap' between words and meaning when it comes to realistic narrative."[44]

While Lindbeck does not rule out ontological truth, the intrasystematic truth of the text or the narrative is obviously preferred. Charles Wood has commented on the "odd sort of veto power" that this constellation gives to the church's texts.[45] These texts finally call the shots, serving as the one guideline that theology really needs. What helps to close the gap between God and humanity, between truth and us, is not simply the assumption that a religion corresponds to reality but the confidence in the texts' ability to overcome the gap between God and us. What rescues the theological enterprise in the crisis of postmodernity, then, are the texts of the church, whether the Protestant emphasis on the Bible or the Roman Catholic emphasis on doctrinal tradition. As Lindbeck points out, "no other foundations are necessary." Much of contemporary life is simply a search for texts that "supply followable directions for coherent patterns of life in new situations." If a text does this, "it can be considered rational to dwell within it."[46]

In Lindbeck's postliberal theology, theological stability, no longer guaranteed primarily by external foundations, finds a secure anchor in the text. The "only major source of theological diversity" is the historical situation. The biblical message, on the other hand, "as classically interpreted is relatively stable."[47] At the same time, the biblical texts for Lindbeck are not completely static. While the biblical narrative is typologically unified and centered in Jesus Christ, there is interaction among the texts that "allows free play to imaginative intertextual and intratextual interpretations which are often not dissimilar to those of contemporary deconstructionists." Lindbeck acknowledges forms such as figuration, allegory, and midrash. He also praises the "gamelike activity of commenting on the biblical text by using it,"[48] practiced by church people and theologians.

Yet how does this turn to language and the text take into account the more pointed insight of scholars such as Ernst Käsemann that the canon is not the foundation for the unity of the church but for its pluriformity?[49]

It is no doubt true that the Bible can help to form consensus and unity in the church. But what about the initial experience of a Martin Luther, for instance, where differing readings of the Bible create tensions in the Christian community? If the turn to the text promotes an illusive unity, it can easily be misused as another cover-up for the special interests of those in power, thereby perpetuating structures of exclusion.

Building on Lindbeck's turn to language and the text that promotes theology as culture-specific activity, Kathryn Tanner has argued that "diversity results not so much from a failure to internalize Christian culture as from a proper socialization into the kind of practice Christianity is."[50] Diversity in Christian thought is not just imposed by pressures from the outside, as Lindbeck seems to assume; the "cultural materials of Christianity" themselves produce diversity. Tanner reminds us of their construction "in the messy course of social relations."[51]

While the standard postliberal account attributes diversity either to corrupting influences from the outside or to insufficient immersion in the language of the church, Tanner proposes an approach that takes the postmodern insight into the breakdown of coherent semiotic systems more seriously and sees differences and even conflicts in the church as rooted in the texts themselves. This perspective gives more room for disagreement and allows for a certain degree of diversity within the church. In addition, it also functions as a critique of the powers that be which stress consensus on their own terms.[52] But the focus remains on the texts of the church. Differences produced not only by the texts but by the exclusion and oppression of others—things that tend to rupture and distort established frameworks of language and text but cannot easily be accounted for on this level without reading between the lines—do not enter the picture.

No doubt the turn to language and the text gets us beyond certain modern forms of individualism. But does it truly help to overcome that narcissism which is so ingrained in our culture? What keeps Lindbeck's community, or Tanner's communities, from developing something like a community narcissism, an *égoïsme à deux*, an egoism of the church? While Tanner's model is better able to resist a certain residual self-referentiality by insisting on the multiplicity of textual communities, what will it take to shock a community into realizing those who are radically excluded from its cultural-linguistic boundaries, be it the human others or the divine Other?

Intratextual Interests in Theology and the Church

The social location of postliberal theology is more difficult to discern than the position of either Schleiermacher or Barth. While Lindbeck's work addresses, often between the lines, what he sees as the fundamental problems of contemporary society, he explicitly refuses to define the social location of the postliberal project. Insisting that postliberals are a "group of collaborators in a common research program,"[53] Lindbeck points out that there are no connections to a particular community or church.

Historically, the postliberal project is located somewhere between modernity and postmodernity. When Lindbeck talks about matters of context he develops broad cultural scenarios. His resistance against the manifestations of late modernity is abundantly clear. Like Barth, he seeks to devise alternatives to the modern self that, he feels, still reigns supreme.[54] He is worried that even in the late twentieth century "psychosocial pressures" continue to work against the postliberal approach, favoring the modern turn to the self. In this scenario religion falls victim to individualism, rapid change, religious pluralism, and other mood swings of the modern self. The turn to the self and its experiential-expressive theories can still be marketed easier, especially with college and university students. Despite its broad cultural impact, however, Lindbeck feels that experiential expressivism has lost ground in the research universities, with the exception of theology departments. "Historians, anthropologists, sociologists, and philosophers . . . seem increasingly to find cultural-linguistic approaches congenial."[55] He sees hope, therefore, not in the postmodern sea of changes at the level of society but in the academic world of the university.

The basic problem that postliberal theology seeks to address has to do with the impression that the lives of most people are no longer shaped by religious communities. The need and the market for the postliberal approach are created by what postliberals see as the progressive fragmentation of society, a result of modern liberal individualism. Even though Western societies have won the Cold War, Lindbeck says, they are in a deep social and cultural crisis. Those societies are now "turning into aggregates of competing special-interest groups." The loss of social cohesiveness is seen as "a problem deeper than wars' destructiveness or the collapse of political or economic systems such as occurred in the East." Lindbeck is concerned that this problem "makes reconstruction impossible."[56]

The only thing that can stop this process is reclaiming a common language, based on the Bible and starting in the church. Special interests need to make way for what might be called "textual interests," for new ways of creating community around common texts. Language is the strongest bond of a society. This bond, according to Lindbeck, held the United States together in the past, even during the Civil War: "Christians who shot at each other with intent to kill did not excommunicate each other."[57] From a historical perspective one would have to add, of course, that the bond of a common language and tradition was not as stable as Lindbeck assumes, since most of the mainline churches already split before the Civil War.[58] Lindbeck's point, however, is to show that a common language and tradition might be a lifesaver in a fragmented world. The concern for structures of exclusion is now relocated on the level of language. Other structures of exclusion, including political and even economic ones, are less important. Postliberals assume that the fragmentation of the contemporary scene can be overcome only through the cohesiveness of a common language and tradition. But what if language itself is shaped by the powers that be? Is postliberal theology able to give an account of that?

We need to take a closer look at the assumption that linguistic cohesiveness as such is able to overcome the structures of exclusion. What if the cohesiveness of the language at use in the church unconsciously reduplicates the cohesiveness produced, for instance, by global business interests, which are now developing their own "texts"? Cohesiveness as such may not always be a virtue and, in the global market economy where cohesiveness is no longer primarily determined by nation or culture but by wealth, it even tends to produce new structures of exclusion. We need to keep in mind that the discourse of the church's tradition never takes place in a vacuum. The theological turn to language and the text needs to realize that there are powerful interests at work between the lines of the text that, often unconsciously, affect and shape the texts and language of the church. How can we resist being pulled into the late capitalist structures of inclusion and exclusion, a sort of fragmentation that has a deadly outcome for 35,000 children every day? This problem becomes even more pressing for theology if the unrecognized exclusion of other people is reproduced in the form of unrecognized exclusion of the divine Other.

Related to the problem of fragmentation, the postliberal approach also resists what Lindbeck calls the weakening of the center of society and the polarization into "left" and "right," with the mainline denominations supposedly moving to the left. Lindbeck is particularly worried about the left since he feels that the remnants of modernity may be hiding out there. This so-called left is seen as merely the avant-garde of a consumerist society focusing on human potential, new age religiosity, and individualistic entitlements."[59] In the churches this has led to an erosion of Christian identity, in turn letting theological education degenerate into a process of "learning to be a very nice person who tries to make everyone happy."[60] At present Lindbeck sees the conservatives on the right as the only ones holding up the decline, due to their interest in preserving cultural identity, transmitting creedal commitments, and preserving communal ties.

Lindbeck's strategies for reclaiming the center (a center that he believes has been constituted earlier in the United States by Protestant neoorthodoxy) can be seen in his ecumenical interests. Here is the heart of his theological thought.[61] He describes his ecumenical commitment as "unitive," concerned about shaping common beliefs. Ecumenical work is about creating a common identity. If Schleiermacher's focus on the self had elitist connotations, Lindbeck's focus on common identity and the text has the potential to reach closer to the grassroots. Virtually anybody can become part of the new identity by learning the language and becoming a member of the church. But Lindbeck remains suspicious of the grassroots. The ecumenical development of a shared theological discourse, he feels, is endangered by another (older) type of ecumenism, rooted in common praxis that grows out of the grassroots. Lindbeck worries that pursuing this type will lead to a neglect of the question of identity. Priority needs to be given to texts and common beliefs, negotiated by the doctrinal experts.[62] Anything else that does not directly have to do with the text is attributed to the modern self's activism, even the praxis of those at the margins who have never shared in the modern self's autonomy and power.

Nevertheless, an insight into the dynamics of language at the grassroots level could have actually helped to flesh out Lindbeck's insistence, in tune with other postmodern turns to language, that the center is not static. At this center he imagines "reconciled diversity rather than uniformity" and "pluralistic unity within the framework of distinctively Christian belief and practice."[63] Such a definition does indeed hold promise for resistance to exclusive structures. The concern for diversity could help to maintain newly emerging concerns for otherness and difference, most forcefully embodied in the postmodern world by the reality of people at the margins, people whose concerns are not being taken seriously by the mainstream. Lindbeck's ecumenical vision, however, is introduced merely as a vision for the future. He bemoans that this model is hardly performed anywhere. Yet there are communities such as the black churches and their commitments to their own traditions or the Latin American base communities and their engagement of the Bible that, if taken seriously, might be more than just examples of a theory. They could contribute to reshaping that theory as well.[64] In these instances the turn to language might provide significant potential for resistance to structures of exclusion. And it is not unimportant to consider whose language we are talking about. Lindbeck's concern for the language of the official church bodies drastically limits his vision in this regard.

For Lindbeck, reaffirming the center has to do not so much with a concern to bring into the center those who have been excluded so far but with an effort to reclaim a better time in which the texts of the church supposedly ruled supreme. While the question as to whether or not a conservative stance is intrinsic to a postliberal approach has been widely debated, the more important question is *what* is to be conserved? Lindbeck is concerned about saving nothing less than Western civilization. The overarching problem is a collective forgetfulness that includes the data of history as well as "the corpus of Western classics."[65] Lindbeck suspects that "the West's continuing imaginative vitality and creativity may well depend on the existence of groups for whom the Hebrew and Christian Scriptures are not simply classics among others, but the canonical literature par excellence."[66] Thus he comes to the conclusion that "the Christianization of culture can be in some situations the churches' major contribution to feeding the poor, clothing the hungry and liberating the imprisoned."[67] This, he believes, is the way it was in the past. But what past? Industrialization in the nineteenth century? Medieval feudalism? The obvious danger of this approach is that, despite the importance of claiming one's heritage, past structures of exclusion are easily romanticized, played down, or simply forgotten, and as a result, insight into contemporary structures of exclusion and their effect on theological reflection is skewed as well.

Lindbeck's conclusion in *The Nature of Doctrine* is surprisingly Schleiermacherian in tone. While he finds that religion in general is an important factor in history, Christian religion has a special place, high up on the ladder of religions. The argument goes like this. Without intentional effort, simply by faithfulness to a text, "biblical religion helped produce democracy and science, as well as other values Westerners treasure." The expectation is that "in similarly unimaginable and unplanned ways . . . biblical religion will help save the world (for Western civilization is now world civilization) from the demonic corruptions of these same values."[68] Lindbeck's stance is no accident. Like Schleiermacher, he does not seem to give much room to the thought that mainline religion itself might have gone awry. The turn to language provides as secure a foundation for theology as the earlier turn to the self.

All these reflections apply, of course, to the First World. We do not need to worry about the Third World yet, Lindbeck proposes elsewhere, since people there still seem to be content with the traditional theological terms "they received from the missionaries." The crisis is in the West. The loss of doctrine is the primary problem, for "nothing seems to be replacing what is disappearing."[69] But even if the turn to the text would take a more radical stance than Lindbeck's, seeking to conserve other aspects of the Christian texts at the grassroots which do not necessarily support the status quo, for example, there remains a similar danger. This danger is that structures of exclusion are preserved without being aware of it, due to a commitment to the text, rather than to the one to whom the text points, or to the ones who do not benefit from the standard interpretation of the texts. Even popular culture is never completely free from structures of exclusion. No wonder it is often being used by those in power for their own purposes.[70]

The philosopher D. Z. Phillips finds that Lindbeck is "the victim of more than one audience and their voices have become confused in his."[71] What Phillips finds in the conceptual realm is mirrored by the reception of Lindbeck's work. Lindbeck has not been associated with a single camp. He has influenced and been influenced by several different developments and persons. One example, of interest because it ties into specific North American ways of doing theology, is the work of Mark Ellingsen who constructs an "American theology" on postliberal grounds. Like Lindbeck, Ellingsen argues that theology "in order to understand ourselves and our world . . . must begin with the Word and the picture of the world rendered by the biblical accounts."[72] Ellingsen fleshes out the location of such a theology at the heart of American society, troubled by the fact that its cultural norms are deteriorating, leaving only a "pervasive preoccupation with self-fulfillment" or "narcissism."[73] This sounds no different from Lindbeck. Ellingsen, however, is more optimistic about the masses and finds hope in the fact that "a majority of Americans may retain loyalty to the old (common sense) values and institutions."[74] The turn to the text matches the American ethos. Based on the fact "that eighty-two percent of the American public deems the Bible to be the inspired 'Word of God,'" Ellingsen concludes that "a truly American theology" could be built on "the authority of the canonical text."[75] For these reasons Ellingsen sees hope in the Religious Right and the evangelical movement. While he insists that this approach "stands on its own integrity," he also displays a number of "'happy' convergences . . . with the American sociopolitical and cultural ethos."[76] Turning to language and the text in North American theology obviously does not automatically guarantee a critique of the status quo.

Recently there have been a number of conversations between postliberals and evangelicals. Both see themselves as back-to-the-Bible movements, even though evangelicals put more emphasis on the realism of the biblical narratives, a point that is repeated over and over in the debates.[77] Evangelicals feel that postliberals may provide the most help in supporting the evangelical movement in its current identity crisis. They see a new coalition forming which resists the conforming of theology to "American culture or Enlightenment epistemology," insisting "that Jesus Christ is not subject to some higher authority."[78] Once more, this position preserves some potential for resisting structures of exclusion: all other authorities, including economic and political ones, are subject to Christ's authority. But what about those challenges to Christ's authority that are not readily visible? Without some kind of relation to those who are actually excluded, the turn to language and the text is in danger of being sucked into that postmodern vortex of textual play, the self-perpetuation of texts ad infinitum.

Others have taken Lindbeck's project in different directions. The African American theologian Theophus Smith has broadened the turn to language in his proposal of ethnography as theology. In a postmodern world where all other foundations are shaken, the African American sacred story is made to perform a " 'rescue' by biblical narrative." Aware of the detrimental effects of modernity and its neglect of those who are different, Smith understands postmodern theology as a turn "from system to story,"[79] taking place in a world where the commonly assumed foundations no longer hold. But is the cultural-linguistic assessment able to pick up the other factor that shaped the texts of the black church, the experience of not fitting in, of being excluded? The pressures at the underside of history that the African American community has to endure do not seem to make a specific difference to this proposal. The turn to story does not promote an account of what is excluded and repressed.[80]

Feminists have taken Lindbeck's impulses in still other directions. So-called reformist feminists, according to Amy Plantinga Pauw, also have used cultural-linguistic arguments. In this way they avoid the problems of a feminism that relies on experience as an ahistorical category. Feminist critique is leveled not from the safe haven of general experience but from the perspective of "fellow pilgrims in the faith." Yet Pauw pushes Lindbeck on the flexibility and dynamic of language. Languages change, she observes, "sometimes even thanks to the practices of outsiders." The apostle Paul is an example of this. What grounds his readings is "the community's corporate experience of the Spirit."[81] Here is a challenge to the "intrinsic conservatism"[82] in Lindbeck's approach, which might provide an important impulse in breaking up the systems of privilege. Unlike Lindbeck, feminists take more seriously the fact that they are participants in many overlapping discourses. Furthermore, due to their own experience of marginalization, feminists seem to be more open to listen to certain openings beyond the text, such as "referent and religious experience," which allows for attention to the "active presence of God in their midst." This experience of God's presence can "infiltrate" or "pry open" the text.[83] Theological questions from the margins, often declared special interest and accused of fragmenting the scene, contribute to the common interest.

The turn to language and the text helps us to understand how the theologian becomes a player in a cultural struggle that can be used to resist exclusivist structures. As Tanner has pointed out, "the more feminist theologians use for their own purposes the cultural elements that have been appropriated by patriarchal interests the greater the feminist claim on theological credibility, and the harder it is for the feminist agenda to be dismissed by those committed to the dominant patriarchal organization of theological discourse."[84] This would guarantee that feminists are recognized as serious participants in theological discourse. But this happens only when the dominant discourses themselves are questioned and reshaped from the perspective of those excluded.

While these fairly different models broaden the horizon of the theological turn to language, all are held together by a fundamental focus on language and the text of the church. Theology begins with the text and, as Tanner's comments show, is basically understood as a cultural struggle over the texts and language of the church. The various shapes of postliberal theological discourse have revealed some of the shortcomings of this model; the feminist contributions show that the turn to language is not sufficient in and of itself.

What is striking in Lindbeck's and other postliberal approaches is the common assumption that contemporary culture is still thoroughly liberal or modern, caught up in the experiential expressivism of the modern self. Yet there is also evidence that this experiential expressivism is vanishing. In a postmodern world, shaped by the logic of late capitalism, the inner life of experience grows dimmer the more we move away from the ideals of the middle class that helped to bring about the modern turn to the self. The complexity of individual religious experience is one of the lost victims of a postmodern mind-set. Modern individualism and narcissism are now more than ever integrated into the trans-individual dreamworld created by collective fantasies, fueled, for example, by the advertising industry. No wonder the Ford Explorer, the automobile for the rugged individualist, is selling at numbers of over 300,000 a year. This is not to say, of course, that the power of the entrepreneurial modern self is overcome. But this self does not necessarily seem to mind certain forms of community and collective identity (even a textual one), as long as its economic and political interests are not challenged. In other words, the postliberal resistance to modern individualism does not necessarily lead us beyond the construction of gated communities. The market may be right for postliberal theology, but it takes additional critical theological guidelines to resist the powers of exclusion and to develop alternatives.

The Confessional Church

The way the turn to language and the text shapes up in the church illustrates what is at stake. The cohesiveness produced by this turn provides an attractive option for churches at a time when the traditional fabric of society, all the way to the structure of the nuclear family, is increasingly challenged. Creating a new community that puts the interests of the text over the immediate interests of the self has theological implications for resisting structures of exclusion. Unlike in liberal theology, God can no longer be assumed to be always on the individual's side. Rugged individualism that subordinates everything to the self is no longer an option. The self opens up to a community.

Yet while God is not automatically on the side of the self, God remains on the side of the text. For the community of faith which remains faithful to its sacred texts, this means that God surely is on its side. But what guarantees that the individualist narcissisms of the modern era are not simply converted into collective narcissisms in the postmodern era? It has been noted that certain forms of the postliberal turn to language and the text work best in well-to-do suburbs where people can more easily afford to separate themselves from the broader structures and benefits of society.[85] Could it be that the turn to language is boosted by the emergence of a global entrepreneurial class that might enjoy the cozy feeling of intratextual groupings of their own choice—feeling reassured in community without having to give up too much of its power? Interestingly enough, the postliberal model has not suffered much damage and indeed may have gained from the celebrated victory of capitalism in the last decade.

Anthony Robinson, a postliberal pastor, notes that people are tired of being "met with a litany of the world's needs or problems and the expectation that they will help shoulder them." On Sunday they feel as if they need to "receive something" and be reminded of "God's grace and presence." Those people are "desperate for meaning, with increasingly few clues about what to tell the kids."[86] The inward turn, in this case the turn to the presence of God in the reality of the church, particularly in its texts and the sermon, is primary. According to postliberal church leaders such as Robinson, the church is "in the business of conversion and formation." Martin Copenhaver, another postliberal pastor, agrees: "Before we can change the world, we must first submit to change ourselves. Call it conversion."[87] No doubt this emphasis on formation and conversion is crucial and has the potential to resist the narcissism of the modern self. But how are people formed? Can the modern self be reshaped by providing some meaning and assuring people of "God's grace and presence" without seriously dealing with the self's discontents?

Using images of the church as lighthouse and lifeboat that correspond to postliberal points of view, Herb Miller, a church consultant, describes the outreach of the church in this way: "Healthy congregations turn on the lights in a dark world by preaching and teaching Christ, but they do more than walk in circles in their lighthouses. They climb down and staff the lifeboats."[88] These images might help to dispel the widespread suspicion that the postliberal church would always end up turning around itself. Miller's rationale works well in the postliberal context. The church is to launch lifeboats in the form of proclaiming its texts, such as the Great Commandment, the story of the Good Samaritan, the parable of the Sheep and Goats, coming to the conclusion that "not caring is alien to God's nature."

But the lifeboat image has its own problems. Miller's suggestions illustrate the difficulty. He proposes that a church talk to social service agencies within fifteen minutes' driving distance, asking three questions: "Which people group in the circle around our church has the greatest needs? What is the most significant need of that people group? What strategy could our church use to meet that need?" The circle seems to be drawn around one's church not merely for pragmatic reasons. The church is in the center; it is the focal point. There is little doubt about the integrity of the church and its people, properly converted and formed, assuming not only that the church can indeed help others in need by reaching out (a mutual relationship does not seem to be required) but also that the church could not possibly be part of the problem that needs to be addressed. Somehow the church is a safe haven. Copenhaver finds that postliberals follow a Jesus who "would rather be odd than relevant," concluding that "when we observe the deceit, violence and greed of the world, why would we want to fit in?"[89]

Even if it does not necessarily have to end up there, what resistance to the church as a safe haven could the theological turn to language and the text put forth? Does not the postliberal church see itself as some sort of a lifeboat, promoting an intratextual reality that is secure and to which only those sitting in the same boat have access? While the postliberal turn to language focuses on intratextual and intertextual aspects, the relation between the texts of one's own and other communities is less clear. Many postliberals display a certain amount of tolerance at the religious level: others are entitled to their own religious stories. But how do different texts interact and relate to each other? How is one text influenced by another, and is it not possible that even the texts of the church and their interpretations are influenced by other, more powerful texts, such as the scripts of the global economy? If this is the case, we need new forms of theological reflection since the structures of exclusion may be reinscribed into the structures of the church without any of the insiders noticing it. Lindbeck's excitement about the story of Western civilization is a case in point. What if the crisis of theology is tied not so much to the loss of the stories of the West but to their crisis, including the stories of its global expansion at the cost of others, starting with the conquest of Latin America?

The ethos of what I call the "confessional church" is also characteristic of many of the newly emerging confessing movements. In a discussion of the United Methodist Confessing Movement, Rebekah Miles points out that, "like other postmodern traditionalists, these confessing groups tend to turn primarily to traditions and ancient communities as authorities for theology." Here, then, is a close parallel to other evangelical groupings. Miles is struck "by the passionate commitment to the Christian faith and to theology itself" of these movements.[90] But her assessment of the danger of the confessing movements that, besides their theological commitment, they have an explicit political agenda, misses the real issue. The problem is not so much the explicit political agenda but the implicit one, hidden between the lines of theological structures that are assumed to be pristine and thus perpetuated unconsciously. To become truly aware of the significance and power of its confessions the confessional church will have to take a closer look at what those confessions do, expanding its sets of theological guidelines.

Conclusion

The contribution to the future of theology by the postliberal turn to language and the text is the recognition of dynamics at work in theology and the church that have been repressed in much of modern theology. Turning to language and the text allows theology to pay closer attention to the actual power of the traditions of the church that modern theology overlooked, to be more attentive to their actual use, and to take more seriously the doctrinal discourses going on in the life of the church, all the way to the grassroots.

To a certain extent, postmodern sentiments are taken seriously here as well. The postmodern concern for language and the text—Derrida's concern for the priority of the written over the spoken word, for example—sparks new interest in the Bible, which is no longer subject to external critique but to be interpreted in its own light. Not only theological reflection but all of reality is now to be reconstructed in terms of the texts of the church. This corresponds to the helpful comments made by two otherwise very different Spanish-speaking theologians, Justo González and Gustavo Gutiérrez, that the Bible reads us as much as we read the Bible.[91] Lindbeck understands this as a paradigm shift that moves "both backward and forward," going "beyond the liberal-conservative polarities of the last several hundred years,"[92] moving beyond a confrontation that, while still in full swing, is no longer helpful.

Postliberal theology develops alternatives to the powerful discourses of modern theology, centered in the modern self. Here is a parallel to the theological turn to the Other. But there remain a number of parallels with modern theology. The texts of the church tend to take over a position of control that strongly resembles the control of the self. On these grounds Lindbeck does not hesitate to formulate universal statements such as the following: "A religion, especially a heavily textualized religion such as Christianity, can be expected to survive as long as its Scriptures are not ignored."[93] Could not Schleiermacher, on the grounds of his confidence in the position of the modern self, have made a similar statement concerning the self's feeling of absolute dependence? When all is said and done, theology is no longer a function of the self but a function of the text.

As with Barth, we might wonder whether Lindbeck's approach can overcome the power structures in place in the modern and postmodern world that exclude those who are different. Is it possible that Lindbeck's approach ultimately feeds back into the power structures of the self? In the theological turn to the self, the incoherences and divisions of the self can be observed fairly easily. The theological turn to language and the text, on the other hand, is based on the assumption that it has overcome the inconsistencies of the self, and thus theology feels free to continue as if nothing had happened. Yet, as Lacanian analyst Robert Samuels points out, the jump into discourses of the tradition often hides the self's vulnerability by pretending to be in charge or by pretending to be in a position where the self's shortcomings can be taken care of and ironed out.[94] Could this approach serve as a shelter for that which it wants to overcome, the modern self? A warning by Gutiérrez, even though formulated at a different time and in a different context, still applies here: "To proclaim a 'postmodern era' while the pillars of the economy are still standing and the representatives of the social class—the bourgeoisie—who sustain the modern ideology are still in charge, is to entertain illusions."[95]

Nevertheless, a theology that puts the tradition of the church in its textual form in such a prominent place does not necessarily have to end up on the side of the status quo. Tanner reminds us that being conditioned by tradition is simply a part of human life. Even one's "imaginative impulses" are produced and conditioned by cultural-linguistic phenomena.[96] We are all shaped by the languages and texts in which we find ourselves, whether we admit it or not. Cultural-linguistic processes are not conservative in and of themselves. But how to give an account of those things that cannot easily be explained according to the turn to language? What about people breaking out of the dominant discourse? What about the ways in which people at the margins are reclaiming the texts of the church? Here a closer look at the theological turns to the Other and to others is important, promoting possibilities for constantly rewriting the texts of the church in the presence of the Holy Spirit, thus keeping them open and in flux.

4

Theology and the Excluded: The Turn to Others

In a context where social and ecclesial structures are deeply shaped by the powers of exclusion, some of the most interesting alternative modes of theological reflection have been developed by theologians who have been in touch with excluded people—or have themselves been excluded. In these approaches we encounter a completely new set of voices. Turning to others, the theological horizon is broadened to include those who have so far been excluded from the theological enterprise, a move based not on a general concern for otherness and difference (as, for example, in postmodernist critiques of modernity) but on actual encounters with people at the margins.[1] Theological guidelines are reshaped in this light. The search for that which has been repressed, a fresh theological move, leads to a constructive reinterpretation of the overall task of theological reflection.

The relationship of God and humanity is now seen in a perspective that is broader yet: there is a close connection between respecting other people and respecting the divine other. But how does this position resist structures of exclusion? How does it contribute to greater inclusivity? And how do churches that are shaped by this model differ from the other models introduced in this book?

The modes of theology discussed in the previous three chapters make up a large part of contemporary mainline theology. Schleiermacher and Barth have long been accommodated as the major protagonists of the contemporary culture wars between liberal and conservative camps, even though many conservatives remained suspicious of Barth. In this context Lindbeck's approach has brought only limited relief. At present those three modes are often discussed as the only viable options available, representing the concern for the human self, the concern for the divine

Other, or the concern for the workings of the church's tradition.[2] The theological turn to others introduces a new voice into that choir.

Contrary to widespread opinion, liberation theologies can never be quite subsumed under one of the three modes.[3] The turn to others provides alternatives to the enchantment of the modern self, the turn to the Other, and the turn to language that have not yet been accounted for by mainstream theology. That liberation theologies have often been classified as special-interest theologies—perspectives shaped by the turn to the self, and the turn to language and the text in particular, have had problems seeing liberation theology as anything else—has further distracted from understanding the significance of the new voice. The far-reaching implications that those theologies might have for new approaches to theological reflection and a new description of the task of theology as a whole still need to be assessed.[4]

Examples of the theological turn to others might be drawn from various global contexts, including both First World and Third World perspectives, informed by tensions on the levels of race, class, and gender.[5] In this book , however, I will limit myself to a North American point of view. A discussion of what's left of theological reflection cannot immediately claim global validity. Feminist theology in the United States, especially where it is becoming more transparent for oppression along the lines of race and class, will serve as an example for a growing awareness of others and its impact on theological reflection as a whole. The concern for the impact of the turn to others on theological reflection is reinforced by the fact that I develop this relation to the feminist perspective as a male theologian. In my own biography observing injustice suffered by women has provided me with an early and existential connection to the dynamics of liberation theologies.[6]

Since this theological mode is less tied to a few select personalities and great theological thinkers than the other modes—in itself an indication of more inclusive practices—I will not focus on one theologian only. Like other liberation theologies, feminist theology includes a variety of different positions that do not hide their tensions and, compared to most mainline modes of theology, is thus less a "school." Listening to different voices in this part, I will nevertheless give special attention to the work of Mary McClintock Fulkerson, where various feminist voices intersect in the context of specific analyses of ordinary women's lives and a dialogue is taken up between two generations of feminist theologians.

While the critical voices grow in numbers, nobody seems to be more aware of the current dilemma of theological reflection than those who have been excluded from the mainstreams of theology. For those at the margins of society and the church, there are few illusions left, and here the most challenging questions are raised. Theological reflections from those perspectives are, of course, never monolithic. At present feminist thought coexists in various shapes, as liberal feminism, radical feminism, reformist feminism, socialist feminism, and so on; lately a number of postmodern forms have been added. Since the 1980s emergence of womanist and *mujerista* theologies that listen to voices of lower-class African American and Hispanic women, these models are in flux more than ever before.[7] At the beginning of the twenty-first century most of the theological turns to others are also affected by the growing number of those who fall through the cracks of the global market.[8]

There are, of course, certain parallels between some of the more established models of feminist thought and the previous three modes of theology. Feminist theology is initially related to the second wave of feminism from the 1960s on, starting with a liberal call for equality. Yet feminist theology never quite fits the existing molds. Feminist and liberation theologies, even where they appear to resemble the other paradigms, provide alternatives to the enchantment of the modern self that have not yet been accounted for by the mainline.[9] The turn to others provides a decisive step beyond what is now commonly summarized under the heading "contextual theology." Context is not what is immediately obvious or what, at first sight, appears closest to home. Context is first of all what hurts, as I have explained elsewhere.[10] A view of context as that which hurts has nothing to do with masochism or with romanticizing pain and suffering; it concerns the need for a greater awareness of actual conflictual relationships. The turn to the self is hardly in a position to deal with this aspect of reality; the turn to the Other, while aware of conflicts between the self and God, often fails to address points of conflict between human beings.

The turn to others, therefore, is not just an adaptation or a modest improvement of any of the other three modes but an entirely new paradigm. Sandra Harding, a philosopher of science, argues that feminist thought is not just a correction of male thought but goes further: it shows the instability of our commonly accepted categories. Harding points out that in the sciences "the destabilization of thought" (the long overdue acknowledgment of conflicts and tensions) by feminist critique "often has advanced understanding more effectively than restabilizations."[11] The turn to others thus helps to broaden the contemporary theological horizon just as earlier revolutions and challenges. What is its potential for resisting late capitalism and the lurings of the economic marketing powers that now affect all of us?

Breaking Up Experience: Critique

Like the turn to the divine Other, the theological turn to human others does not start immediately with a search for the possibility of theology but starts with a critique. Following the trail blazed by the early feminist theologians, Fulkerson finds that in place of the arguments for the intelligibility of theology to the modern mind, provided by liberal theology from Schleiermacher on, feminist theologians offer arguments for "the unacceptability of the enterprise as it has traditionally been done."[12]

This observation provides an initial challenge to the frequent equation of feminist and liberal theologies:[13] While the reference to experience and the self's connection to God plays an important role especially in early feminist theology, it is no longer at the center of recent debates. Many of the differing camps of feminist theology seem to come together precisely at this point. Rosemary Radford Ruether clarifies this issue in the new introduction to her classic, *Sexism and God-Talk*: "The starting point for feminist theology . . . is cognitive dissonance. What is, is not what ought to be." From an Asian American feminist perspective, Rita Nakashima Brock makes a similar point. Letty Russell explains that women's experience "is primarily of the old creation and of the structures of patriarchy in church and society. We do not yet know what real live children of God will look like (Rom. 8:19)."[14] Many other contemporary feminist reflections on experience go in the same direction.[15]

Despite some striking similarities between early feminist theologies and liberal theology, this move is diametrically opposed to the liberal turn to the self. Schleiermacher's notion of experience is tied to what is, rather than what is not. The feeling of absolute dependence detects harmony and peace rather than tension and conflict. The "whence" of this feeling is secure: experience connects with God. Feminist experience, by contrast, grows not primarily out of an equation between humanity and God but out of a tension. A significant aspect of women's experience in the late 1960s and early 1970s (even for those who talked about this experience in liberal and essentialist terms) had to do with not entirely fitting in.

Here is a strong parallel to writings of women from the Third World who tend to identify experience of suffering as the starting point of theological reflection. From a Latin American perspective Consuelo del Prado relates the notion of experience to the "just claim of the silent or neglected aspects of ordinary speech."[16] María Aquino argues that spirituality "springs from conflict and connects formally reflected practice, mysticism, and our behavior in daily life." In sum, "the divine presence is felt within this tension between death and life, oppression and liberation."[17] Critics of colonialism and neocolonialism have added new perspectives on the notion of women's experience. The so-called subaltern study groups emerging in various contexts all around the globe have insisted that the diversity of people at the very bottom raises new questions and must be recognized and studied.[18] Laura Donaldson, a Native American scholar, points out that "colonialism problematizes the category of women's 'experience.'" In the colonial context, gender is no longer clearly definable, and needs to be related to other forms of oppression.[19]

Experience is therefore not primarily that which provides a safe foundation for theological construction but that which reminds us of the tensions that mainline theology often overlooks or covers up. In other words, experience—and this is a most subversive move in a feel-good culture—is that which hurts. This form of experience produces resistance. Rebecca Chopp suggests that the agreement among otherwise very different proponents of feminist theology "may well rest on a common struggle to live in, resist, and transform the metanarrative of history that informs Christian theology."[20]

The theological significance of this turn to the experience of those who are put into the place of the "other" by the powers that be has to do with the connection between the exclusion of other people and of the divine Other which has already been shining through in the previous chapters. In closing one's eyes to those who live through suffering and pain, chances are that the vision of the Other also remains impaired, an insight that feeds into the critical task of theological reflection.

Encounters of women who are different, like the encounter of African American and Anglo American women in the United States, further clarify what is at stake. Susan Thistlethwaite wonders: "What happens when the *differences* between black and white women become the starting point for white feminist theology?"[21] This encounter supports a new look at experience. The existential differences of women become more important than their "essential" biological similarity.[22] Contrary to the turn to the self, one's own experience is no longer made absolute. Experience is therefore not the Archimedean point upon which the theological enterprise grounds itself but an open-ended sense for differences, conflicts, and tensions. Thistlethwaite observes that women, who have usually been socialized to avoid conflict, are now empowered to face conflict for the first time.[23] The turn to others, becoming aware of oppression not only in one's own life but also in the life of others, does not lend itself to a reconstruction of modern liberal theology and its search for identity and harmony. In this mode differences can finally be taken up constructively; they only become problematic when they are covered up. A "hermeneutics of connection," relating people from all walks of life, is crucial, but it can only follow a hermeneutics of suspicion. In Thistlethwaite's words, the formation of connections needs to be "kindled by conflict."[24] Communities and relationships that do not give an account of difference tend to reproduce exclusionary structures, as my analyses of the projects of liberal and even postliberal theologies have shown. Many theological efforts to be more inclusive fail because they do not understand the all-pervasiveness of the structures of exclusion.

The increasing awareness of the interconnectedness of oppression is setting new standards for the critical task of theology, introducing a newly conceived, self-critical moment. The way this is fleshed out in the work of womanist and *mujerista* theologians may serve as an example. Delores Williams, a womanist theologian, pays close attention to the faith experiences of African American women, but she is also aware that theology must not "romanticize black women's Christian faith."[25] Pointing out that it is not possible to ignore that this faith has also been shaped by what she calls "colonization of female mind and culture," Williams specifies the limits of theological reference to experience. She describes the experience of black women as a "wilderness experience."[26] This is exactly the opposite of the experience of the modern self, which is built on a position of control. The experience of the oppressed creates a self-critical perspective. Womanist theology, shaped by oppression along the lines of gender, race, and class, is strongly aware of the fragmentation of experience: "As black women retrieving our experience from 'invisibility,' each of us retrieves from the underside of the underside partial facts about ourselves and partial visions of missing parts of our experience." The theological task, then, becomes not to identify the dominant experience and to follow its lead, as in liberal theology, but "to connect these pieces of fact and vision. Like a mosaic, these 'colored pieces' will eventually make many designs of black women's experience."[27] Experience is not monolithic and for that reason needs to be double-checked and reconstructed in communities that open up to those who are excluded.

Ada María Isasi-Díaz, a *mujerista* theologian, starts theology with autobiographical reflections. She does so, however, not to render her own position absolute but to deal with the limitations of human experience:

"Long ago I learned to distrust those who claim objectivity, which in my view is merely the subjectivity of those who have the power to impose it on others." *Mujerista* theology cannot be reduced to the self. The self is not the "foundation" of this theology.[28] *Mujerista* theologians insist that experience is always communal. Isasi-Díaz points out: "I not only listen to grassroots Latinas but share with them what I write and say about them."[29] On occasions, she reports, Latinas have corrected her. Experience is shared, diverse (related to the reality of *mestizaje* and *mulatez*, the mixture of white and native people and the mixture of black and white people), and transitory and incomplete. At the core of the everyday experience of Hispanic women is difference. As in womanist theology, this type of experience is not a metaphysical category that would provide a shortcut to God.[30] Isasi-Díaz talks about "embracing ambiguity, something those of us who live at the margins know much about." For traditional theology this would mean to challenge the security of "its impermeable and immutable center." And, I need to add, for liberal theology this challenges the authoritative position of the self. From the perspective of the underside, the self is not fixed. Isasi-Díaz makes it clear that "Latino men as well as men and women from other racial/ethnic groups can also opt to be *mujeristas*."[31]

With theology turning to others, important elements are added to its critical potential and ability to identify ideological distortions. In liberal theology since Schleiermacher the experience of the modern self, its sense for how things really are, supplied the critical tools for theology in the modern world. Even revisionist theologians in the tradition of Tillich's modifications of Schleiermacher (Schubert Ogden, Edward Farley, and David Tracy, for example) have followed this path. These theologies are not naively modern in that they would be "asituational" or "acontextual." Responding to liberation theologies, these theologians admit that power and human limitations have an impact on theological reflection. The problem is, however, in Fulkerson's words, "they are unable to problematize their own writing other than to note its fallibility."[32]

Schubert Ogden's definition of ideology, introduced in chapter 1, is a case in point. He sees ideology primarily as the justification of positions already taken. Yet how is this position able to address the justification of positions that one is not even aware of? Clearly, a more self-critical perspective is needed. Exclusive structures, especially where they are pursued on unconscious levels, cannot be challenged by merely admitting our fallibility and by claiming more inclusivity. Self-critique in the true sense of the word is only possible where the self gains an outside perspective on itself. Inclusion becomes possible only in relation to those who are excluded and—this may be the hardest lesson to learn for mainline theologians—implies challenging those who do the excluding.

The turn to others also adds to the critical awareness of the theological turn to the Other. While the turn to the Other also provides an outside perspective on the self, allowing for a critical stance, the turn to others adds the self-critical awareness of the actual impact of the self's power on other people. The turn to others helps to understand that ideology is a false understanding of one's social location which, whether realized or not, shapes theological reflection. Theological reflection needs to incorporate a critique of ideology as the justification of positions that one is not even aware of. We need a deeper recognition of our own, often unconscious, complicity with the powers that be.

Even fairly rudimentary encounters with people who are different can produce new opportunities for theological critique and resistance to structures of exclusion. Encounters with people at the margins on mission trips or in soup kitchens are sometimes the beginning of new theological awareness, even though theologians, pastors, and churches alike still barely know what to make of this. In Fulkerson's words, Christian theology must grow out of "attention to the continual tendency of . . . the church *not-to-see* things." The questions are, "Who is the stranger?" and "Who is 'unintelligible' now?"[33] Theology needs to deal with the fact that, as Fulkerson reminds us, loyalty to God and loyalty to the stranger go together in the tradition of the church, as far back as ancient Israel.

In this approach to theology receptivity, listening, and reflecting are more important initially than establishing foundations and identities. This insight provides a challenge to identity politics—politics based on the assumption of a common essence in which marginalized groups share.[34] Understood in this way feminist theologies are not automatically "the substitute 'correct' ideas for the wrong ones of critical modernist (or traditional orthodox) theologies," as Fulkerson points out. These theologies raise questions about, for example, "the social practices that support Christian reflection" and challenge "pretensions of intelligibility."[35] Theological reflection in this model starts with a position of listening, broadening the field of theology by including questions that are normally overlooked or actively excluded.

What early on might have looked just like another turn to self, this time putting the female self in control, has opened the door for new theological horizons. Now it is finally possible to reconstruct the modern self's claim to universality in more effective ways, and thus to gain a sense for its limits. Second-generation feminist theologians have explored the implications of this approach further, describing the implications of destabilizing the self in the context of a greater awareness of otherness and difference motivated by the turn to others.[36]

Most crucial is the self-critical factor. The point is not to destroy the self, Christian faith, or even theology. More than just reconstructing others' mistakes, the point is to acknowledge one's own complicity and to understand the constant temptation to join the status quo. In this respect we need what Fulkerson calls a "thicker account of fallibility" to understand not just *that* theology is fallible (already critical modern theology knew that well) but more importantly *how* it is failing. The fundamental problem is that the temptation to succumb to the pleasures of the status quo and the promise of certainty may prevent even feminist theologians from responding to "alternative wisdom."[37] Theology turning to others needs to take seriously the fallible and ambiguous character of its own visions.

In relinquishing the power of the modern self (particularly the power to exclude), the theologian becomes open to acknowledge the wisdom of those who are different. Mainline middle-class theology lacks precisely this sensitivity. Theology, in order to overcome its crisis in the current capitalist world, needs to begin by reshaping the mechanisms that allow theological discourse to cover up contradictions and difference. Theologians can no longer afford to close their eyes to life—as liberal theology already knew—but even more important, unlike the liberals, we can no longer afford to stay within the comfortable safety of our own contexts. This is the new challenge. In this new paradigm the self is not eliminated but redefined in relation to others.

This leads to a surprising reversal. Modern theology, insisting on the universal qualities of experience and the self, is in fact less universal than those positions that promote openness for others who are different. The modern claim to universality, as we have seen, fails to give an account of the special interests of the modern self. Acknowledging diversity, on the other hand, being aware of the limitations of one's own position, may be the only way to maintain the initial concern for a certain universality, through the discernment of common or shared theological interests. The critical task of theological reflection, in sum, depends on recognizing difference rather than eliminating it. A self-critical attitude is crucial in order to resist the invasion of the structures of exclusion into the theological enterprise. Feminist and other theologies that turn to others in such a way that they combine the positions of the oppressed and their oppressors need to ask time and again, Is there room for those at the very bottom? In this process theology finally moves away from the conservative-liberal paradigm and the vicious circles of competition between the authority of the self and the ecclesial texts in the church's culture wars.

There is, of course, always a certain danger of exploiting the victimization of other people. Writing from the context of women in Asia, Rey Chow cautions that we must not once again take over the place of others and pretend that we could be agents or witnesses for them.[38] Yet turning to others does not have to mean that we would now be in a position to speak and act for them. Taking seriously the experience of others begins by listening and adds a new theological impulse only when it takes seriously the contributions of those who have not been included in the theological enterprise. In this process of listening there is no need to romanticize others or press them into the role of the modern self that sees itself at the center of theology.[39]

Fulkerson is right: "Experience is not the *origin* of theology in the sense of the evidence for our claims, but the reality that needs to be explained."[40] Relying on experience as origin, as in the turn to the self, means that theology does not need to account for the forces that produce experience. In the turn to others, however, feminist and liberationist models help to uncover those hidden presuppositions and identities that shape experience and, by dealing with them, provide new openings for the divine Other.

A Theo/acentric Journey: Authority

The turn to others continues to transform feminist theology. Much of early feminist theology still oscillates between deconstruction and acceptance of the premises of liberal theology. Ruether's early work is a case in point. In *Sexism and God-Talk* she claims that "the uniqueness of feminist theology lies not in its use of the criterion of experience but rather in its use of *women's* experience."[41] She understands that liberal theology is unaware that it has not been built on universal experience but on the experience of men. Yet while she critiques Schleiermacher's belief in the authority of universal experience, she in turn seems to universalize the authority of women's experience. In this way the "liberal" and "modern" bent of Schleiermacher is maintained and the myth of the modern self perpetuated: experience continues to function as guide.

More recently feminist theology, continuing its initial impulse of turning to others, has started to move beyond the liberal paradigms. In the new introduction to *Sexism and God-Talk* Ruether herself acknowledges new challenges, including the "multicontextualization of feminist theology across ethnic, cultural, and religious lines."[42] Feminist interpretations of the authority of women's experience now take into account the fact of the plurality of experience. This initiates a new listening to voices that have been excluded. In this context new ways of listening to others open up new ways of listening to the divine Other as well. Unlike Barth, however, feminist theology, closely tied to the social location and subject position of women, turns to the Other in a way that does not reject the importance of the self and experience. Yet the self in this case differs from the modern self on various counts, most importantly in its connection to a position of marginality which points to the gaps in theological discourse. According to Fulkerson, "a dominant discourse is contested and even modified when spoken from the subject position that exposes its distortions."[43]

Here new encounters with God emerge which are exactly the opposite of liberal theology's encounter with God through the religious experience of the modern self, an experience unconsciously shaped by positions of control. When Williams talks about the experience of black women as a "wilderness experience" she explains that it is precisely out of this "near-destruction situation" that "God gives personal direction to the believer and thereby helps her make a way out of what she thought was no way." We can see the dramatic difference to the liberal approach as Williams's interpretation continues: "For both Hagar and the African-American women, the wilderness experience meant standing utterly alone, in the midst of serious trouble, with only God's support to rely upon."[44] In light of the wilderness experience of oppression and suffering, God's support is central. Here is another indication that the centerpiece of the turn to others is not the other person himself or herself. These others, persons who face "near-destruction situations," point away from themselves. In the process self-critical listening to other people may lead to new listening to the divine Other as well.

Out of this process emerges a new focus on God, related to the fundamental realization that the others to which theology now turns are not in positions of absolute control.[45] There is a significant difference between the experience of the self that claims to be in touch with the way things are and the experience of those who are constantly reminded of their limits by the fact that they are not in control of things in everyday life. Encounters with these others help to dispel the two related myths that the modern self is the image of universal humanity (the myth perpetuated by the proponents of the turn to the self) and that theological turns that are concerned with humanity always end up usurping God's place (the myth perpetuated by the opponents of the turn to the self). These others are usually not in a position where playing God is an option. There are other sins that haunt those in the position of the "other," but pride and self-centeredness are not primary.

A common misunderstanding of the turn to others is exemplified by a sympathetic reviewer of Fulkerson's book *Changing the Subject*, which calls for further reflection on what is theo/alogical rather than anthropological, linguistic, and sociological about her argument.[46] While this aspect will indeed need further clarification as feminist theology develops, the fundamental theological challenge has to do with a general sense that the encounter with others opens new visions of the Other.

At the heart of theological reflection in much of feminist theology is the understanding of God. Russell explains that, rather than appealing to experience, feminist Christians appeal to the future as the source of authority, more precisely to "God's future action" which is already present in the action of God through the people of Israel and through Jesus Christ.[47] Fulkerson argues for what she calls a "theo/acentric character" of feminist theology. The specific question, parallel to Williams's comments above, is "what it means in this age for a theologian to confess that God alone saves."[48] Unlike modern theology, this theo/acentric emphasis is not interested in defending the existence of God. From a liberation perspective the question of the existence of God has always been of lesser interest than the question of who God is and what God is doing. The feminist experience of God, not unlike the experience of God in most liberation theologies, grows out of encounters with God in the tensions of life and in new encounters with God related to communal experiences such as worship that include those who have been marginalized in society and church.

The turn to others reminds us that theological reflection can no longer be done apart from those communities that seek to serve both God and neighbor and work to overcome idolatry. Yet even in those settings no theological achievements can ever be fixed. Any position, theological or otherwise, can only be preliminary. No human being can claim to be an absolute match of the image of God. Neither can the meaning of the texts of the church be fixed once and for all. This does not mean that the search for images of God and attempts to understand the texts of the church are futile, but we need to rethink how we search for more appropriate images of God and how we arrive at alternative readings of the texts.

While the theo/acentric approach displays some affinity to Barth's critique of the liberal domestication of God in terms of the self, feminist theology introduces another challenge. In connection with a new appreciation for the Otherness of God, we need to examine whether our theology opens up the worth of others. Alternative visions of God and alternative visions of humanity are closely connected. The focus on God leads to a new awareness of the self and to the confession, that we know little about the nature of human beings.[49] Encountering God, theology must realize that it cannot define humanity in any universal or a priori way; the opening up to others becomes an ongoing theological challenge. This insight applies not only to the knowledge of others but also to self-knowledge.

The theo/acentric perspective helps to resist the position of the controlling subject and to develop alternatives. If theologians, not having a "God's-eye-view," cannot "represent" others, they must give up a good deal of control.[50] More specifically, they must learn to give up both control of God, the fundamental theological problem of modernity which has detrimental consequences for the relation to others, and the control of others, the root of the problem of exclusion at the beginning of the twenty-first century which has detrimental consequences for the relation to God. Mainline theology, whether turning to the self, the Other, or the text, can learn a great deal from this critique, but feminist theology explicitly includes itself here. This implies a much greater risk, of course, for feminist positions can now no longer establish their own identity in terms of the universal subject-position of "woman."

Theology as a whole benefits from listening more closely to other voices. This process of listening sharpens the self-critical mode of theology and leads to a better understanding of one's own limits. The turn to others, charting the terrain for a theo/acentric turn to the Other, promotes new respect for what is different. Aware that even well-meaning attempts at identification and solidarity can once again lead to the domestication and exclusion of others, Fulkerson proposes a "feminist theology of affinity."[51] Without realizing it, the modern search for identity mirrors the structures of exclusion, as we have seen. The notion of affinity, on the other hand, acknowledges the inability to know others. Once again, this respect for human others teaches respect for the divine Other as well. The turn to others, therefore, does not rival the theo/acentric perspective but supports it. In Fulkerson's words, the hope is that "the terms of good news we might receive if we were formed to receive from the other will surprise even those of us who tell stories about the oppressed."[52]

One of the biggest surprises might be that the new openness to the voices of excluded others and the voice of the divine Other is also manifest in a new openness for the texts of the church. Critics of feminist theology and other theological turns to others often fail to realize the profound implications for fresh encounters with the biblical and other ecclesial texts. Unlike the turn to the self, the turn to others resists control and points away from itself. Realizing that we need to take seriously other subject positions than our own, the self is reconstructed in relationship. Deconstructing the modern self as center of theology, theology turning to others insists that in dealing with the biblical texts both readers and texts transform each other. The reader is no longer in a position to tell the text what it can say and what it cannot.[53]

The turn to others introduces new dimensions into the relationship of readers and texts. Liberal theological emphases on the central place of the self, universalizing their own concerns and discounting others, were simply not listening closely enough. The relationship between the reader, the text, and others means that the texts of the church definitely must not be read in the abstract, as liberal theology already knew so well. But neither must the texts be read in contexts that are confined to the egocentric world of the modern self. The texts open up only in contexts that are receptive to the deeper tension of life in desperate situations.

Where the self is relativized in these encounters with others the text can be perceived once more in its challenging aspects, opening up the closed circles of both church and self.[54] Yet the text is no longer the "thing itself" either. The texts of the church cannot be substitutes for God. The others' reminder of a new center away from text and self, the theo/acentric dynamic, needs to be taken seriously. Like the self, the texts are subject to critique at the point where they, often unconsciously, cover up exclusive structures and thus become smokescreens that cover up the immense suffering of large parts of humanity and creation under the conditions of the global economy. The most important challenge of the theological turn to others is its understanding that, as Fulkerson puts it, "liberation theologies emerge from particular gaps in faith's reading of reality—the 'fissures and cracks.' "[55] The encounter with others challenges the control of self and text and opens up the theological enterprise, creating new space for encounters with the Other.

As a consequence, theology that incorporates the perspective of others does no longer start in a linear way. Feminist theologians realize that "something new is cobbled together out of the necessities of the time read with the practices of faith, and it is not possible to say that one precedes the other."[56] Encounters with others remind us of the dynamic character of the theological enterprise. At this point, the process of theological reflection changes profoundly: There can be no monolithic or coherent starting point, be it the experience of the modern self which is still at the center of liberal theology, or the certainty of a clearly defined and reasonably secure world of texts, as postliberal theology seems to assume.

In sum, the turn to others demonstrates that theology can no longer afford to talk about the divine Other in isolation from the other person. Theology begins in relationship, as modern theology knew so well. But this relationship needs to be broadened so as to include those who are left out, those who fall through the cracks even in a world that prides itself to be globally connected, and needs to include new encounters with God that cannot easily be packaged in terms of the self or the text.

No Other without Others: Doctrine and Truth

The turn to others creates room for a new concern for the doctrines of the church. Doctrines are no longer a function of the self, as in liberal theology. Yet they are not the exclusive focus of theology either, as in postliberalism. Feminist theology reminds us that the church's doctrines are not isolated from life and from history but are produced by the church in specific historical contexts. Two things are clear now: neither the self nor the texts of the church are in a position to usurp the place of God. The referential character of doctrines therefore needs to be reconsidered, for doctrines do not provide immediate access to the reality of God. Theology that takes into account the position of others can take Lindbeck's critique of the propositionalist theological model in new directions. A propositionalist understanding of doctrines not only is cumbersome (Lindbeck's point) but is idolatrous since it pretends to have privileged access to God, an access that God alone can grant. This critique applies also to the liberal defense of doctrine grounded in the security of the innermost recesses of the self.

Far from displacing the significance of doctrine, the turn to others helps to refocus its importance. At the point where the authority of the self is called into question, doctrines acquire new space as (never infallible) pointers in the search for truth. Various aspects are involved: First, the reach of doctrine is extended to the grassroots, a move that has already been prefigured to a certain degree in the postliberal turn to the text. Doctrine is no longer limited to the formal statements of the church alone. Theology needs to investigate different "discursive communities of Christians," not just different, officially recognized traditions as in postliberal theology but also the doctrinal traditions of different classes and races.[57] Second, since doctrinal discourse never exists independently of other discourses, its intersections with other aspects of life need to be taken into account. In the encounter with others new awareness of these intersections emerges. How is the doctrinal discourse of the church shaped by other powerful discourses? More specifically, how is doctrine shaped by the powers of exclusion? As Fulkerson reminds us, theology and, by implication, doctrine are both "determined by and determining of the larger world."[58] The new vision of doctrine does not promote doctrinal pluralism. The meaningfulness of doctrine depends on what difference it makes in people's lives in relation to the powers that be. Finally, Fulkerson formulates an important insight made possible by the turn to others, namely, that "any narrative is co-constituted by those it excludes."[59] Even where theology begins to encounter others, a feminist or liberation theologian can never assume that doctrinal discourse is no longer in need of critical reflection. We must constantly examine how the formation of doctrine keeps others in places of oppression and remains open for transformation.

In a postmodern age, when questioning truth and the value of foundations has become fashionable, it is often overlooked that theology turning to others challenges absolute truth claims and foundations for specific reasons. The philosophical reasons on which postmodernity operates are not primary. The trouble with absolute claims to truth is basically that they do not match the reality of everyday life. Early feminist theologians, while challenging the universal claims of mainline theology, had themselves to be reminded of that by their womanist, *mujerista*, and Third World sisters. Not even the category of "women's experience" can contain the notion of truth.[60]

Feminist attention to brokenness and incompleteness makes a difference in our understanding of doctrine and truth. God's own liberating actions have to be sought in the gaps and fissures of actual events. It goes without saying that this position calls into question the genre of systematic theology, in its modern sense of the production of philosophically coherent systems or secure identities. The postliberal reliance on the stability of the narratives and texts of the church is also challenged. Feminist theology listens precisely to the cracks and openings in the totalities of systematic theology. In this context second-generation feminist theologians such as Fulkerson find post-structuralist theories helpful insofar as they give a better account of sin than representational theories of language and help to counteract sin by destabilizing both subjects and texts. Chopp talks about the "iconoclastic shattering of all finalities."[61] Going beyond post-structuralist theories, however, theology turning to others finds that any totalizing discourse creates specific closures and outsiders. Turning to others, feminist theology looks precisely for these. It is here that it finds important clues in its search for truth, no longer as something that can be preserved but as something that is always new. Discernment of truth needs to pay attention to the particular and the flow of power.

While truth understood in a foundationalist fashion as a secure Archimedean anchor is challenged, the insight into relativity does not have to end up in relativism. In fact, theology turning to others senses that the problem of relativism can only be addressed by embracing relativity, not by refusing to admit it. From the perspective of Hispanic women Isasi-Díaz points out that women's everyday experience is not an "anything goes" attitude. "That attitude is possible only in those who feel their world is completely stable, that nothing needs to change and that nothing will change." The experience of people at the margins, on the other hand, is an awareness that all knowledge, including theological knowledge, "is fragmentary, partisan, conjectural, and provisional."[62]

Theology turning to others does not give up on the notion of truth. But glimpses of truth occur where they are least expected, where one's own relativity is acknowledged in the midst of brokenness, in the lives of actual communities. Those glimpses are real, yet the miracles that occur, such as healing relationships or newfound respect for others, point beyond themselves. Theological truth, therefore, is always unfinished and in progress, not systematic or complete. Any vision of truth needs to take into account breaks and disruptions of our knowledge, always open to self-critique. What is lost is not truth itself but a God's eye view of truth. Absolute claims about truth, whether totalitarian or relativistic, remain caught up in this God's eye view, unable to transcend it.[63] The claim to own the truth and the claim not to have any truth at all are pretty similar in this sense. Susan Secker has put it this way: "The reason we women are insisting upon the truth of our experience is because of a fundamental 'contrast experience' we encounter as we do our theology."[64] Truth is not grounded in the way things are, in male or female essentials; truth is related to an experience of the limits of the way things are. It can only be acknowledged if the voices of those who have so far been excluded are admitted and if multiple visions are considered.

Chopp formulates a similar concern for broadening the notion of truth: "God may well operate . . . in a particular construct of textual tradition, but what about the rituals and feasts? What about the prayers and practices of women? What about the subversiveness of slave narratives that did not transgress the master's Christian language but carefully transformed it to make it expressive of African American religious praxis?" In order to gauge truth claims the doctrinal tradition needs to be assessed "in terms of how texts functioned in historical situations as often counterproductive and even harmful to present and future 'truth' of the survival and flourishing of women, and men, and the earth."[65] Truth is not just to be found in written Christian tradition but also in the traditions of those places at the margins where we often fail to look. The notion of truth is not watered down here (as is often suspected by mainline critics) but expanded.

Chopp describes the parallels and differences to the postliberal model. She notes that feminist theology also takes seriously the theological turn to language and the text. It shares with the postliberals "a sense of symbolic logic of faith in the sense that the symbols of Christian faith provide the threads of continuity and transformation of piety, social witness, worship, the life of the community together, and the life in the world." In agreement with the postliberal critique of foundationalism of modern liberal theology, feminist theologians nonetheless add that the texts of the church are not beyond critique either, since "the faith has itself been faulted and corrupted by patriarchy."[66]

In the modern turn to the self, truth is to be discerned from the inside out. The self's feelings and experience serve as a guide. By contrast, both the turn to the Other and the turn to language insist that truth can be discerned only from the outside in, where either Godself or the sacred texts of the church serve as guides. The turn to others introduces yet another perspective. Neither experience nor the texts can be absolute guides anymore. Their function is to provide openings for the Other, but they cannot guarantee truth. Yet neither can we assume that we can connect with God directly, as the turn to the Other might hope. Truth is not to be found in claiming identity with God in any form but in gaining a sense of our own limits.

As we have seen earlier, with Schleiermacher theology started the move away from metaphysics, becoming a hermeneutical enterprise. From a feminist perspective Mary Gerhart points out that the hermeneutical concern that started with Schleiermacher might still be helpful since it challenges the positivist search for certainty and stability.[67] Both Barth and Lindbeck have, in their own ways, proceeded further along those lines and challenged even the more limited certainty of modern hermeneutics. Recent feminist theologies continue to pry open the still narrow gates of hermeneutics, going one step further.

First, the availability of a unified text or body of texts is called into question. Biblical and doctrinal texts are read as open-ended. One implication of this is that the Bible can no longer be defined as either completely oppressive or absolutely liberating. Fulkerson points out the problematic assumption of a "given" of hermeneutical theory which assumes that there is one Christianity that can be unearthed.[68] The view from the margins resists the projection of an unproblematic unity, a common fantasy of those who are used to calling the shots. Second, the biblical and doctrinal texts are no longer read by seemingly autonomous selves. The position of the reader or interpreter needs to be questioned. Fulkerson calls into question the hermeneutical reliance on a "unitary understanding subject" like the one we have encountered in the work of Schleiermacher, even when this subject position has been broadened so as to include somehow women or the marginalized.[69] The turn to others does not imitate the turn to the self. Third, even a "communal hermeneutic," now highly popular with postliberals and others, fails since such a hermeneutics often presupposes homogeneous communities where any distinction between dominant and subordinated voices is missing. These images of community, as we have already seen in the previous chapter, often mirror the concept of the autonomous self. As a result, the modern hermeneutical dialectic between fairly stable selves and texts is merely replaced with a dialectic of fairly stable communities and texts.[70]

According to Fulkerson, the task is to "articulate a relation between scripture and Christian communities that does not begin with a closure of meaning on either end."[71] It is not surprising, then, that she no longer uses the term *hermeneutics*. What must be done is to trace a temporary stability of meaning "by way of conflicts and desires and the meanings these trigger." What are the effects of such discourses, both in terms of the oppression and the liberation they bring? The hermeneutical move proposed by the turn to others promotes critical attention to "living practices of particular communities" in relation to "their willingness to attend to (or to occlude) the political horizons of their practices."[72]

At first sight, feminist theology seems to fit what Stephen Bevans has called the "praxis model of theology," a model that is defined as taking "its inspiration neither from classic texts nor classic behavior but from present realities and future possibilities."[73] But this argument misses the point if it pits the texts of the church and the present situation against each other. While feminist theologians indeed remind us that neither the texts of the church nor subject positions are fixed—both are constructed and constantly reconstructed—we must not forget that the "present situation" is not fixed either. At the same time, both "classic texts" and "classic behavior" continue to matter. This position takes Scripture and doctrines more seriously than the modernist approaches since it better understands the limits of the modern middle-class self, which can no longer claim to control the true meaning. In this sense Fulkerson, unlike some other feminists, argues for the need of a "scripture-shaped community"[74] where Scripture continues to be a living word, reread time and again, aiming at the reconstruction of tradition.

Taking Scripture and doctrines more seriously also includes an honest account of their limits that is sometimes missing in the theological turn to the text. The Word of God cannot be reduced to the biblical words. Neither Scripture nor doctrine provides secure guarantees for absolute truth. It makes little sense, for instance, to think of the Bible in black-and-white terms as either oppressive or liberating literature. The oppressive aspect of the Bible can only be understood when it is seen in relation to other powerful discourses, such as patriarchy and capitalism. By the same token, it is easy to miss the liberating aspect of the Bible if one fails to take into account the minute openings that are created, for instance, even through its use by women who do not consider themselves feminist.

Theology turning to others finds a new dynamic in the texts of the church where they are read from the margins. Paying attention to the gaps and silences, the texts can be read in constructive fashion, resisting their misuse as cover-ups for oppressive situations, and shaping human life constructively. Turning to others in this way, theology is developing new approaches to the Bible as well as to the doctrinal tradition of the church.

A new attitude of listening develops here that, more sharply than the other theological modes, is able to filter out the distortions of the powers of the self. In this way the turn to others promotes a new concern for the doctrines of the church, reminding us that doctrines and truth do not need to be the functions of those in power. In the process of relating doctrines and truth to the experience of people at the margins, they are purged of a great deal of their invisible ideological baggage and thus become relevant once more for the church as a whole. The turn to others does not promote another special-interest theology. Feminist theology is not just for women, black theology is not just for African Americans, Hispanic theology is not just for Latinas and Latinos, and so on.

Providing a fuller account of the distortions and structures of exclusion that sneak into the church's command of doctrine and truth is intended not to tear apart doctrines but to understand the instability of particular readings of doctrines, especially of those built on the backs of others. The theological tools developed by the turn to others allow for theological self-critique which is relevant for the church as a whole. No one is excluded from this task. The turn to others does not do away with the self but puts it into a new context. While the theological turn to the self never excluded others completely, it now becomes clearer that theology needs to be developed not only for those who are different, but together with them. In the process paying attention to those who are excluded helps to reshape those who exclude as well. The turn to others promotes the development of a new self, and ultimately this perspective helps to acquire a deeper understanding of God's work in the world of the global economy, moving through cross and resurrection.

Beyond Special Interests in Theology and the Church

Due to the lack of historical distance, the social and historical location of theology turning to others is trickier to evaluate than the location of either Schleiermacher or Barth. At the same time, however, this theological mode gives much more specific information about its own social location than Lindbeck's postliberal approach and most other contemporary theologies. The previous modes of theology required an analytical reading between the lines to understand the relation of theological reflection and social location. In contrast, theology turning to others is better positioned to give its own accounts of this relation, having increasingly become aware that theological reflection needs to pay attention not only to the texts and doctrines of the church but also to "more ordinary sites of religious meaning,"[75] including people at the margins.

The most obvious reason for paying attention to the marginalized has to do with the fact that theology has not yet recognized their contributions to the Christian faith. Christian thought is shaped not only by theologians and the elites but at the grassroots, among those who have no voice. To develop a broader understanding of the Christian faith, listening to the marginalized is not optional. In fact, at a time when new voices are being added to the theological chorus and theological reflection is broadening its horizons, fragmentation can be resisted not by shutting down others but by listening to those who normally escape the attention of the mainstream.

Theology turning to others is more than a common research project or another theological school. It is the attempt to reconstruct theology in connection to what has existed only in repressed form in the dominant theological discourses. This concern sparks new theological investigation of the various shapes of repression and exclusion—womanist and *mujerista* theologies are among the more recent arrivals—but at the same time also pulls them together. Unity, however, is not achieved by giving up differences. Feminist theology is one particular manifestation of the turn to others, and it is becoming increasingly clear that its reach is much broader than those who explicitly reflect on feminist issues.

Even though theology in general is not completely unaware of the existence of structures of oppression and exclusion, the lives of people who are excluded call for more realistic assessments, forcing us to take the reality of exclusion seriously in all of its dimensions. Chopp, for instance, gives expression to a reality of women's lives that is often hardly noticed by men. She argues that "rape names the ontic condition under which most women live most of the time." The connection of this condition to theological reflection can no longer be neglected: "Rape, for women, forms how we feel about ourselves, how we understand the connections and boundaries between ourselves and others, how we experience and speak of God."[76] The oppression of Latin American women goes one step further by adding the ever-present dimension of death. Theology—and this insight can hardly be overemphasized—literally becomes a matter of life and death.

Nevertheless, as I have now pointed out repeatedly, in turning to others there is always a certain danger of romanticization. Paula Cooey has helped to push feminist theology beyond what she calls "theological innocence."[77] She identifies a polarization where one side romanticizes women by considering them incapable of evil and the other demonizes them. This polarization can also be observed when women who harm others (for example, neglecting or abusing their children) are demonized, while all other women are excused. In order not to romanticize others we need a more specific look at who they are. Theology cannot be done in ahistorical fashion, which is a constant temptation in theological reflection even where theology becomes more interested in matters of context, and one of the common problems of the previous modes of theology.

The romantic version makes matters worse for everyone involved. Coupled with a certain class bias that pretends that harming others is an underclass problem, romanticizing women "masks middle-class women's vulnerability to frustration, rage, and subsequent guilt in respect to their child rearing." Cooey suspects that the idealizations which prevent a "good mother" from "acting like a mature adult subject to moral and emotional complexity" may actually contribute to women's violent reactions. The others to which theology is turning cannot be fully understood in the black-and-white opposition of terms such as *victim* or *agent*. Cooey concludes that "feminist Christian theologians need to provide strong representations of women as complex subjects" and "to capture the full tragedy of what it means for women to resist circumstances only to be destroyed by them . . . just as we attend to the grace of what it means to survive and to transcend the damage others have done."[78] The others are real persons, in all their complexity, sharing in human sinfulness as well as in the offer of God's grace.

Theology turning to others points to the need for broadening the horizon of those who, even though they share in the plight of others at some level, are in positions of privilege. Jeanette Rodríguez, a Latina theologian, notes that "a woman from a dominant culture does not have to learn my point of view to survive, but Mexican American women have to know the ways of the dominant culture."[79] For theological reflection, this means that the view from the underside is broader, an insight that must come as a shock in a discipline that, like most mainline commonsense thinking, assumes that the better views are always to be had from the perspectives of the elites. The turn to others reminds us not only that we need to broaden our horizons but also that the view from the top needs to be reconstructed. The blindness—and this is one of the major lessons for theology in crisis today—is greatest at the top. Those at the top are, already as children, told by well-meaning adults that the others, those who are not quite part of our social status, are "just like us." We never look at it the other way around. Secker draws the obvious conclusion: "We look at someone who is different from us and come right back to ourselves."[80]

Theology turning to others begins to realize what it means that the view from the top is epistemologically crippling. It is impossible for those who identify with the powers that be to cut through the illusions of the reality they have constructed. This form of blindness does not apply in the same way to those at the margins. Using Hegel's terminology of master and slave we can put it like this: In being forced to serve the master's desire, the slave comes to learn about the "underside" of the master's consciousness and power, while the master is, as Fredric Jameson has observed, "condemned to idealism—to the luxury of placeless freedom"[81] and his or her own idiosyncrasies. For the majority of academic theologians and most middle-class church people, the turn to others does not first result in the liberation of the oppressed others, but in their own liberation.

Here is a major difference with the other three modes of theology: Theologies turning to others draw from a broader spectrum of human reality, recognizing the wisdom among those who are both culturally and economically marginalized. The turn to others, therefore, promotes not just the special interest of a certain group (as the proponents of the mainline often falsely suspect) but the common interest of all. Theology can no longer afford to disqualify the knowledge of those at the margins. The shift from the "cultured despisers of religion" (Schleiermacher) to the nonpersons is not optional—even in First World theology.

As academic theologians, aware of the limitations of our own social location, we can show respect for the marginalized by admitting their questions and challenges into our communities. No doubt, as Fulkerson has argued, this will help to "destabilize our identity as theologians."[82] Theology will be reshaped. Ultimately the marginalized themselves become part of the theological enterprise. The debate around the notion of experience in feminist theology has shown what is at stake: early feminist theologians, while trying to overcome the control of the modern male self, have introduced notions of experience that in some ways imitated the dominant model and, while claiming universality for women, were still fairly narrow. Yet growing awareness of, and encounters with, the many different locations at the margins have broadened and diversified the notion of experience. One of the most important moves of recent feminist theological work is to listen to women who have not yet been included in the thought of feminist theology.

Fulkerson gives accounts of lower-class Pentecostal and middle-class Presbyterian women who try to respect difference and promote new forms of listening. Theology turning to others invites us to take more seriously the contributions of people who, even within the context of our churches, have never been taken seriously. Fulkerson explains that "categorical respect" for the practices of other women is necessary since this has not been well developed so far in feminist theological accounts.[83] The future of theological reflection depends on this. Different women resist patriarchal structures of exclusion in ways that are often overlooked by feminist theologians. We miss the reality of Pentecostal women, for instance, by simply looking at their language or their ideas. When these women confess that they are nothing, when they attribute agency to God rather to themselves, for example, they do not just follow the scripts of patriarchal theology but protect women's activities from male oppression. Fulkerson summarizes: "Their liberating practices are found in the cracks where discourses of self-worth can be forged and where new lines of life-giving flow can still be found on an old plant, the Pentecostal system."[84]

The feminist deconstruction of the modern middle-class self does not abandon selfhood but leads to a broader awareness of it. Feminist theory has at times distinguished between sex, referring to the anatomical differences of bodies, and gender, a construct. Selfhood is not a given, as the modern turn to the self and liberal and radical forms of feminism had assumed. The gendered self is constructed, an insight that might also be affirmed by postliberals in principle. This creates room for questions and transformation. In addition, feminists have learned that, like gender identity, gender domination is constructed differently for other women of African American, Asian, or Latina descent. Fulkerson and others go one step further, pointing out that even the notion of sex has a history and is therefore not unchanging. Only in modernity has the sexual, together with gender, been equated with the essence of the self.[85] The problem is that here another structure is introduced through the back door which supports the control of the status quo, sorting out what fits into the value structures of a given context and what does not. Modern theology is not therefore "genderized" by the emergence of feminist theology but just the opposite: feminist theology addresses the unrecognized genderization and the gender bias of modern theology. The problem is not necessarily the traditional construction of gender as binary in specific situations. The problem is the fixing and naturalizing of this relationship that produces structures of exclusion.

The basic theological question that arises here is whether the identities that we construct "are identical with that about the gospel which is changeless and constitutive."[86] The presence of homosexuals in the church, for example, might be a unique opportunity to think through the question of what really matters, breaking open conventions that are not related to the heart of the gospel and creating new room for the power of God.

The Liberation Church

The way the theological turn to others shapes up in the church illustrates what is at stake. Women and other marginalized people are active participants in the life of the church but, in the words of Chopp, we often think about church "as the official actions to such an extent that we overlook the church of the people, especially the women."[87] Even when we do pay attention to people at the margins, however, we often forget that a church which is truly inclusive is measured not necessarily by the numbers of marginalized people in its ranks (usually the majority of members, if one considers the situation of women) but by the roles those people play. Churches that take seriously the turn to others know that there is a difference between who sits in the pews and who is active on the boards. They are also aware of the difference between diversity as fun and a more challenging form of diversity that attempts to take the neighbor seriously.

A church that truly becomes aware of others not only provides safe havens but also develops relationships of mutual give-and-take, establishing two-way streets where others are no longer just recipients (as in the liberal turn to the self) but also the ones who give and act. Successful resistance to the structures of exclusion is directly related to whether others are permitted to critique the self-image of those in power, however benevolent it may be.

Marjorie Procter-Smith puts the challenge as follows: "What would happen if a whole church of women told the truth about their lives? What if the men heard them? Would the church split open? Perhaps then we could begin, men and women together, to spin and weave a new world and a new church."[88] The turn to others requires both telling the truth and a willingness to listen. This church no longer plays the morally superior prophet, merely indicting the world for its racial, sexual, and economic bigotry, but learns to see how it is part of the problem. Here resistance to the greatest challenge of the present is developed, the unconscious perpetuation of structures of exclusion by well-meaning people, starting in the church itself.

In the process of developing alternative church structures, feminist theologians have also talked about "women church." It is often overlooked that this is not an exclusive club, promoting the special interests of a certain group, but a reality in which women find themselves at certain times and which helps them to deal with the church. The term itself was initially created in light of the exclusion of women from ordained ministry in the Roman Catholic Church. It is surprising, only at first sight, that at a time when the church has lost most of its steam in many First World locations, women's liturgy groups flourish and experience new life.[89] While people often see very little in the church worth "laying down one's life for Christ," here is something that makes a difference.

The separatist tendencies in certain models of women church may be necessary at times since they create safe havens. But there is always a danger of getting stuck in the mechanisms described by the turn to the self. The turn to others has the potential to reach beyond this impasse.

Observing that women are already marginalized in the church, Procter-Smith argues that "we do not need to move out any farther," a move that perhaps might be seen as a parallel to the modern self's move into the suburbs. She continues: "If we are to *exodus* it must be an exodus out of marginality and into the center."[90] At stake is not the formation of a private church—another special-interest deal—but the transformation of the church as a whole. Moving into the center of the church, reshaping patriarchal authority and other oppressive systems, women witness to the church's ongoing need for conversion. In this context it becomes clear that the church can only be the church "insofar as it is continually struggling to overcome its patriarchy and androcentrism, only insofar as it openly confesses and repents of its sexism, racism, and classism, only insofar as it challenges patriarchal structures in the world."[91]

As we have seen, the church's turn to others, resisting the self-serving tendencies of the turn to the self, does not do away with the texts of the church. Instead, the texts are now put in a broader context. Procter-Smith talks about one aspect of feminist liturgies as "the active remembrance of our collective past as seen through women's eyes and experienced in women's bodies. This is necessary, not to fragment further the Christian community, but to restore to it that which has been missing from it. Only by recognizing the particularity of such remembering are reconciliation and wholeness possible."[92] The liturgical and doctrinal texts of the church are thus remembered, reclaimed, and reappropriated in constructive ways. The basis is a new spirituality that, "before it is particular disciplines of prayers, is a way of being in the world: a way of living, of knowing, of seeing and hearing."[93]

Last but not least, the church informed by the turn to others does not need to claim to be the perfect community. Just as the marginalized as such or the experience of women does not exist, so the liberation church as such does not exist.[94] The position of others reminds us that the church always needs to pay attention to those who are left out in specific situations, never to be content with the integration of one group or another. This church knows that it is on the way, a community in process constantly being opened up to new encounters with both other people and the divine Other.

Conclusion

Rather than promoting the special interest of certain groups, the turn to others is broadening the horizons of theology as a whole. At a time when more and more people are pushed to the margins, theology needs to learn how to deal with the structures of exclusion that define the world today and how to resist that which unconsciously shapes its own disciplines. There is a certain danger, of course, that the turn to others gets stuck in a hermeneutics of suspicion. The most recent examples of this attitude in postmodern thought illustrate the problem when the self and its agency are dismissed at a time when many women and other marginalized people have never even had a sense of self.

While the critical potential is important, especially where it turns into self-critique, the theological turn to others leads beyond the critical mode. Something positive is produced, but one has to listen for it. Theological authorship in this position is very different and cannot be equated with general notions of authorship in modern theology.[95] Sharon Welch makes a helpful suggestion when, in response to Michel Foucault's well-known critique of authorship, she comments that "what is dead is not the author per se but the author who can assume the mantle of universality."[96] In other words, liberation thought primarily challenges not the struggle for identity in itself but the process of universalization in which such identities become controlling and oppressive.

The self does not disappear in the turn to others but is reconstructed in relation to them. Feminist and other theologies from the margins understand that even the self of those in power, whether aware of it or not, is always co-constituted by that which it excludes. Paying attention to the gaps, to the place of the marginalized, the turn to others is not lost in an endless swirl of otherness and difference but enters into a constructive dialogue with the church and its traditions. In this context references to experience do not promote an "anything goes" attitude but invite sustained attention to that which hurts. Thus the turn to others extends theological respect for diversity without falling into the trap of relativism.

By focusing on what the other three modes of theological reflection repress, all four modes can now be seen in a new light without having to claim an easy synthesis. Each mode serves as a reminder of a set of concerns that cannot easily be given up. But it is the turn to others that reactivates those concerns at a time when theology is in deep crisis and when even the most respected theological guidelines are crumbling under the force of the growing gap between those in control and those left out.

Rather than abandoning the self, the turn to others contributes to a new awareness of the specific shape of the communal nature of the self and the relation of self and others. At the same time, the turn to others opens new insights into the complexity of the turn to the Other. The respect for the Other is related to our ability to respect others and needs to be practiced and trained in this context. Finally, turning to others contributes both to a more focused appreciation and critique of the turn to language and to new encounters with the texts of the church.

5

Interconnections, Blind Spots, and Unconscious Desires

Suspended between God and the excluded, we can no longer afford to perpetuate theological segregation. Instead, we need to understand the links and connections between differing ways of theological reflection and their combined potential for resistance to the major threat of our day, the powers of exclusion. The thought of the French psychoanalyst Jacques Lacan, while not theologically normative, is helpful here in two ways. First, his analytical framework of the "four discourses" parallels the four modes of theology we have discussed and helps to examine their interconnectedness. Lacan reminds us that no discourse is complete in and of itself. Second, Lacan also develops tools that enable the search for what is repressed and excluded by each of the discourses, that is, their blind spots. Far from being a peripheral topic, what is repressed and excluded points to hidden truth, to that which moves people, without which no progress can be made.[1] The search for truth connects the two central issues of this chapter: the search for the location of authority (that which moves people unconsciously, desire) and the search for blind spots. Unless we can reconnect with what we have repressed and excluded, it will always come back to haunt us. As theologians we still need to realize that what our theologies are asking for is only one indicator as to what they actually produce. Lacan's attention to blind spots and related repressions will be particularly helpful in uncovering what drives a specific discourse and where its unconscious desires are located.

The relevance of Lacan's four discourses to contemporary theology does not simply depend on certain parallels in the realm of ideas and concepts. More important is the fact that both share in a common historical location. Lacan's work as a whole is often misunderstood because it is assumed that he tries to describe the human being in general. Feminist critics have been among the first to voice this suspicion. But Lacan's interest is focused on the specific alienations and fragmentations of humanity at the apex of modern society—with a special interest in North American phenomena. Lacan writes at a time when the modern self has finally won most of its battles for autonomy and fortified its positions of power, authority, and control. This is the so-called ego's era. He raises in his own way the question that is at the basis of the current theological dilemma, of "the place man assigns to himself at the centre of the universe."[2] Lacan leaves no doubt about his criticism of the milestones in the history of the rise of the modern self, from Descartes's "*Cogito*" through Hegel's idea of an "Absolute Spirit," all the way to North American "ego psychology" which, in its efforts to smooth over rather than deal with the tensions of the modern self, has come to dominate our culture through its impact on pop psychology.

The Lacanian notion of the ego's era describes the modern self as caught up in narcissistic structures that manifest themselves not only in personal relationships but also in the economic and political realms where this self has managed aggressively to draw everything into its force field and to exclude the rest of humanity.[3] Here are some parallels to other influential critiques of modernity that deplore modern self-centeredness, individualism, and arrogance. Unfortunately, these matters are often treated in a moralistic way by condemning the problem and implying that we could be different if we only tried,[4] a mentality that is also shared by much of contemporary theology where it is assumed that the modern turn to the self can be replaced easily with other turns. No wonder some of these turns are pulled back into the turn to the self and its dreams of being in control. In this context Lacan's work is absolutely crucial because it reminds us that truly resisting the ego's era and the established structures of exclusion will not be possible by repressing it or by smoothing over its discontents. We need a deeper understanding and reconstruction of what really motivates the modern self.[5]

Lacan developed his theory of the four discourses in the late sixties and early seventies, times of crisis all over the world.[6] The student movements started to question the established discourses of the university and other powers that be, and the ways in which they transmit knowledge. Arguing that the established forms of transmitting knowledge had taken on forms that were totalizing, restrictive, and in the service of the powers of the status quo, the revolutionary students wanted to free discourse from all constraints. Yet their revolution, Lacan predicted, was threatened by merely replacing the old masters with new ones. To change the rigid discourses of the university and the tradition, he argued, we must develop a deeper understanding of the way they function. Only then can the system truly be transformed.[7] The four discourses are of particular interest because they take up important aspects of the visions of modernity and postmodernity while offering a critical analysis of their limitations in light of the phenomenon of exclusion.

The Discourse of the Self

Theological reflection in modern times is reconfigured in terms of the religious genius of the modern self in the process of learning how to shape its world. What happens to theological discourse when the modern self is put in such a prominent place? Some of the characteristics of liberal theology, representing the basic presuppositions of classic liberal theology, are mirrored in what Lacan has called the "discourse of the hysteric." To keep the designation as open as possible, I rename this discourse here the "discourse of the self." The "hysteric" to whom Lacan refers is in fact not an individual in need of help but the modern self as we know it today, born in the Enlightenment and the emergence of the middle class, asserting its powers in various political revolutions and the development of capitalist market economies during the past 250 years. This discourse is the most typical discourse in the modern world, the ego's era.

The discourse of the self is shaped primarily by the interests and concerns of the modern self. Lacan designates the self with the symbol "$." The S is crossed through since the modern self, without being aware of it, is not truly the master in its own house. The modern self is divided; its confidence, identity, unity, and autonomy are on shaky ground. In the discourse of the self, the self takes on a leading function over the other three elements, which Lacan identifies as the master signifiers or key words or concepts ("S1," dominant in the discourse of the master), language or tradition ("S2," dominant in the discourse of the tradition), and the repressed object of desire, the other ("a," dominant in the discourse of the marginalized).

In each discourse a different element takes on leadership. In the discourse of the self, the self assumes this place. The other three elements occupy the following positions (see Diagram 1).[8]

Here the self's ($) primary activity is to put to work the master signifiers (S1). In other words, the self shapes the key concepts of its world, its central ideas, its main slogans. This constellation leads to the production and reconstruction of language and tradition (S2). As a result,

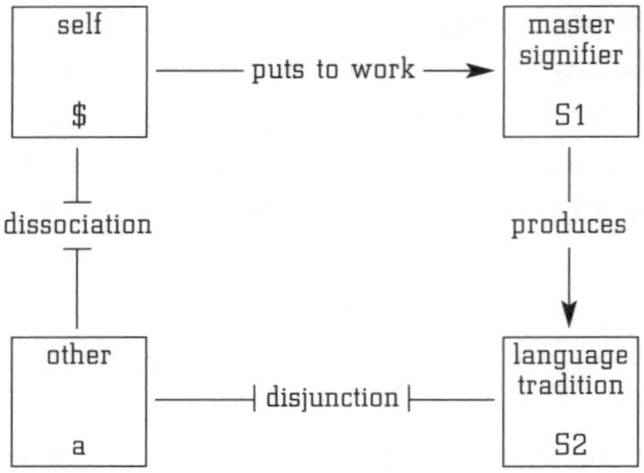

Diagram 1

both master signifiers (S1) and language and tradition (S2) are now functions of the self ($). The most direct impact of the self is on the master signifiers (the relation on the upper line of the diagram). The self here is in a position to determine the key concepts and mottoes of its own discourse, one of the declared goals of liberal theology. Equally important, however, is the place of the elements on the lower line of the diagram, starting with a specific language or tradition (S2). This language/tradition is "produced" and shaped by the very master signifiers that the self has chosen.

This setting provides us with a first grasp of Lacan's analysis and its usefulness in expanding the postmodern horizons of contemporary thought. While Lacan agrees with the general postmodern sentiment that has called for an end of the classical search for Archimedean points (including all external referents and foundations), he continues the search for that which is not located immediately on the surface, for a deeper level of meaning "between the lines." In much of postmodern discourse all that matters is what is produced by relationships at the surface level, as post-structuralism and structuralism suggest and now even postmodern advertising seems to confirm: Soft drinks, for example, are no longer the "real thing," as the marketers of Coca-Cola used to claim; soft drinks are now sold under slogans such as "obey your thirst," as advertisements for Sprite proclaim. The reference to underlying realities is abandoned. A similar phenomenon can be observed in the stock market, increasingly governed by its own internal rules, rather than by external referents (such as the actual performance of the market, unemployment, and so on). Lacan, while taking up these insights, nevertheless also reminds us of deeper levels of meaning. The discourse of the self, for instance, does not involve only the surface relation of the self ($) and its master signifiers (S1), on the upper line of the diagram; another dimension must be accounted for below the surface, represented by the lower line of the diagram.[9]

Part of what is at stake here can be explained in terms of the Hegelian master-slave dialectic: what the master (the self, in the discourse of the self) really wants is not the slave (here the master signifier [S1]) but the product of the slave's work (language and tradition [S2]). As the diagram shows, there is one more element located below the surface. Analysis inspired by Lacan requires yet another even more radical reading between the lines, as we will see in a moment.

It is widely recognized that Schleiermacher's theology is a grand attempt to reconfigure the master signifiers of theological reflection (S1), most importantly the theological concepts of God, the self, and the world. But, according to Lacan's analytical framework, what the self ($) really wants is not the master signifiers (S1) but their work or product, in this case the reconfiguration of the church's language and tradition as a whole (S2). By reshaping the central master signifiers and key concepts of the Christian faith on the grounds of the self's authority, what Schleiermacher really wants is to arrive at a new dogmatic. This is the goal of liberal systematic theology: the whole range of dogmatics must be rewritten on the grounds of the self's selection of key signifiers of theology.

Mark Bracher, a Lacanian analyst, finds that the discourse of the self represents a number of discourses that express resistance, protest, and complaint, "from the plaintive anthems of slaves, to the yearning lyrics of lovesick poets, to the iconoclastic rhetoric of revolutionaries."[10] They all share in common the fact that here people are beginning to shape their own master signifiers. Repudiating the letter for the spirit, the discourse of the self bears within it the potential for protest and for revolutionizing the status quo.[11] Revolutionary movements driven by the middle class tend to perpetuate this discourse in their own ways, putting tremendous pressures on the master signifiers of the mainstream that, in the example of the student movements, can still be felt more than thirty years later. A certain restlessness, characteristic of the discourse of the self, is also part of liberal theology. Even the Social Gospel is a manifestation of the discourse of the self: here social involvement is based on the transforming potential of the middle-class self.[12] Lacan worried that the revolutionary students of the late 1960s and other middle-class revolutions, perpetuating the discourse of the self, would end up merely replacing one set of master signifiers with another. I will show later, however, that the discourse of slaves and other oppressed people can be better understood as part of another discourse and that a fundamental difference exists between liberal and liberation theologies.

So far, Lacanian analysis parallels my interpretation of Schleiermacher and the general consensus among his interpreters, a fact that confirms the usefulness of this model. Yet Lacan compels us to add one more step to our evaluation. We need to take into account the other element on the lower level of the diagram.[13] Here we reach the limits of the discourse of the self. Looking below the surface, we realize that something is repressed here beyond recognition. According to the diagram above, in the discourse of the self, the self is dissociated from the other. The other is in the place of what Lacan calls the "truth." The fact that the truth is isolated and repressed does not mean, however, as many postmodernists quickly tend to conclude, that there is no truth at all and that relativism rules the day. It simply means that truth cannot be easily uncovered at this point. Here is the blind spot in the discourse of the self. Nevertheless, even though the self cannot reach its own truth, this truth shapes the discourse of the self in powerful ways. The things that drive the self unconsciously, its innermost desires, are located precisely at this point.

In the discourse of the self the position of truth is occupied by the other, which Lacan calls the "object a." Of the four elements this is the most difficult to grasp. The place of the "other (a)" is best described as an empty space, a void, something that has no existence in and of itself. Whatever occupies this space has been put there by mechanisms of repression. Things repressed from the level of consciousness, for example, get consigned to this place. Yet while the things deposited here are stored out of reach, they have a significant impact on everything else. Lacan also calls the "other (a)" the "object of desire," indicating that that which is repressed paradoxically has a most powerful effect on shaping our deepest desires and dreams. As something that is repressed the Lacanian other can be compared to the position of the marginalized other. Marginalized people do not exist as marginalized in and of themselves. In other words, their marginalization is not their own fault. They are put into this position by other factors. In patriarchal society the position of women exemplifies this odd mixture of marginalization and desired object. Lacan provides a strong reminder that this position needs to be taken seriously. People in marginalized positions relate differently to the powers that be, often aware of things that theologians and other people within the system cannot see. In the broader picture the position of the other as object of desire signifies a position of receptiveness, openness, and listening, the ability to pick up repressed signals that escape everyone else, and the ability to read between the lines. Lacan therefore terms the discourse where the other is in charge the "discourse of the analyst" (I will call it the "discourse of the marginalized").

In the discourse of the self, the truth to which the self cannot get is represented by the other (a), the repressed object of desire where various things are stored that unconsciously motivate or haunt the self. In late capitalism many powers compete to fill this unconscious void. After all, this is also the level that the advertising industry is trying to reach, pushing its message into areas that cannot be consciously controlled and thus are all the more influential. More significantly, however, the place of the other as repressed object of desire is also the level of the marginalized, of all those people who are repressed by the self.

Even though it is constantly searching for its hidden truth, the self never really knows exactly what it wants. Not only is its subconscious truth located below the surface where it cannot reach, the other that occupies the place of truth is itself subject to constant shifts and readjustments determined by the signs of the times. No wonder the self is restless, displaying at times even revolutionary tendencies, never quite satisfied with the traditional status quo and the master signifiers it offers. There is a constant urge to innovate and to change, to transform the dominant master signifiers and to rewrite the tradition. Yet without a deeper look into its own truth, the discourse of the self's search for stability and security—supported by the fact that the self is in power in the world of late capitalism—leads only to the ongoing production of more new masters (S1) and belief systems (S2).

The result is something like a revolution from above, a revolution by those in control. Without recovering that which has been repressed, however, such revolutions can easily take on narcissistic forms. While certain master signifiers and traditions may be transformed, the system stays the same. The self ends up turning around itself and its own interests, determined to shape everything else in its image. Theology built upon this foundation always runs the risk of turning into special-interest theology, pursuing primarily the interests of specific groups of people in charge, however benevolent and charitable they may present themselves at the moment.

It is not surprising that there is a certain neurotic potential in the discourse of the self which is multiplied if the links to the other elements, such as already established master signifiers and the tradition of the church, are loosened. (The reference to neurotic structures here and to other clinical terms such as *psychosis* in the following chapters may help us to understand the specific issues at stake in the various modes of theology and is not meant to discredit certain forms of theology.[14]) In his earlier work Lacan has pointed out that the problem of the neurotic is that "the Word is driven out of the concrete discourse which orders the subject's consciousness."[15] Unlike in psychosis, where the "Word" (a master signifier) is in charge, in neurosis the authority of the Word is removed from discourse. As we have seen, the discourse of the self is not ordered by the Word but by the functions of the self, particularly its intuitions and feelings.[16] Yet what if the self is never quite "master in its own house" (Freud's famous insight) despite pop-psychological and other political and economic efforts to maintain this mastery? No wonder that, in the words of Jameson, the position of the self can easily become "a most unreliable space," often not producing much more than "nostalgia or instinctual Utopianism,"[17] forms of idealism often promoted by those who feel they do not need to deal with the deeper challenges and hardships of the present.

Here is a very real danger in liberal theology. As Ellie Ragland-Sullivan has pointed out, "the neurotic's myth . . . avoids the Real in favor of living out fantasies or promoting symptoms."[18] While not every self falls squarely into the category of the neurotic, it is clear that the self can no longer function as an unambiguous guide. In contrast to Descartes's reassuring motto "I think, therefore I am," Lacan expresses the predicament of the self in this way: "'Either I do not think, or I am not.' There where I think, I don't recognize myself; there where I am not, is the unconscious; there where I am, it is only too clear tha[t] I stray from myself."[19]

Lacan is hopeful that the shortcomings of the self can be made up by more emphasis on the Word, the master signifiers (S1). Theology, too, has sensed that a turn to the Word could help to transform and reshape a theology built on the discourse of the self. In the case of the neurotic, however, that Word is "driven out" and thus cannot easily be brought back into the discourse. In this situation neurotics are left in a vicious circle, unable to pull themselves up by their own bootstraps. The self ends up constructing its own world, caught up in its own idealistic fantasies.

These narcissistic tendencies help us to understand the lack of inclusivity that we have found in the theological manifestations of the turn to the self. The self, even if it promotes ideals of inclusivity and participation, is simply too preoccupied with itself to pay sufficient attention to others at the margins. In addition, the location of marginalized people in modern and postmodern societies is precisely that of the other, the repressed object of desire. Repressed from the places where things are happening, they nevertheless help us to understand what the self really wants, including the self's desire for admiration and even gratitude from those less well off.

The discourse of the self is, of course, not the only form in which theology can develop idealistic blinders. There is another disorder, where the words take over (rather than the Word), which is even less able to recognize its idealistic illusions since it regards itself on objective grounds. In the neurotic situation, however, there is at least some remaining sense of a gap between the self and the "thing in itself." In other words, while there is a danger of the self turning in on itself as a result of its ongoing search for identity, the idolatrous confusion of the self and God is not always a necessary consequence. The self, while unaware of the seriousness of its divided nature, knows "that something is wrong in knowledge, something is missing in Symbolic order myths."[20] Theologies that follow the turn to the self are usually quite aware of the fact that humanity is not perfect and that there are limits. But, like the self, they are never quite able to see what precisely those limits are. Most significantly—and this brings us back to the main problem—the exclusionary tendencies of the turn to the self go unrecognized. The self has a hard time recognizing others, those who are repressed. This impaired relation to the repressed others also puts some limits on the relation to the divine Other since the self is focused primarily on its own interests. One of the fundamental blind spots of this position is the way it is coupled with the exclusion of the marginalized others. Resisting exclusion is therefore not optional but key for developing more adequate theological guidelines.

Another Turn

In the discourse of the self, as we have seen, the self is unable to understand what really moves it. The self can come to its truth only by leaving the position of leadership. When this happens the self leaves its own discourse and enters another discourse, in this case what I call the "discourse of the marginalized" (to be discussed in more detail below). The truth about oneself can be discovered only a posteriori, in the move to another discourse formation where the self is put to work by the other, its previously repressed truth. Countering the structures of exclusion is therefore much more than the attempt to be charitable and kind to the marginalized or to help those who are in need: without going against the grain of the structures of exclusion, we cannot see the truth.

Diagram 2 illustrates the process, introducing the relation of "transference."

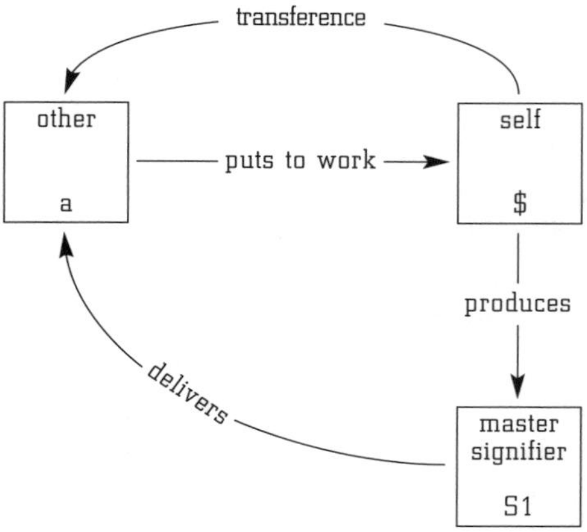

Diagram 2

Here the self is put to work by what it had repressed so far: the other (a). At this point, the self and the marginalized others can finally begin to enter into a relationship. Relations between the self and those who have been repressed or excluded now go beyond the one-way streets of charity and handouts, so typical of the modern turn to the self. A two-way street opens up and a dialogue begins in which the self is transformed in its encounter with marginalized others, thus learning how the structures of marginalization and exclusion might be overcome.[21]

Put to work by the marginalized other (a), the self ($) produces new master signifiers (S1). Those signifiers are delivered back to the marginalized other, who is now in a position of knowing what he or she did not know a priori, namely, the hidden truth of the self. Through the process of transference this knowledge is delivered back to the self as self-knowledge. Getting to know oneself in this way is not always pleasant, of course, a fact that accounts for resistance to this approach especially in liberal theologies and churches. In very simple terms, transference in this case is what allows the self to glimpse that which is in the position of the other (see diagram).[22] This process finally leads to the recognition of previously hidden truth. This is not simply an epistemological or hermeneutical matter. Truth shapes an entire way of life and action; knowing it and reflecting on it can lead to the possible change of praxis as well.

Does modern theology, putting the self in such a prominent place, have to turn out narcissistic? Schleiermacher wants to keep the self as open as possible. He is aware that the self can become all-controlling. The Christian self must understand that there is something else: "While morality always shows itself as manipulating, as self-controlling, piety appears as a surrender, a submission to be moved by the Whole that stands over against man."[23] The Christian self has some sense that there is a reality that it cannot control, a reality that stands over against it. Schleiermacher realizes that the problem for most modern people is that "God is obviously nothing more than the genius of humanity. Man is the prototype of their God." He affirms, therefore, that religion transcends humanity when he confesses that "humanity is not everything to me." Schleiermacher wants to leave open the place of the infinite.[24]

No doubt the modern self is dimly aware that there are things which go beyond its control. It is driven by unconscious desires that transmit their impulses in various ways. The modern self, in moments of honesty, could always sympathize with Paul in Rom. 7:15: "For I do not do what I want, but I do the very thing I hate." But can we take for granted that in the midst of all of these impulses there is still an impulse which points directly to God, such as the "feeling of absolute dependence"? The only feeling of absolute dependence that seems to be left at the beginning of the twenty-first century is related to ever more powerful webs of economic relationships which are now global. In modern liberal Protestantism feeling absolutely dependent is, of course, no longer in fashion. Now it is feeling good about oneself that suggests a close connection to God.[25] But the basic theological problems remain the same: Is the self able to determine God's place?

At this point, we are clearer about the dangers of this position. The self is unable to understand itself fully. Feelings and experiences, and the objects of desire that determine our lives, do not always point us to God, even if they seem religious. To sort out feelings and the hidden roots of desires, theologians need the wisdom of other theological discourses. Liberal theology's turn to the self cannot guide theological reflection in isolation. Schleiermacher's God remains strangely vague, having lost the reference to important traditional and biblical images, perhaps most importantly the connections with the Old Testament.[26] In the end, God is still pulled into the force field of the self.

The dilemma cannot be resolved at this point. For a fuller account of the relationship of the self ($) and its repressed other (a), we have to wait until we can take a closer look at the discourse of the marginalized at the end of this chapter. We shall see that the turn to others produces a critical reconstruction of modernity that is even more forceful than the postmodern turn to language.

The Discourse of the Master

Theology turning to the Other no longer needs to be tied to the feelings and dispositions of creative selves. Theological reflection is now initiated by new encounters with God as the Wholly Other. What happens to theological discourse when the encounter with the Other is put into such a prominent place? The discourse of the master contains a strong critique of the discourse of the modern self, even though it may not be completely independent from its powers.

This discourse is dominated by what Lacan calls the "master signifier" (S1). A master signifier can be anything in which a person invests his or her identity.[27] Master signifiers can be key words or concepts, but they can be also meaningful objects, persons, or names. A master signifier is anything that assumes the status of an end in itself. In Barth's theology the end in itself is God, the Word (developed in terms of the Trinity of Father, Son, and Holy Spirit). Thus there is no need to give further proof of the existence or reality of God. In the context of modernity the discourse of the master can be conceived as a challenge to the powers of the modern self. Where the master signifier takes over the leading function the self ($) is put in the least active position, becomes virtually invisible, and appears to be completely deprived of its powers. Even in this repressed position, however, the self remains part of the picture. The four elements occupy the positions in Diagram 3.

In this discourse the master signifier (S1) "puts to work" the language of the Christian tradition (S2) and reshapes it. In a next step, tradition is now in a position to reshape the other (a), what Lacan calls the object of desire. As a result, both the tradition and its product, the other, become functions of the master signifier. This dynamic helps to reinforce what is ultimately at stake in Barth's work. Both moments belong together in Barth's theology. The surface relation of master signifier and tradition in Barth's theology is widely recognized. Here the turn to the Other delivers what it promises; in his writings Barth indeed rebuilds a whole "universe of discourse" from scratch, thus setting the course for future generations of theologians.[28] The thousands of pages of *Church Dogmatics* are proof of this effort to shape dogmatic discourse. This is the neoorthodox tendency of Barth, that is, orthodoxy with a twist: the doctrines of the church are not just perpetuated but reshaped in light of a specific set of master signifiers.

In Barth's discourse the encounter with the Otherness of God, the Word of God, reshapes the words of both Bible and doctrinal tradition. As we have seen, theology turning to the Other is not content with establish-

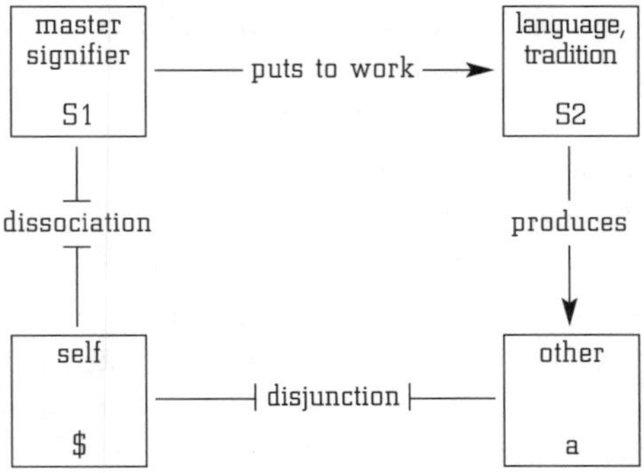

Diagram 3

ing a list of existing doctrines. Theology is built on doctrines that are reshaped in the encounter with their origin, God in Christ. If Barth were in fact a neoorthodox theologian, he would stop here, with the production of language and dogmatics that is faithful to its master signifier. But something deeper is at stake.

The Lacanian paradigm helps us to understand that Barth is interested not just in a new dogmatics but also in the formation of the other (a), the object of desire, that which drives the human being. Dogmatics is not just a cognitive enterprise, getting the doctrines right; dogmatics aims also at a deeper transformation that reshapes the secret preferences and desires of the theologian and the whole church. More than Schleiermacher, Barth understands that this will require hard work. What Barth really wants is the formation of theological identity at the most existential level in the midst of a sea of dogmatic (in)difference. The theology that grows out of the encounter with the master signifier not only reshapes the language and traditions of the church but also reaches into matters that touch the identity of the theologian and the church.

The significance of the theological turn to the Other, the turn to the master signifiers, lies in the fact that it seeks to provide an alternative both to the modern self in its self-centeredness and to a traditionalism which gets stuck with the texts of the church. The discourse of the master seeks to instill in the theologian a much-needed respect for and sense of the divine Other. If all goes well, an encounter with the Other, presented by the master signifiers of the church, leads to the initiation of the theologian into the language of the church and, vice versa, helps to make the language of the church meaningful to theologians.

Jameson points to the dynamic nature of the discourse of the master when he associates it with charismatic authority. This discourse introduces "a freshness of conceptuality" and "the authority of the word, or even prophecy,"[29] all aspects that are clearly visible in the theological turn to the Other. Teaching and political discourse, for example, often proceed initially by promoting specific master signifiers. Lacan is fully aware of the power of the discourse of the master in the political realm since the revolutionary students of the late 1960s have appropriated it for their own purposes. But herein also lies the problem: The revolution of the students is limited since they merely replace old master signifiers with new ones. The system stays the same.

Realizing the limitations of the discourse of the master, Lacan compels us once again to add another step to our evaluation. A first look below the surface (at the lower line in the diagram) has helped us to understand the goal of Barth's theology that has been fairly clear to those who read his work carefully. In the discourse of the master, however, the master signifier is also separated from its unconscious and repressed truth, the modern self ($). This repression points to a question that has arisen ever more clearly in the previous chapters. Is it possible that Barth's critique of the theological influence of the modern self might lead to a repression of the problem rather than to its resolution?

It appears as if in Barth's work the self is critiqued to such a degree that it is virtually phased out. Barth's reception of the modern theological concern for religious feeling or experience is a case in point. As we have already seen, religious experience cannot be something a person owns, something that is part of a person's nature. The experience Barth considers relevant for theology is exclusively shaped by the Word of God. Experience, as "determination of human existence by God's Word," must not "be confused with a determination man can give his own existence." Barth concedes that "this experience ceases to be an experience." Experience leads to the "real perishing and dying of man."[30] Experience, as Barth uses the term, is merely a function of the master signifier. Barth could not be clearer that the self cannot serve as a warrant for the theological enterprise. While the modern self strives for autonomy, the self in Barth's theology—if it appears at all—is completely heteronomous. But does he forget to take into account the ways in which the modern self is still present?

By doing away with the self, the discourse of the master merely seems to repress its own troubles, creating the illusion of being whole, undivided, self-identical.[31] But when the self is merely repressed, rather than reconstructed, it comes back to haunt us. What is worse, those promoting the master's discourse have even more trouble seeing where they, too, become subservient to the special interests of the modern self. This suspicion is supported by Ragland-Sullivan's observation that the discourse of the master "unconsciously perpetuates the suppression of the person's own division," a move which "enables him or her to retain an unchallenged belief in her or his autonomy."[32] There is a danger that the modern self, now in repressed form, continues to determine the shape of the master signifiers in unconscious ways. Even in the discourse of the master, for all its liberating potential, the powers of exclusion, based on the power of the modern self and supported by the structures of the global economy, are not yet fully overcome.

Some Lacanians have talked about the "tyranny of the all-knowing" in the discourse of the master. This is a latent danger which all master discourses need to face. [33] If the turn to the Other is to be a helpful theological move, theology needs to understand that we never have access to a pure master signifier. To keep with its own intentions, the reference to the Wholly Other needs to face its unconscious truth. It cannot shy away from the painful process of exploring what actually drives it and in which ways it is still influenced by the power structures of the modern world and thus continues to mirror the modern structures of exclusion.[34] The modern self, those in power at the present, have a way of interfering even with the purest theological intentions. In other words, we begin to suspect that the power of the modern self cannot be overcome simply by putting something else in its place. To use an example that can be easily verified by nontheologians as well, even the postmodern global market still reflects the power structures of modernity. The flow of profits shows that, despite all the gains by minorities and women, and despite much postmodern rhetoric about the disappearance of the self and the valuation of otherness and difference, middle- and upper-class white males of the First World are, by and large, still in charge.

In this discourse there seems to be a certain potential for a condition that resembles the psychotic constellation. The problem worsens the more the master signifier is made absolute. In psychosis, as Lacan has discovered, master signifiers are free-floating, cut off from their relation to the other elements of the discourse. The psychotic's words (S1) are not anchored in, or in dialogue with, any language (S2) other than the psychotic's very own. In light of the structures of exclusion, this looks like a particularly troublesome case of special-interest theology, worse than in the neuroses and narcissisms of the modern self. The words of the psychotic have primacy over any language and the communities that speak it. Lacan talks about an objectification of the psychotic self in a language without dialectic, treating its own words as the "thing in itself."[35] Psychotics, alone with their words, tend to assume that the questions of the real and of truth are already answered for them. Worst of all, they are unaware that they might have substituted their own words for the Word and confused the two.[36] From a theological perspective it is clear that this is a powerful basis for idolatry. It is like Paul says in Rom. 1:25: "They exchanged the truth for a lie and worshiped and served the creature rather than the Creator." Barth escapes the trap of the psychotic constellation insofar as he ties his strong emphasis on the master signifiers, the Word of God, to the doctrinal tradition, the words of the church. In this way the master signifiers are not completely isolated or free-floating but bound to a larger whole.

Another Turn

How does the Barthian discourse of the master help us to face the powers of exclusion manifest in the struggles and the suffering of people at the margins of the global economy? The turn to the Other, it seems, can be misused for other purposes. According to the Lacanian model, the master signifiers can come to their truth only by leaving their dominant position. In this case we enter the realm of another discourse, coming back to the "discourse of the self." It is not without irony that precisely the discourse which the discourse of the master sought so much to overcome (Barth struggled with Schleiermacher and liberal theology all his life) can help us to understand its shortcomings.

Once again, we are making use of the process of transference (see Diagram 4). Put to work by the self ($), the master signifier (S1) finally recognizes the truth that was hidden and repressed in the discourse of the master. Engaged by the self ($), the master signifier (S1) produces a specific language (S2) that delivers back to the self new insights about the master signifier. Having received this message, the self is able to mirror back to the master signifier the signifier's incompleteness, its own repressions and unconscious truth. What comes in transference back to the master signifier as its truth and secret desire is the modern self in all of its ambiguity.[37]

In other words, even the turn to the Other is still driven, if only unconsciously, by the modern self. What if the Barthian search for new theological master signifiers were simply another manifestation of the modern self's search for a safe haven? The actual master signifiers that Barth chooses do not seem to support this suspicion, but challenge the security

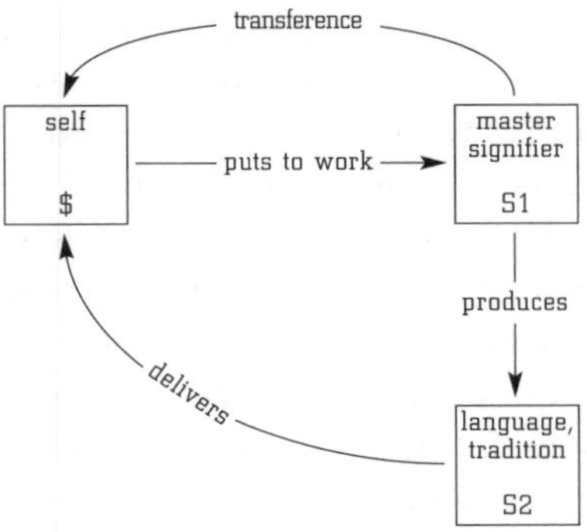

Diagram 4

of the modern self and suggest alternatives. At the same time, however, the discourse of the master is unable to deal with its unconscious as part of its own identity. There is a tendency to dismiss the unconscious, that which is repressed, "just as patriarchy dismisses the mystery of Woman as anything to be taken seriously outside a private context."[38]

In Barth's case the problem is not so much that he would give in to the modern self as such as it is a certain inability to deal with the modern self as part of the identity of his theology. To more effectively reconstruct the modern self, and the special-interest deals that have produced its power in the conquests of the modern world, theology needs to better understand its own complicity and come up with alternative images for the self. Barth is aware that he might not have been able to transcend the modern temptation completely. But he is less clear about where to look in order to provide more effective alternatives.

In order to keep up the critical momentum of theology we are now aware that we must pay closer attention to the self since, even when liberal theology is dismissed by the turn to the Other, it continues to have considerable influence on the master signifier.[39] In other words, theology, especially if it is written in a First World context, needs to understand more clearly that, despite all of its protest in the name of the divine Other, it is never completely unrelated to the power of the modern self and the structures of exclusion. If this is clear, we come to understand that any encounter with the master, the Wholly Other, no matter how powerful and inspiring it might be, must still be subject to theological analysis. Such theological analysis must include not only scripture and tradition, as Barth has argued, but a deeper look into the elements that go into the production of theological master signifiers, including the hidden challenges of the powers that be.

It does not take a theologian to see what happens when master signifier and God are equated. Nestor Braunstein, a psychoanalyst who equates the master with God, reaches the conclusion one would expect, namely, that "God is dead, that He was always dead." Lacan knew that the master is not the ultimate reality either, that, in Freudian terms, "the Master is castrated." The psychoanalyst understands that this news "can free the church, the university, and psychoanalysis of the everlasting turns of the wheel of repetition."[40] Ultimately no concept or master signifier, not even the notion of the Wholly Other, can stand in for God.

All would go wrong, however, if the theological production of master signifiers were seen as a closed circle. In the ongoing process of the discourse of the master, master signifiers need to understand their limits; since discourse cannot stop here, however, other master signifiers will be and need to be produced in the future. The discourse of the master is most interesting for theology when it maintains a certain openness. Only in this way will the Word of God continue to shine through, an encounter that goes beyond what psychoanalysts can account for. The eternal relevance of the Word of God, expressed in such biblical passages as Isa. 40:8 and 1 Pet. 1:25 which claim that "the Word of the Lord endures forever," is not static but part of a process.

The Discourse of the Tradition

Postliberal theology, rejecting modern foundationalism, turns to textual and linguistic phenomena. What happens to theological discourse when the biblical and traditional texts of the church are put in such a prominent place? The Lacanian "discourse of the university," set in relation with the other three discourses, will help to understand better both the advantages but also the limitations, blind spots, and related repressions of the theological turn to language. Rather than talk about the "discourse of the university," however, I will talk about the "discourse of the tradition." Others have also talked about this discourse as the discourse of the priest or the professor.[41] What sets the pace in the postliberal mode of theology is precisely the tradition of the church, in Lindbeck's case most importantly the Bible and the creeds as they are used by the community of believers.[42] To be a Christian here means to be "traditioned," shaped by tradition.

The discourse of the tradition is governed by systems of knowledge or belief, which receive the symbol S2. According to Lacan, both knowledge and belief are developed on the grounds of languages that a person learns to speak and that, in turn, also speak to that person. This discourse is perhaps the most typical discourse in the postmodern world where the powers of the self are called into question on various levels. In many postmodern schools of thought the modern self's loss of authority is compensated by the turn to language. In academic circles formalism, structuralism, and post-structuralism are among the better-known examples,[43] but postliberalism fits here as well.

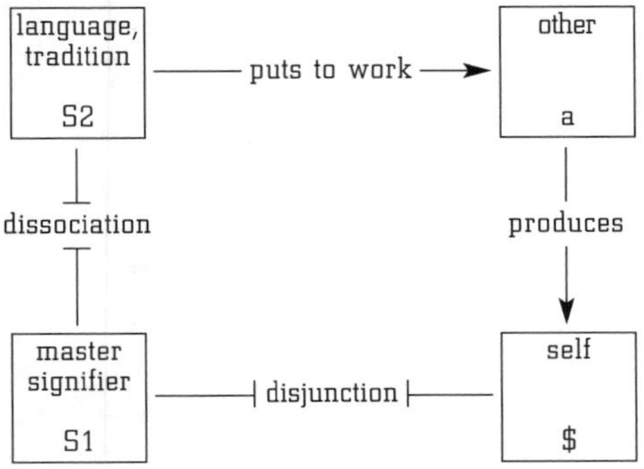

Diagram 5

In this discourse the four elements occupy the positions in Diagram 5. Here the place of authority is assumed by tradition, represented by a specific set of texts or a language and its grammatical rules (S2). These texts put to work the other (a) in a constellation which ultimately leads to the production of a new self ($). In this model the other and the self become the function of a given language. The most direct influence of the signifying chain here is on the other. This matches Lindbeck's declared goal: The biblical text is supposed to assume the world into its structures. A first step in this project is no doubt to form the other, those positions that guide our desire and ideals. The primary concern of the text is to reshape our deepest desires and experiences according to the goals of the text. The place of desire, initially an empty place, as we have seen, is to be filled out by the constructs of the text. This leads us beyond the narcissistic blindness that is characteristic of the individualistic self, unable to connect with, let alone shape, its own object of desire. In a postmodern world where there is increasing competition about who has the power to shape desire—and the capitalist market economy through the powers of advertising is the prime contender—the postliberal approach addresses an important aspect of life.

In another step the discourse of the tradition also leads to the formation of a new self. It is now clear how Lindbeck's project is diametrically opposed to the liberal theological paradigm. While in that paradigm the self sought to restructure the language of the church, here the language of the church aims at reconstructing the self. Lindbeck's model self-consciously opposes the discourse of the self, dominant in the modern world, where "selfhood is experienced as a given rather than as a gift or an achievement."[45] What the discourse of the tradition really wants is the "subject being built up as insufficiency,"[46] a self that it can teach and mold into its own image. The self shaped by tradition is what postliberal theology really is after. The goal of this model is to integrate the uninitiated (students, non-Christians, and so on) into the system, enabling them to repeat and reproduce the language and tradition of the church. The overall purpose of the discourse of the tradition, according to Lacan, is the production of culture.[47]

The discourse of the tradition has its place in every human life, perhaps most clearly visible at the beginning of the life of the individual. Lacan points out that we all begin life in the position of the other, being the object of desire, for example, of our parents.[48] In this discourse the declared goal is the formation of the other, as, for example, the education of the uneducated or the civilization of those seen as savages. Here the other is subjected to a coherent system of knowledge in order to produce a self that fits into the overall structure of the discourse of the tradition. In this process the desired result of the discourse of tradition is delivered: conformity. According to Lacan, this discourse is found in such places as education and bureaucracy, both aimed at the formation of particular types of subjects.[49] Jameson identifies this discourse with "the authority of the letter, texts, doctrine; the scholastic weighing and comparing of juridical formulas; the concern with coherency and system; and the punctilious textual distinctions between what is orthodox and what is not."[50] There is, no doubt, also a certain affinity to those voices who at present want to preserve the traditional Western canon or certain traditions of the church with as little change as possible. But the discourse of the tradition can also be driven by alternative texts that do not fit that particular canon, asserting their difference in terms of gender, class, and race.[51] The significance of the theological turn to language and the text lies in the fact that it puts to use these dynamics in the development of new theological guidelines, creating an alternative to the turn to the modern self and, whether or not postliberals are aware of it, to the Barthian turn to the Other as well.

Lacanian analysis contributes to a better understanding of the general concerns and programs of Lindbeck. What is often neglected, however, especially in postliberal positions that have more radical postmodern leanings, is that while ontological and other referents are not central here (tradition is sufficient in and of itself and does not need to seek anxiously what grounds it), there is a hidden point of reference which must not be ignored. We need to add another step to this evaluation, giving an account of the moment of truth that remains inaccessible and hidden for those within the discourse. Some of Lindbeck's interpreters have sensed this blind spot in postliberal theology. James Buckley, for example, argues that in Lindbeck, while the word is prior to the Spirit, "the rules for the *perichoresis* of Word and Spirit are unclear."[52] This is not surprising since the power of the Spirit (connected to the master signifiers [S1] and at the heart of the Barthian turn to the Other) is precisely what is repressed by the discourse of the tradition. Miroslav Volf, too, finds that Lindbeck disregards the question of the power of the Holy Spirit: "The Holy Spirit has created flesh-and-blood people connected by a semiotic system as well as by nonsemiotic relations" to Christ.[53] The problem is, as our analysis that it is simply not possible to define the relationship of word and Spirit from within the system. It is clearer now why Lindbeck has little sympathy for Barth's concern for the encounter with the Wholly Other. As we have seen, he rejects Barth's prolegomena in the first volume of *Church Dogmatics* as bad epistemology. The question of master signifiers, those powerful symbols that shape and at times disrupt the metonymic flow of language, is not even raised in the postliberal theological mode. The orderly relations of the signifying chain take over.

In this discourse the emphasis on language can become problematic. According to Lacan, there is a basic antinomy between language and the word: "As Language becomes more functional, it becomes improper for the word, and as it becomes too particular to us [i.e., as it becomes word for us], it loses its function as Language." Many years before he develops the four discourses, Lacan finds this problem where a "subject loses his meaning and direction in the objectifications of the discourse."[54] This is diametrically opposed to the domination of the master signifier discussed above. Whereas in that case the word was played off against language, here language becomes the decisive factor. In both instances the modern self takes the back seat, since "the subject is spoken rather than speaking."[55] Basic interests, habits, and attitudes of the self are located not within the self but in the structures of language. This is Lindbeck's basic point as well.

This, then, translates into a certain ability of the discourse of the tradition to resist the powers of exclusion produced by the modern self. But what if the master signifiers that unconsciously influence this discourse are also shaped by late capitalism? Lindbeck's admiration for Western civilization points to a master signifier that influences his theological discourse, sheltered deep below the surface and thus avoiding any serious theological critique. Furthermore, the discourse of the tradition might create its own structures of exclusion, which far transcend the often useful tendency of the text to establish limits and boundaries. In the case of the psychotic domination of the master signifier, discussed in the previous part, words (substituted for the word) become decisive as basic symbolic units. As a result, master signifiers create their own language. In the discourse of the tradition, on the other hand, language takes over and represses the intimacy of the word. Both the self and the other become functions of language. Yet when everything is subordinated to language and tradition, virtually no place is left from which a given language or tradition might be questioned or transformed. In this situation discipline becomes excessive. The possibility of resistance against the governing discourse, whatever it may be, is lost. Lacan calls this phenomenon "normalcy." As Ragland-Sullivan has pointed out, *normalcy* means "repressing well (as in being a 'good citizen')," but normalcy (not unlike neurosis and psychosis) can also be problematic since it "demands blind submission to the social order and the eschewal of unconscious truth."[56]

Lacan hints that "here is the most profound alienation of the subject in our scientific civilization."[57] Many other postmodernist thinkers would agree. According to Lacan, there are barely "any assignable limits to the credulity to which [the subject] must succumb in that situation."[58] This observation applies to our submission to the laws and rules of science and technology, structures that are so influential that they are often taken for granted and accepted without question. The fact that these rules operate at a subconscious level makes them all the more powerful. This observation also throws light on the theological turn to language and texts. While it is indeed possible to be shaped by traditions to such an extent that the self is transformed, how does this theological mode avoid the credulity that Lacan is talking about that seems to go far beyond the demands of Christian discipleship?

The discourse of the tradition is the very opposite of the discourse of the self that constantly asks the question of truth. This is not to say that there is no concern for truth, but for postliberals, for instance, this is simply not the main issue. Truth can primarily be dealt with in an intratextual way without having to leave the discourse of the tradition. The specific blind spots of this discourse, the inability to recognize its master signifiers, are not of major concern. This observation also throws light on those critics of postliberal theology who focus on the question of truth alone, especially in the more conservative camps. Arguably, they are more strongly caught up in the modern turn to the self and its concern for certainty and truth than they realize.

Another Turn

The discourse of the tradition helps us to resist the powers of exclusion insofar as it creates room for alternative traditions. But even the good intentions of the tradition can be misused for other purposes, serving other gods and masters without even being aware of it. As in the previous discourses, in the discourse of the tradition there is no clear understanding of what is repressed, even though this is in many ways the most powerful element. As Braunstein observes, the discourse of the tradition "exercises a subtle strategy. It is the doctoral, the doctrine's discourse. Since . . . God keeps Himself silent, the S2 takes his place and speaks from there."[59] The tradition can come to its truth once again only by leaving the position of dominance. Here we are back at the previous discourse, the discourse of the master (see Diagram 6).

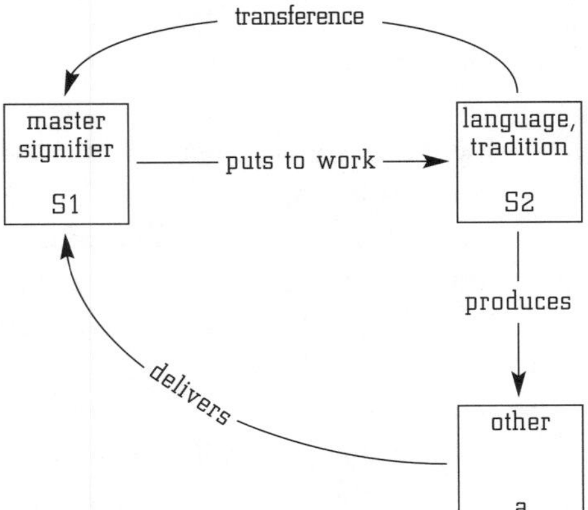

Diagram 6

Once the tradition (S2) is put to work by what it had repressed so far, its master signifiers (S1), it delivers back as its product the other (a). In this way the tradition (S2) can at last find out who its real master is and which gods it is following. The apparently self-sufficient (and self-referential, as the postliberals would add) signifying chain of the tradition can now realize whose gospel it is actually preaching, and in whose interest its work is really done. Paraphrasing Braunstein, we can say that the tradition never speaks for itself; it proclaims the news of the master signifier that spoke first, for example, in the flames of the burning bush or on the benches of the laboratory.[61] Are theologians turning to language and the text aware of what ultimately drives the languages and texts they are dealing with? To be able to resist false gods—the gods of late capitalism, for example, who exclude most of humanity—and to better worship the true God this area needs to be explored further.

The self-critical perspective that grows out of this exploration feeds into new theological guidelines which allow for a deeper appropriation of language and text and the necessary adjustments in direction. At the same time, this of course implies a certain loss of influence for the texts of the church since the discourse of the tradition is no longer the sole authority. Authority is now shared with the respective master signifiers. Yet, as we have seen in the previous chapter, those master signifiers are not absolute in themselves either; their authority is in turn shared with the discourse of the self. None of the discourses can function without the other.

Mark Bracher summarizes Lacan's point when he explains that the discourse of the tradition, "functions as an avatar of the master discourse, promulgating master signifiers hidden beneath systematic knowledge." Resisting the absolute control of the discourse of the tradition would therefore mean to "expose the master signifiers that underlie it and constitute its truth."[62] The theological turn to language and the text will have to face the question about what it is that drives its chains of signification. Unless this question is addressed, there is always a potential for false gods to have a say in how the traditions of the church are shaped. At a time when economic structures permeate more and more of our world, take over God's own place, and shape our master signifiers, we need to take more seriously than ever before the possibility that even the discourse of the tradition might, without ever being aware of it, give shelter to the gods of Mammon.

The Discourse of the Marginalized

Theologies turning to others have further broadened the horizon of theological reflection by paying attention to a factor that has not yet been considered in modern theology and has rarely surfaced in the almost two thousand years of Christianity: the reality of the repressed others. What happens to theological discourse when the position of others, the marginalized, is put in such a prominent place? The Lacanian "discourse of the analyst," set in relation with the other three discourses, will help to understand better both the advantages but also the limitations, blind spots, and related repressions of theology turning to others. Lacan's designation of this final discourse as "discourse of the analyst" is misleading, however, if it is taken to imply another elitism. In the Lacanian model the analyst is not the one who is in control and has all the answers but the one who is able to listen from the position of the repressed.[63] The analyst's task is to relate to that which is repressed and marginalized. This is why I designate this discourse the "discourse of the marginalized." Not knowing the truth in advance, all the analyst can do is be in solidarity with this position and listen. This is without a doubt the hardest discourse for both psychoanalysts and theologians who find themselves in the position of what Lacan calls "the subject supposed to know."[64]

The discourse of the marginalized is determined by what is most often forgotten in reflections on discourse, including its theological varieties, and is certainly the most elusive to grasp: the other (a). The other, or the object of desire, as I have already explained, is best understood as an element that fills a deeper lack or emptiness. This emptiness is not unrelated to the turn to the Other's insight into the fundamental lack of humanity, its inability to connect to the divine. But there is also a parallel to the openness of the human self to God promoted by the turn to the self, realizing that humanity is not complete in itself. Lacan insists, however, that humanity cannot stand to leave this place open. What is put in place of the void, according to Lacan, are products of human repression. If this is true, both the turn to the Other and the turn to the self need to connect with the repressed others.

What is repressed may differ, yet in any given society structures of repression already exist. In patriarchy, Lacan notes, women are put into this position. In capitalism it is the working classes and the poor. The challenge for us at the beginning of the new millennium is to become clearer about the mixed forms, combining gender repression with class and race repression. The repressions that produce the other point to one's hidden desires.

Lacan has given a detailed analysis as to how women are made into repressed objects of desire. In a patriarchal context women do not occupy the position of the self in charge (represented by the discourse of the self).

For this reason one cannot speak of "*the* woman." Women exist only as that which is repressed, excluded.[65] At the same time, women are constantly idealized by men and made into objects of desire.[66] In this way they are incorporated and made into functions of the powers that be. The mystification of women can only be resisted by the recognition of the constructed reality of women. This is the meaning of Lacan's often misunderstood statement that "*the* woman does not exist" which, as Jacqueline Rose has pointed out, "means, not that women do not exist, but that her status as an absolute category and guarantor of fantasy [for those in power] . . . is false."[67] This is related to what feminist theologians have gradually discovered: There is no female experience in general. Universal notions of women's experience can also be oppressive to women, especially for those at the margins.

The advantage of this position, according to Lacan, is that women, unlike men, can never be made to fit completely into the system and are thus not simply functions of the powers that be. In patriarchy only women and those who adopt their point of view are able to see beyond the limits of the status quo.[68] The turn to others is therefore not merely a turn to passive victims. Those in the position of the other, although they experience repression, also point beyond repression. The other is not only the marginalized but also the analyst, the only one who is in a position to figure out the repressed truth of the status quo. In other words, the other is also in the position of leadership and agency. Yet the other as agent is profoundly different from the modern self, just as the position of the subject in feminist theology is fundamentally different from the subject in liberal theology: the self is not the autonomous individual, in control of others, but someone aware of the web of the often oppressive relationships within which she or he lives. A definition of the self by Fulkerson works well in this context: "Our definition of subjects must begin with the historically created situations of disparity and subjugation."[69]

The discourse of the marginalized goes against the grain of the other discourses. It is the discourse of those who are nothing in themselves, those who are pushed to the underside and into positions of recipients in the dominant discourses of modernity and postmodernity (just follow the position of the other in the previous three discourses), and who point to a truth that has not yet been fully acknowledged. At a time when the structures of exclusion threaten to suffocate not only the poor but all of life and even the Christian faith, this discourse is both the most self-critical and the most constructive one. But that does not mean that this discourse supersedes the others. In Lacan's words, the discourse of the marginalized "loops the dizzying loop of the three other discourses but does not resolve it."[70] While the conflict between the different modes of theology is not resolved here, it might be opened up just enough to allow for a reorientation. In this way, that which has been left out of theological reflection helps to reactivate theology at the beginning of the new millennium.

In the discourse of the marginalized, the other (a) appears in the role of the agent (see Diagram 7). In this constellation the other (a) puts to work and engages the self ($), which in turn produces and reveals its master signifiers (S1). At this point, we come to understand better that both the master signifiers and the self are not as independent as they purport to be in their respective discourses.[71] Both are shaped in specific ways by the other, their object of their desire. Yet this can only be seen from the perspective of the other itself, particularly the people who are forced into this position, people at the margins including women, the poor, or ethnic minorities, and those who maintain solidarity with these positions, the analysts. Lacan presumed that the position of the analyst, the one who identifies with the other, could be taken up not only in relation to individuals but also in relation to social structures.[72] From this perspective it is now possible to observe both the fundamental identifications and unconscious desires of the self and its master signifiers.

In the evolving triad the analyst, who has put herself in the place of the other, can retrieve what she was actually looking for, namely, the master signifiers—the gods—which the modern self follows without knowing it. Theology turning to others is able to give a sharper, more challenging and perceptive reading of liberal theology than the other theological modes since the other is in the position of the unconscious truth in the discourse

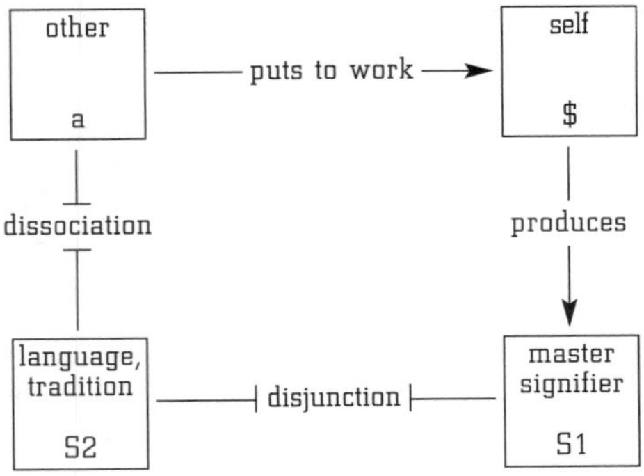

Diagram 7

of the modern self and knows things that the self prefers not to know. Yet if the self is put in a position where it has to listen to its own truth in relation to the theological turn to others, theology might finally be able to enter a new age, opening up the limits of contemporary theological reflection. Here everything starts coming together.

From the perspective of the modern self the exciting but nonetheless anxiety-provoking news is that, being confronted with what it had always repressed, it can finally get to know itself better. Theology turning to others is now in a position to challenge and transform the power and authority of the modern self. Feminist theology's concern for reshaping the self, for example, has been widely recognized yet is still too often misunderstood in terms of the liberal turn to the self.[73] This misunderstanding is mirrored by Lacan's interpreters as well. Bracher also locates feminist thought under the discourse of the self: "Feminism has led the way in freeing criticism from its enthrallment to master signifiers and systems of knowledge by introducing the personal into the public, political arena, where System dominates, and thus confronting the S1 and S2 with the $."[74] At best this describes older types of feminism. As we have seen, more recent generations of feminists are going beyond this focus on the self to a new awareness of others. Here is also the challenge for the North American reception of liberation theologies from "south of the border" which, imported into a context squarely located in the ego's era, has at times confused the discourse of the self and the discourse of the marginalized.[75] Unlike liberal theology, liberation theology is no longer preoccupied with the self.

The discourse of the marginalized helps us to see that both the self and the master signifiers are reshaped in an encounter with the repressed other. Here we can clarify some common misunderstandings of the theological turn to others. Feminist theology is not exclusively preoccupied with the formation of a new self. According to the above diagram, what the other desires is not simply the relation to the self ($) but also the work of the master signifiers (S1). In other words, what feminist theology really wants to do is not to abandon the master signifiers of Christian theology in favor of the self, as mainline theologians frequently suspect, but to reformulate them in ways that bring out their freeing and liberating potential for all. This corresponds with Chopp's identification of three leading principles in feminist theology: (1) the reinterpretation of Christian symbols and doctrines (the master signifiers, S1); (2) the development of a feminist ethic (new selves, $, communal and accountable); and (3) the reconstruction of the nature of the church (this relates to the tradition, S2).[76]

Jameson associates this discourse as "a position of articulated receptivity, of deep listening," and of "some attention beyond the self or the ego." Observing that contemporary political thought is unable to articulate this discourse, he argues that "the active and theoretical passivity, the rigorous and committed self-denial, of this final subject position, which acknowledges collective desire at the same moment that it tracks its spoors and traces, may well have lessons for cultural intellectuals as well as politicians and psychoanalysts."[77] Theologians, too, might have a lesson to learn. Nestor Braunstein points out that, unlike the other discourses, the discourse of the marginalized "does not express propositions that would have the pretension of speaking the truth." While the other discourses transmit a truth already constituted, the function of the discourse of the marginalized "is not to speak the truth, but to make the truth work and produce in the other of his discourse."[78] The goal of Lacanian analysis is not so much to speak but to listen and, in this way, to make others speak. Here a connection to Barth's concern for the divine Other can be identified, but now in inverted form: listening to the Other (the master signifier, S1) may not be possible without learning how to listen to marginalized others (the other, a).

In this model the most problematic area is the relation to the tradition (S2). No wonder liberation theologies have at times been accused of trying to do away with the tradition of the church. But we are now able to see the fundamental misunderstanding. What really drives the discourse of the marginalized is precisely a tradition (S2). In other words, while there is a real danger of overemphasizing the poor and thus distorting everything, a closer look at the discourse of the marginalized reveals that this is not inevitable.[79] Nevertheless, the specific shape of the tradition (S2) is hidden from the other (a). Just like in the three previous discourses, there is a blind spot.

At this point, however, we are in for a surprise. While the three modes of theology that we have discussed earlier have not been able to deal with their blind spots, theology turning to others seems to be doing a better job. This mode of theology appears to be more capable than other theologies of reading between the lines and envisioning what is repressed. Fulkerson's work is a case in point. She is aware, for instance, that "discursive processes . . . construct subject positions."[80] In her work there is a good deal of reflection on the relation of the tradition and marginalized people. In this sense feminist theology proves to be in touch with its truth in a way the other theologies are not. Most importantly, however, Fulkerson pays attention to conflictive discourses. In this way she helps us to understand better the nature of tradition. Tradition is not as clear-cut and monolithic as some of the postliberals have led us to believe. In the life of people at the margins various traditions are intersecting. People are not simply the products of a single tradition. This insight helps to acknowledge the existence of differences among the marginalized as well: no group is the product of an exactly similar constellation of discourses.[81] This also invites more research into the diverse functions of the tradition in theology.

The three discourses introduced above manifest conditions such as neurosis, psychosis, and normalcy that Lacan has analyzed early on. There is a fourth distortion, related to the discourse of the marginalized. Once again, the problem has to do with an overemphasis on the element that determines the discourse. The problem occurs where the repressed others, such as women in patriarchal societies, are made absolute and thus turned into idols. This happens in various psychoanalytic practices, vigorously opposed by Lacan, that aim at curing the analysand by trying to settle his or her desire. Rather than keep the place of the other, the object of desire open, and flexible as a place where listening and self-reflection become possible, this place is defined (for example, as biological sexual desire for women or men), fixed, and thus supposedly overcome. In this case, rather than listen to the analysand's desire, the analyst "plays God," solving the unsolvable and pretending to have the one right answer. There is a certain parallel to psychosis, where the object of desire is identified with a thing, but psychotics are completely caught up in this madness. Analysts, on the other hand, impose their knowledge from outside the system.

Here is a potential danger of theology turning to others as well. A new authoritarianism could emerge where the theologian who identifies with the marginalized plays God, putting certain things such as "*the* poor" or "*the* woman" into an absolute place of authority. This move puts the theologian, as the one who identifies the object of desire, in a position of absolute power. In this case theology turning to others would have no need for self-critical reflection since, knowing the facts, it is exempt from the interrelation of the elements of discourse, knowing all the answers without really having to listen to the details. In this scenario desire is not examined as to the specific repressions that have produced it, and then perhaps transformed, but "cured." As a result, the marginalized are romanticized and presented as autonomous selves just like the theologian. Lacan notes the problem: in this constellation the subject is expected to conform to the analyst's ego,[82] mirroring once again the already discussed problems of the discourse of the self.

At the same time, however, this discourse offers an "effective means of countering the psychological and social tyranny exercised through language."[83] This is not to say that here all discursive processes end. Producing new and transformed master signifiers, a new round of discourses takes off. This time, Lacan hopes, "the master signifier will perhaps be a little less stupid," but also a little less powerful.[84] The real revolutionaries, according to Lacan, are therefore not anarchists but analysts.[85]

In sum, the discourse of the marginalized resists the powers that be. Unlike the turns to the self and the text, the turn to others does not first promote stability; rather, it promotes the transformation of static systems in light of their unconscious repressions, raising the question of who our God really is. In the words of the Lacanian analyst Bracher, "What must be done, essentially, is to reveal to the subjects of a society that what they are asking for (and perhaps they think they are getting) in their values, ideals, conscious desires, and identifications is not the only expression or even the most truthful embodiment of what they really want."[86]

In the current crisis of theology the theological turn to others is able to respond more constructively to the powers of the modern self and the contemporary crisis of theology than the other turns. Moreover, the theological turn to others combines and further defines what Rita Nakashima Brock describes as two of the formative stages of feminist thought, "Women as Victims" and "Women-Centered,"[87] and reminds us that both belong together: The position of the repressed object of desire shows how women are not only victims but also agents of change and transformation. Identifying with those who are excluded points us to new sources of energy that are overlooked in the other discourses, thus reconstructing theology as a whole.

Another Turn

How does the discourse of the marginalized help us to face the powers of exclusion? Despite a deep sense of oppression and injustice, marginalized people in the position of the other have trouble understanding what really moves them. To come to the truth we need to advance the elements of this discourse one more turn. Here we are back at the discourse of the tradition. This step reminds us that neither the marginalized nor the analysts must occupy the place of God.[88] While they can help the modern self understand its hidden truth, they are still separated from their own truth (see Diagram 8).[89]

When the other is put to work by the tradition, the reaction is not to usurp all attention but to open up a new encounter with the self. The

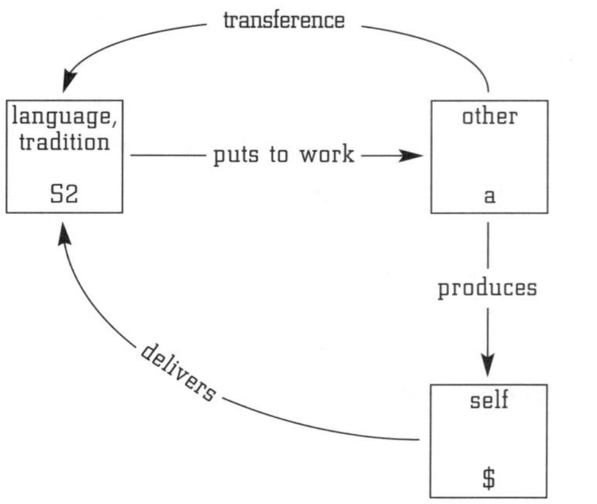

Diagram 8

analyst in the position of the other gains knowledge only at the very end of the process, through transference. There is no a priori way of knowing truth in and of itself. Analysts are not all-powerful and omniscient, a fantasy imposed on them that they sometimes find hard to resist; analysts depend on being put to work by various stories and traditions. Knowledge comes only through listening: "The analyst takes the place of the other, of the ignorance, to whom the discourse of the [tradition] is addressed."[90]

The discourse of the marginalized invites us to raise the question of the function of the tradition in new ways. It may come as a surprise that it is the discourse of the tradition, the concern for the texts and language of the church, which helps to uncover the unconscious truth of the discourse of the marginalized. Yet feminist theology has been well aware of this fact, which has two sides: Women need to understand, first of all, what drives them unconsciously. This raises the question, What narratives have been most detrimental for them and have contributed to misshaping them? Being marginalized is not a virtue, and the idealization of people at the margins is problematic, especially if one takes a look at who might be interested in that.[91] Yet, secondly, women have also found support from certain aspects of the tradition. As we have seen, after liberal theology's demise of the text, women have found new ways of taking the biblical texts seriously. Increasingly they also take each other's stories seriously. In Fulkerson's words, "For those of us in different subject positions, dispositions to receive from new 'masters' must be formed."[92] Consequently, at the point where the other listens to the tradition, there needs to be an evaluation. Where are the blind spots of the discourse of the marginalized? What elements unconsciously shape the other? What elements are liberating in that they help to keep this position as open and flexible as possible?

Feminists know what postliberals and their rather one-dimensional view of the tradition overlook: In Fulkerson's words, "narratives are always marked by silences, intertwined with recognized or obscured narratives of the social order." She wonders whether, "given the gaps and multiplicity of discourses," there can be a story in liberation theology. She answers her own question in the affirmative, adding, however, that it will be a "strange story."[93] It is a story—or tradition—that can never be fixed, that must always be newly told, not just re-told, taking into account its gaps and repressions.

But this does not mean that the turn to others would put tradition at the mercy of the marginalized. Bracher does not quite get it right when he argues that in the discourse of the marginalized the subject can finally "produce its own new master signifiers."[94] We must not forget that the marginalized are not autonomous, the position in which the modern self is used to see itself, but are always already shaped by specific traditions. The new signifiers that are produced in the discourse of the marginalized are therefore part of a larger whole, thus reconstructing the nature of the church in a response to those traditions. Theology needs to make sure that this response is critical and accountable.[95]

Lacan puts it this way: "When offering itself to teaching, analytic discourse puts the analyst in the position of an analysand, that is, in the position of not producing anything masterable, except as symptom."[96] In this model the marginalized not only are the objects of the powers that be, but assume a new kind of active role that differs from the controlling actions of the self, thus opening the way for a reconstruction of the all-pervasive powers of exclusion.

Conclusion

As Jameson has pointed out, it is not possible to avoid foregrounding and privileging one of the elements of the four discourses to the others in any given situation.[97] But none of the elements must become the norm all by itself—an important clue for theological thinking. In addition, the four positions are not fixed once and for all. Lacan himself kept playing with them, making multiple associations. He developed this model less as something to be understood than as something to be used.[98] In Lacan's own words: "Do not expect anything more subversive in my discourse than not to have the solution."[99]

In the model of the four discourses there is no state of absolute truth or of absolute balance. The challenge is to maintain a constant act of balancing and relating the different discourses. We need to pay more attention to what the discourses can learn from each other: What are the master signifiers that are given to us today? What are the traditions? Where do we need to listen most passionately? And what selves do we want to become? Separating any one of the discourses and treating it as the only one has disastrous consequences; contemporary theology serves as a model for this warning. Each discourse has its own strengths and advantages that need to be taken into consideration, helping to alleviate the blind spots of the other discourses. Nevertheless, in the ego's era some things come more naturally than others. We need to learn to inhabit especially those discourses that are most neglected.

Where all four discourses come together in light of what is repressed, theological reflection becomes a form of listening, of reading between the lines, and of receptivity to that which usually goes unnoticed—a novel approach to the field of systematic theology. Here new forms of listening emerge that promote not only listening to others but also listening to the texts of the church, including the Bible, and listening to God as Other. This approach bears promise for leading us on a more efficient path of overcoming the contemporary theological crisis, since the mainline approaches often have little effect, based alternately on what Bracher describes as "merely asserting a new system of knowledge and belief" (the discourse of the tradition), or "insisting on new ideals or values" (the discourse of the master), or "lamenting or protesting the current state of affairs" (the discourse of the self).[100] Theology turning to others—still the most neglected and misunderstood theological discourse—is able to explore parts of reality not accessible to the other theological modes. It is only from this perspective that the utter seriousness of our situation becomes visible. In the process new visions of God (new turns to the Other, S1), new dogmatics (new turns to language and tradition, S2), and new selves (new turns to the self, $) emerge.

Ultimately being in solidarity with others can help theologians gain a new sense of the diversity and complexity of human life in relation to a new sense of the diversity and complexity of God's own work. The other in general does not exist. While we have been making progress (as the feminist-womanist encounters show, for example), there is still a lot to do. Closer listening to the traditions and texts of the church from the perspective of the marginalized in light of God's own work will be the major task ahead for theological reflection. This gives new meaning to

David Tracy's point that the voice of postmodernity is the voice of the other, a claim which only makes sense as a description of the work that is before us.[101]

The debate that has occupied modern theology for centuries of where to start the theological enterprise once and for all, acting as if we had to jump on the bandwagon of either of the four discourses, is over. Having gone through the four discourses, the theological circle starts anew, hopefully, however, on a different level since the knowledge gained in analysis differs from the knowledge of the starting point. This is related to the self-critical potential of Freudian and Lacanian thought which contains the power to return back upon itself and question already settled knowledge and truth.

6

Opening the Floodgates: A New Paradigm

Theological developments are often decided in response to intellectual trends and the concerns of those who are in charge. But in light of the most fatal crises of the present, reaching from the suffering of large parts of humanity all the way to environmental issues, what is left of theology in the tension between God and the excluded? The crisis that only a few decades ago erupted into the Holocaust taught us that "no statement, theological or otherwise, should be made that would not be credible in the presence of burning children."[1] Unfortunately, we often act as if such lessons would apply only to select groups of people or specific periods in history. But what happens to theology if those in charge realize that their concerns are tied up with the concerns of those who are excluded, some of them kept in place on the underside by glass ceilings, some of them in dismal poverty, and over 30,000 children still dying every day from hunger and preventable diseases?

For theology in the twenty-first century, a lot more is at stake than the modern theological quests for credibility and respectability. We need to understand how we might be part of the problem and we must become aware of our potential complicities. Is theology, without being aware of it and even though it means well, helping to perpetuate the structures create the crises of the present?

In this chapter I take up the basic structure of chapters 1–4 and complete the development of the constructive argument of the book. Working out the foundations for a new theological paradigm, my argument picks up the basic interconnectedness of the four modes and moves on to develop theological guidelines that provide resistance and alternatives for a more inclusive future. Here emerge several crucial impulses for a new constructive theological proposal. Theology is reconfigured in light of those who are crushed by the global market and a postmodern world in which difference and the loss of foundations are not primarily celebrated ideas but manifest in structures of exclusion and everyday marginalization, suffering, and oppression. The new paradigm, which reconstructs the main concerns of all four modes, will have to be developed in relation to the call of the (divine) Other who challenges structures of exclusion and whose concern for the margins and the (human) others in all shapes and colors, who is manifest in a good number of (often repressed) texts of both the Old and the New Testament, cannot be taken lightly. This will be the ultimate challenge for not only modern theology and the self but postmodern forms of theology as well, having to rethink once more the character of potential interfaces between humanity and God. As the analysis of the previous chapter has shown, we can no longer assume that one mode will have all the answers or that it will be able to deal with its own blind spots. A contemporary approach to theological reflection that is truly constructive will therefore have to develop the habit of listening in new ways.

No doubt one of the greatest weaknesses of Christian theology at present is its inability to recognize the complementary character of the various modes. But attempts that simply try to add up the different approaches or establish a middle road will not do. The relationships of different theologies need to be seen in greater relief, including a whole new set of insights into how different modes of theology reconstruct each other in light of the challenges of the present. In the search for connections one of the most difficult things to acknowledge is that other modes of theological reflection may hold the key to understanding the truth about one's own mode. We can no longer afford to work in isolation.

In the process it will become clear in which ways those different modes might work together in reshaping theology and resisting the powers of exclusion, serving the interest not only of one group of people or another but of all people. Encountering the four modes of theology in the midst of the new global pressures, the question for theology is this: How can these approaches help to overcome both the notorious exclusion of others that has become so characteristic of contemporary life and the related but even less noticed displacement of the divine Other so that we can follow once again the movement of the Spirit?

Self-Critique: Reconstructing the Critical Task

How does theology keep itself honest? Each of the four theological modes has given its own answer to this question. Taken together, the various elements create the more comprehensive perspective that I develop here. But nothing would be gained without a deeper understanding of the challenge. We need to pay closer attention to those factors that shape the production of theology unconsciously, including the social, political, and economic pressures and conflicts that have not yet been accounted for in mainline theological discourse. In the process theology realizes that it is indeed a matter of life and death.[2]

One of the major lessons of the newly developing sense for the deeper challenges of our time is that ideological factors that distort theological reflection are more than the justification of positions already taken. Ideology has to do with the justification of positions of which one is not even aware. The Lacanian paradigm helps us to uncover the blind spots of each of the modes.

Theology is commonly defined as "the critical reflection on the witness of the church." This definition is all too easily appropriated by each of the theological modes. Theology turning to the self offers critical theological guidelines shaped by the idiosyncrasies of the self; theology turning to the Other develops a theological critique in terms of a specific perception of God; theology turning to the text allows certain texts of the church to critique the church's witness; and theology turning to others finally elevates the position of the marginalized as critical principle. But this move fails to take into account the blind spots of each of the turns. We need a new approach. What if theology is understood as the *self*-critical reflection on the witness of the church, a form of critique that includes a retroactive moment? This definition creates room for an awareness of the respective blind spots, cover-ups, and repressions of each of the modes without giving up the critical task of theology.

The theological turn to the self is arguably still the most influential but, in many ways, also the least self-critical mode of the four. This turn can easily be pulled into the powers that be since the critical stance of modern theology does not extend to the position of the self. In this situation "contextual" theology becomes problematic since the self is unable to transcend its own context that by default becomes normative.[3] Narcissism is one of the biggest challenges for those theologians and churches that begin by focusing on themselves and their own needs. In this context concerns for other people, the divine Other, and even the texts of the church all become functions of the position of the self. The self determines its favorite texts, promotes its own images of the divine, and gets a boost out of helping others. These narcissistic tendencies cannot be overcome in a moralistic way by simply condemning the problem and implying that we could be different if we only tried.

In the global economy, driven by the interests of the middle and upper classes, theology turning to the self, even where it tries to make a difference and to help those who are left out, is easily assimilated. Liberal theology, even though promoting openness and more democratic participation, can be a hideout for the structures of exclusion since others never become fully part of liberal theological reflection. The modern middle-class self, however well meaning it may be, remains firmly in control.

In this context the self can assume a more productive theological position only if it begins to relate to that which is repressed in modern theology: the position of the marginalized others. Understanding that people at the margins are able to reflect the truth about ourselves, revealing who put them in their place to begin with, becomes a question of theological significance. Respect for the repressed others opens up new respect for other elements of theological reflection as well. In other words, without a self-critical encounter with its repressed truth, the self's relation to the texts of the church and even to God is also distorted. A new awareness of the self, in turn, can throw new light on the turn to the Other (a constellation where, as Lacan has taught us, the self takes up the position of the repressed truth).

Step one of self-critical theological reflection at a time when the modern entrepreneurial self is still in control, not only of economic but also of theological relations, is therefore to develop an understanding of the web of relationships in which we find ourselves by opening up to others. This may well be the hardest step for contemporary theology, especially for those of us who are closer to the top of the food chain, since it means giving up control and facing our tendency to use others to support our own position. But only when this happens can we realize that we are not autonomous and that even our innermost experiences, feelings, and intuitions are shaped in relationship with other people, our languages and favorite texts, and God, in ways that we would never otherwise recognize.

The turn to the Other, although propagating a more radical theological critique of the status quo, can also be incorporated into the powers that be. Here the problem is not outright narcissism but a form of escapism that leaves the narcissistic structures of the modern world basically untouched. The focus on God's majesty and power has at times led theology to neglect a self-critical evaluation of its own unconscious relations to worldly authorities and powers. Do not many of our Sunday morning worship services get stuck precisely at this point? But even where the opposition of God's power and human powers has been more clearly addressed, as in the Confessing Church during the Third Reich, a certain blindness for those at the very margins of the system remains.

The turn to the Other has been designed to lead theology back to its roots, creating space for new awareness of God's work. In this way it displays strong iconoclastic tendencies: uncritically accepted images of God must go. Here is a parallel between Barth and feminist theology.[4] While this move is absolutely critical, the structures of exclusion are perpetuated in ways that may be even more dangerous than the turn to the self, if the turn to the Other fails to take note of its own blind spots. The interests of the modern self, of those in charge of political and economic structures, are now at work, hidden from view below the surface in a sheltered place but no less powerful. Reminders of God's majesty that do not challenge the majesty of those who tend to put themselves in God's place by stepping up the pace of exclusion in our market economies exemplify the problem.

The turn to the Other can become productive theologically only if it understands the ways in which it is still influenced by the powers of the modern self. Being aware of who benefits from theological turns to the Other becomes another question of theological importance. Do those benefit who are the recipients of God's promises, including the strangers, the widows, and the orphans?[5] An understanding of these dynamics then leads to more faithful living in and with the texts of the church[6] and, equally important, to new awareness of the position of the marginalized.

Step two of self-critical theological reflection is therefore an understanding of who benefits from our theological turns to the Other in global capitalism. Since the economic powers that be crave theological justification, especially in the North American context, any turn to the Other needs to seriously consider what determines our images of God below the surface.[7] Only if this is clear will the turn to the Other make a difference and be able to initiate resistance to the idiosyncrasy and egocentricity of our First World market societies.

The turn to language and the text, offering another useful critique of theology in the modern world, is often pulled into the powers that be when it seeks out those texts of the church that are most convincing and powerful at the moment, especially if there is little awareness of the hidden motives that authorize those texts and their interpretation. The dominant discourses of Western civilization, for example, while frequently promoting Christian themes, are not automatically sound at the theological level. The Spaniards' attempt to serve God in the missionary conquest of Latin American in the sixteenth century is an obvious example, but even contemporary discourses that promote now-popular themes such as "compassionate conservatism" or a communitarian ethic cannot pass without theological scrutiny. Is not a communitarian logic easily appropriated to encourage middle-class efforts to form gated communities? And what is compassionate about a conservatism that proposes that churches and other charitable institutions tend to the victims of an economy that is left unregulated?

In this situation theology turning to language and the text, even though it intends to reshape the still powerful modern turn to the self, needs to learn more about the hidden elements (specific images of God, for example, or other master signifiers, as Lacan's analysis has shown) that govern particular appropriations of the language and texts of the church. Often the promoters of this approach assume that they are able to provide alternative community structures. But what if those alternatives are sucked into the powers that be without realizing it? The crucial question is, Which gods are those communities serving? Even the well-intentioned turn to the orthodox traditions of the church can, without being aware of it, be assimilated by the dominant gods. At a time when even economists admit that the market has become god we need to be clearer about who our gods are than ever before.

The language and the texts of the church can assume more productive theological positions only in conjunction with an exploration of what ultimately motivates and drives them. Clearly this is an ongoing concern. No text is ever secure enough that this question would not have to be raised. The problem with theology turning to language and the text is that it, like the liberals, does not give much room to the thought that Christianity itself might have gone awry. But only if this possibility is faced can theology begin to shape the world, the self, and others in more constructive and truly revolutionary ways.[8]

Here Hal Foster's distinction between a "postmodernism of reaction" and a "postmodernism of resistance"[9] is instructive. The former critiques modernism merely to return to "the verities of tradition (in art, family, religion)" while the latter counters not only modernism but also a self-congratulatory postmodernism. Barth in his own way says as much when he reminds us that not only the theologian but also the biblical witness itself has to come to terms with a fundamental lack: "Why and in what respect does the biblical witness have authority? Because and in the fact that he claims no authority for himself, that his witness amounts to letting that other itself be its own authority."[10] A sense of God's Otherness helps to double check the ideological powers of the text.

Step three of self-critical theological reflection is therefore an analysis of which gods our uses and interpretations of the language and the texts of the church are ultimately serving—an ongoing challenge. Life in the texts of the church must not become a fool's paradise, a community gated by linguistic means for those who can afford it. Only if this is clear will we be able to move further into the world of the text and also encounter those texts and traditions of the church that have been covered up.

The turn to others, finally, offers the most radical critique of contemporary theology in the ego's era—a time when the liberal theological emphasis on the modern self still permeates the field and, on an unconscious level, even the work of its critics. This mode of theological reflection offers a crucial impulse for a new constructive theological proposal in that it helps to expand the questions raised by the crisis of theology in a context in transition from modernity to postmodernity. Theology will have to change in response to the challenges of a postmodern world in which difference and the loss of foundations are not only a set of ideas (celebrated by some and rejected by others) but manifest in everyday marginalization, suffering, and oppression.

But even this turn can be undermined where it mutates into special-interest deals. Closely related to this problem are the romanticization and idealization of marginalized groups, where each group closes in on itself and pursues its own business. The social and intellectual fragmentations that result from such a misunderstanding of the turn to others are widely realized and denounced.[11]

The main danger in our current situation, however, is not necessarily fragmentation itself but the fact that in this fragmentation the turn to others is pulled into the dynamics of the turn to the self. Narcissistic tendencies among the marginalized would be only slightly noticed and would have little appeal if they were not riding the wave of the narcissism of the dominant group. Feminist theology, for example, has had to deal with this problem when women who were not part of the white, academic middle class started to raise questions about who was really in charge in the early feminist turn to women. Here the turn to others was in danger of being taken over by the powers that be.

The position of others can become productive theologically only if we gather more insights into what is at work below the surface—in this case, as Lacan has observed, the various languages and texts that shape the others and remind them of their limits. Theological encounters with others also need to be aware that the other is not the "thing in itself." If this is clear, theology turning to others provides a useful critique of the powers that be, beginning with the position of the self, occupied by those whose interests drive the current agenda of the global economy. In this way the turn to others leads us back to the beginning, throwing more light on the turn to the self since it occupies the position of repressed truth in the turn to the self. Here theology can find a new handle on how to resist the reach of the powers of exclusion and how to promote new encounters with the divine Other, with the language and the texts of the church, and especially with those who have been pushed to the margins.[12]

The fourth step of self-critical theological reflection is therefore to become aware of the existence of others. In this context we then need to find out both who put the others in place (the powers of the modern self, in the ego's era) and what shapes them and keeps them there (specific relations to repressed textual realities as, for example, the marginalized texts of the church). This is the major challenge for mainline theology, but the various liberation theologies need to continue to work on these issues as well. Even theologies written from the perspective of the marginalized have to be reminded that, as Gutiérrez puts it, the poor also need to make an option for the poor.[13] Many, and this is especially true in the North American context where the organizations of the lower classes are weak, make an option for the rich.

All four steps work together in keeping theology honest. To uncover the truth that became inaccessible when any of these discourses was made absolute, the four discourses must be in constant interrelation with one another. In this context the actual interrelation and "complicity" of theological approaches will need to be analyzed. It is of no use, for example, to continue playing off against each other Schleiermacher and Barth, or liberal and postliberal theology, with all the obvious relations of such debates to the two camps of the culture wars that are still raging in both church and society. Constructive theology in the present cannot be done without being in dialogue with multiple approaches and abandoning the two-dimensional worlds of the status quo. In this effort closer encounters with marginalized others shatter our closed worlds and remind us of the reality of difference. Encountering those outside of our mainline theological worlds enables us to realize that we must learn how to deal not only with multiple perspectives but also with conflicts and exclusion. Constructive theology, while searching for new relations and connections, cannot pretend to produce easy syntheses.[14]

Having reviewed the distortions produced by the blind spots and unconscious desires of the various approaches, it is now clearer why the standard definition of theology as critical examination of the witness of the church will not do. Talking instead about self-critique implies a radical reconstruction of the theological task. What keeps theology going is neither the evolution of the self's religious genius nor the steady intratextual flow of texts. Theology takes shape between God and the excluded, in the cracks and the fissures, where the tensions and repressions of the life of the church are addressed and reconstructed, thus opening up a new sense for God's own work. Neither a method of correlation grounded in a basic harmony between God and humanity nor its opposite, the radical separation of God and humanity, can produce this.

In the effort to free theology from the distortions that are produced at various levels, we must learn how to listen in new ways. Karl Barth has taught us that theology as self-critical reflection is the attempt to identify the ideological distortions of the Christian message and, in this way, to open up to what God is doing. From a different angle Fulkerson describes the challenge as "being able to hear from rather than explain the Other."[15] The ultimate question to be put to the four modes of theological reflection is this: In which of these modes can God break through and challenge us, from our secret objects of desire all the way to the most vicious structures of exclusion that we just as unconsciously perpetuate?

Opening Up to the Spirit: Authority

Having clarified the critical task of theological reflection, we can now take a closer look at what authorizes the pursuit of theology. What compels us to engage in theological work? Keeping in mind the often overlooked fact that people will not do theology unless they have to, we need to take a closer look at what moves theology at the beginning of the twenty-first century.

No doubt all theologians would agree that ultimately it is Godself who authorizes theology. But how does this happen? How is God's authority manifested? What are the most important means of communication? Here lies the other important contribution of Lacan's model of the four discourses that goes beyond the analysis of blind spots, providing a framework for understanding how certain discourses move people. While this model helps us to listen in new ways, there is no need to pretend that it could explain the structures of theological authority in one way or another (a temptation for Lacanians and theologians alike).

Taking up the conclusion of the previous part, the theological question that imposes itself is this: How can new openness to both God and neighbor emerge, enabling theology to follow the movement of the Spirit that appears to be silenced where any of the elements—be it the modern concern for self, the postmodern concern for linguistic structures, or the concerns for the divine and human others—rule supreme? In which ways does this happen? In the following I will seek to integrate the contributions of the various theological modes to this question, while trying to respect and preserve their differences.

The modern entrepreneurial self, having passed through self-critical reflection, is finally in a position to understand that it is not in control. Realizing its relation to marginalized others, the self has to deal with the fact that it is always part of a wider web of relationships that transcend the familiar circles and gated communities in which it tends to move. In this context the fundamental concerns of the turn to the authority of the self in modern theology become important once again—theology turned to the self not to usurp God's place but because it became clear that it is impossible to talk about God in Godself. We can only talk and think about God in relation to us.

At this point, the self becomes open to listening in new ways. While there is no longer a guarantee that the self's intuitions and feelings always connect to God, in learning to respect people who are different and resisting the structures of exclusion, new openness and new respect for God's Otherness can develop. While the self in control is hardly in a position where it can notice a God who is different and radically challenging, the new self—self-critical and open—may be in for surprising encounters with God where it would least expect them. Giving up claims of identity between God and the modern self and the control over the divine that goes with them, we may be able to listen to God in new ways. We do not need to produce these encounters with God. God is at work all the time. But we need to become open.

The deepest theological problem of our time is closely linked with the tendency of the selves in control to accommodate, and to perpetuate, the structures of exclusion. The common assumption that God is always on our side shows the deep influence of a misshaped turn to the self, unable to recognize and respect the social and theological location of others. Shutting out others presents problems for our relation with the divine Other as well. Trying to reshape others in our own image does not provide a helpful ground for dealing with God, and the modern tendency to control others—often for well-meaning reasons—shows our inability to listen to anybody who is different. Without a shift in our relationship to others, a new relationship with the Other may not be possible, a matter that has far-reaching consequences, for example, for how we conceive of spiritual formation.[16]

Turning to the authority of the self in a self-critical mode provides new insights into the ways we shape our images of the divine Other and into the formation of the traditions of the church, and creates openings in which those images and traditions can be reshaped. All of our images and texts are shaped by human beings and thus are in need of transformation. None of them has ever fallen straight from heaven.

Turning to the authority of the Other is a vital theological move. Only through fresh encounters with the Other can theology break out of the limits of the status quo and, in turn, contribute to the transformation of both church and world. Yet this turn to the Other can be truly effective only if it has passed through theological critique. Theology turning to the Other needs to realize that its vision can easily be distorted. Unless there is a basic level of self-critical investigation into one's blind spots, almost anything might be interpreted as an encounter with the divine Other. Without taking into account the ways in which the powers that be influence our conception of God, theology tends to fool itself. No wonder the turn to the Other is easily sucked into the structures of exclusion.

Self-critical awareness is therefore not a restrictive move but the first step in opening up to God's power. In the process it becomes clearer that God is often at work where we least expect it. We encounter God's work—as the biblical witnesses already knew—primarily at the points where God descends into the "utter depths" of life, where people need help the most and are most oppressed and where Godself resists the powers of exclusion.[17] Once the turn to the Other is freed from the domesticating efforts of those in control, rejecting the constant temptation to be in sync with the powerful, something new can take shape. In other words, developing resistance to the powers of exclusion becomes a move of theological import: the turn to the Other can easily fail without it. The Other, as theologians such as Luther and Barth knew to a certain extent but many Lutherans and Barthians overlooked, can never be claimed as warrant for the status quo. The turn to the Other is always surprising, revolutionary, and radically reshaping the way things are. In the process the self-critical turn to the authority of the Other creates new awareness for the way our ecclesial traditions and our most secret objects of desire are shaped and, equally important, provides direction as to how they need to be reshaped.

The turn to the texts of the church invites us to take the authority of the church's traditions and the Bible more seriously. Yet neither the traditional texts of the church nor the Bible itself provide a divine deposit that can be owned as a commodity. The apostle Paul puts it this way: "But we have this treasure in clay jars, so that it may be made clear that this extraordinary power belongs to God and does not come from us" (2 Cor. 4:7). Only if it is clear that there is no room for textual triumphalism do ideas such as the primacy of the Bible, which many Protestant traditions claim (and for which my model leaves plenty of room), make sense.

The texts of the church are not divine and cannot stand in for God, or else they become idols. While it may seem paradoxical at first sight, the texts of the church can be taken more seriously if they do not have to fill in for God. If the texts are not God, there is no need to cover up their obvious limitations and tensions. In fact, we are now in a position to realize that the texts themselves are not static but grow out of a struggle to serve the true God, a concern that led to the canonization of the biblical writings in the fourth century.

The biggest problem with the turn to the text is the temptation to use these texts as "proof texts." Yet reference to the texts of the church is not the end of theological reflection but its beginning. Theology that takes the texts of the church seriously needs to commit a thorough investigation of which gods are being served by a particular use of the texts. Which readings are in the service of the God of Israel and the God of Jesus Christ? This process of raising questions encourages a new listening that is better able to appreciate the vitality and authority of the texts of the church—their power to shape the Christian life and the Christian faith and, through it, also the world.

Even our interpretations of the most sacred texts of the church are never unaffected by the powers that be and their exclusionary tendencies. From slavery to Manifest Destiny and the global economy, everything in North American history has been justified in the name of the texts of the church at one time or another. Yet the awareness of those dynamics does not need to result in an abandonment of the texts: it can help us to become newly aware of their liberating powers in the midst of situations of oppression. In the process suppressed texts of the church's tradition emerge out of the cracks and fissures of dominant discourses and may assume new life and importance, as events such as the Protestant Reformation of the sixteenth century or the more recent rediscovery of the biblical concern for the poor and marginalized in the theologies of liberation show.

The turn to the authority of language and the text, when pursued in this spirit, allows for much-needed insights into the formation of our secret objects of desire and into the formation of the self. Selves and desires can be reshaped, of course, only if the texts are able to speak in ways that provide alternatives to the value structures of market capitalism and the resulting structures of exclusion.

Finally, an encounter with people at the margins that does not romanticize them and force them into the positions of authority and control occupied by the self in liberal theology can teach us a lesson that has eluded theology so far. To deal with the authority of the self, the Other, and the texts of the church more constructively, we need a new position of receptivity.

Without being forced to give up control in the confrontation with people at the margins, the self will always end up worshiping projections of its own power, a problem that the early critics of liberal theology have already realized.[18] Without developing respect for human others, talk about the divine Other easily misses the mark: What sense does it make to claim respect for the divine Other if we are unable to respect our neighbors? Likewise, without gathering a broader understanding of the texts of the church that includes the repressed texts and the texts of those who are repressed, the theological turn to the text easily ends up perpetuating the status quo.

In the ego's era, where the control mode of the turn to the self also tends to shape the other modes of theology, the turn to others broadens our theological horizons, bundling together the various turns and opening them up in constructive ways. New images of God and alternative approaches to the text are set free that have the potential to reshape the ways we turn to others.[19]

The new receptivity that develops here is stifled when the structures of exclusion rule supreme. Even the unconscious exclusion of other people in well-meaning liberal theologies challenges theological receptivity, as I have shown. My accounts of the failure of theology, however, need not lead to despair. Just the opposite: at the point where structures of exclusion and oppression are uncovered and analyzed, room is created for new encounters with the Other. In traditional theological terms, where sin is identified and confessed, grace intensifies. The ideals of the turn to the Other cannot be accomplished without new awareness of others; that is, no Other without others.

Here the deeper challenge of theology turning to others becomes clear. Merely turning to one excluded group or another, as if we could choose just one preferred field of oppression, is not possible. The turn to others includes all who are affected by exclusive structures along the fault lines of race, class, and gender. Feminist theology has begun to understand the problem. Where the turn to others returns to the identity politics of the self, celebrating the romanticized qualities of specific marginalized groups and their identity with the divine and thus joining the rules of the mainstream theological market, we are in trouble.

The turn to the authority of others, finally, helps us to understand better how both our selves and our images of God are shaped and, more importantly, reshaped. In giving up control in the encounter with repressed others, certain images of God that reflect our own misuses of power break down. The same is true for our images of the self. In the encounter with others the new self becomes the open self, and at this point the process starts all over again.

In these four steps theology as a whole is redefined in new forms of listening that include new receptivity to the texts of the church, new openness to others, as well as new forms of awareness of the self and Other. The pattern that develops here can also be expressed in the interrelation of four elements that represent the most commonly debated types of theological authority: Bible, tradition, experience, and reason.[20]

The turn to the self relates to the notion of experience. While postmodern thinkers have reminded us that the self's experience is not in control (Lacan talks about the self as split), experience in our consumer society is still mainly geared to feeling good about oneself, thus reaffirming the position of the self. Here God is easily identified with what makes us feel good. Yet the experience of the new self is different. Encountering its limits in relation to others, the Other, and the texts, the process that Schleiermacher mistakenly assumed would be natural, happens at last: experience is opened up and led beyond itself.

Turns to the Other often take shape as turns to the Bible. Luther and Barth are among the classical examples, but similar dynamics can also be found in the more recent histories of the base communities of Latin America and elsewhere. In these cases the Bible is not so much a book of rules or a book that contains all the right answers as it is a reality that is challenging and empowering. The Bible is not primarily personal devotional material but something that moves the people of God. The Bible does not provide a coherent theological system, as postmodernists remind us and as those who actually read the book have known for a long time. In fact, like all encounters with the Other, biblical texts are most challenging where they not only mess up our most beautiful and coherent theological systems (as Barth knew so well) but also open up spaces for those at the margins of the system—the widow, the stranger, and the orphan.

Tradition is, of course, represented by the turn to language and the text. This tradition is not primarily something that is in the past but something that is alive in the church. As such it is not primarily some deposit that can be safeguarded and controlled. Listening to the various strands of tradition, the most interesting theological insights emerge at the place of dissonances and tensions, in the encounters with what is repressed in the dominant traditional discourses. Tradition will only make the kind of difference for which postliberals such as Lindbeck hope where it stays alive and enters into relations with other elements.

Reason, finally, is completely redefined in the turn to others. We can no longer follow the models of controlling reason that operate within the safety of closed systems and on the grounds of Archimedean points. Whether foundations exist or not—which is one of the big debates between modernists and postmodernists—we need to admit that we do not have immediate access to them and cannot own them. This is true also for people at the margins even though their horizon may be broader in certain ways. New processes of theological reasoning must go through the trouble of the circle of the other elements, learning to let go and to open up. Here reasoning means to develop a new position of receptivity and listening.

In our search for a constructive approach we might take a clue from the old Barth as he envisions a future theology of the Holy Spirit. In this context all four elements—Bible, tradition, experience, and reason—can be taken more seriously, since neither needs to be identified directly with God. Each of the four turns appears in new light when seen in this context. The openness for which I am arguing here matches the openness of the Spirit: Barth conjectured that this concern for the Spirit might already have been the concern which drove Schleiermacher, although unconsciously.[21] Nevertheless, a theology of the Holy Spirit is not a theology of identity.[22] A theology of the Holy Spirit might also be what, equally unconsciously, already drove the early Barth in his insistence on the autonomy and activity of the word of God. As such it might be the missing link that relates the differing approaches discussed in this book.[23] Yet the radical challenge of the Spirit still needs a clearer profile. Lindbeck, too, knows that ultimately it is the power of the Holy Spirit which is necessary to make theological connections: "The hearing does not occur without the reading, but it does not happen . . . except in the power of the Holy Spirit." As it is in Schleiermacher's theology of identity, identifying God-consciousness and Spirit, it is difficult to distinguish between reading and Spirit in Lindbeck's approach.[24]

The turn to others might help us to move to the next step in carving out space for the Holy Spirit. Here theology is built on neither the identity of humanity and the divine nor a guaranteed connection between the texts of the church and the divine. Theology has to do with "hearing from the Other," as Fulkerson puts it, and with expecting help in a situation of utter defeat, as Delores Williams has argued in the context of African American women. This move takes up the turn to the Other, but with a twist: without some form of openness for others, openness for the Other—for the Holy Spirit—can easily become just another theological buzzword.

Telling the Truth: Repositioning Doctrine and Truth

In all four modes of theology there are glimpses of God. No matter how overbearing the self and its texts become in the ego's era, God's concern cannot be eradicated completely. But can we decide on matters of truth? How can we distinguish glimpses of God from wishful thinking?

At first sight, foundationalist notions of truth might look attractive. "Give me a point on which to stand and I will move the earth," the Greek philosopher Archimedes claimed. This type of truth is especially alluring to those who, in the transitions at the beginning of a new millennium, seek to preserve their positions of control. If I (and perhaps some of my friends) have access to this Archimedean point, we can move the earth without collaborating with others who are different and without having to immerse ourselves in the tensions of our times. The theological problem with such notions of truth is reflected in the fact that here truth allows for positions of control: what is controlled, of course, is not only other people but ultimately Godself. "Give me a point on which to stand" and my images of God will ultimately be sucked into the system as well.

Trying to get a secure handle on matters of truth is not just a harmless fantasy. Controlling notions of truth prevent us from encountering God and end up perpetuating the structures of exclusion. This is true even for the other extreme, the fierce revolutionary who seeks to overthrow the system by proclaiming radically alternative images of God, an approach that, as Lacan has taught us, merely leads to a reshuffling of the powers that be.

The theological question here is, How can theology interpret the witness of the church and its truth in such a way that it does not dominate that which is interpreted? What is the status of the doctrines of the church in this context? In the process of exploring these issues I will show how theology can approach matters of truth in ways that avoid both foundationalism on the one hand and pluralistic relativism on the other.

Theology turning to the self reminds us that doctrines are always related to people's lives. Doctrines do not live a life of their own as unrelated documents that somehow have "fallen from heaven" or that are imposed on the church from the outside. Doctrines take shape as people reflect on their relation with God. The earliest christological confession in the Gospel of Mark (8:29) is an example. Peter's awareness that Jesus is the Messiah grows out of his and the other disciples' walk with Jesus.

Problems develop when the self takes on a position of control in matters of doctrine, a position that I have argued is reinforced by the exclusion of others in the global market. If doctrines become merely functions of the self's concerns and interests, they lose not only their integrity but also their ability to make a difference and transform people's lives.

Understanding that doctrines are related to people's lives can therefore no longer mean that doctrines are determined simply by whatever people in power feel is appropriate. The initial encounters with Jesus show how people learn to give up control in the relation to an other, someone who is really different and represents divine Otherness. Recall Simon Peter's response to his first encounter with Jesus in the Gospel of Luke (5:8): "Go away from me, Lord, for I am a sinful man!" The doctrines of the church come alive in the relation to selves that are reshaped in the encounter with others, representing the repressed truth of the self, but also in the encounter with God as Other and the texts of the church.

Likewise, the turn to the self reminds us that truth is not some abstract deposit that exists in and of itself. Truth is always related to people's lives.

Truth is contextual not in the sense that it is primarily a function of a particular context—any context, as the pluralists maintain—but in the sense that it aims at making a difference in people's lives. Liberal theology understood in part the contextual nature of truth. But there context itself is often either universalized, especially in the older liberal approaches, or atomized into a pluralistic "anything goes," the preference of current liberalism.[25] Yet only when the self encounters its unconscious truth, others, does it become clear that matters of context do not vanish into relativism. Here truth becomes a dynamic concept that cannot be settled once and for all but invites ongoing investigation and research into specific contexts tied to blind spots and unconscious desires of the self.

The turn to the Other reminds us that the doctrines of the church point away from themselves to God. According to Barth, there always has to be "a theological warning against theology, a warning against the idea that its propositions or principles are certain in themselves . . . and are not rather related to their theme and content . . . which they cannot master, by which they must be mastered if they are not to be mere soap-bubbles."[26] Yet problems develop when doctrines point away from themselves in such a way that they merely leave behind and forget whatever they point away from. Doctrines that merely "transcend" the context in which they arise in order to point to the Other easily become cover-ups. While the contemporary situation in all its exclusiveness and oppressiveness is perhaps transcended in this case, it is not reconstructed.

Nevertheless, doctrines that open up to the divine Other do not have to promote transcendence in terms of dropping out. In opening up to the Other, doctrines and the contexts in which they arise are radically reshaped. Barth, unlike some of those who claim to be Barthians, was aware that the Otherness of God did not primarily refer to God's otherworldliness but to God's challenge of all human (and ecclesial) contexts and decrees. God is not Other in the sense that God passively observes us from far away; God is Other in the sense that God is at work where we least expect it, on the underside. As Mary the mother of Jesus (and Hannah long before her) realized, God has a tendency to bring down the powerful from their thrones, to lift up the lowly, to fill the hungry with good things, and to send the rich away empty (Luke 1:52-53, paraphrased; see also 1 Sam. 2:1-10).

The turn to the Other reminds us that the doctrines of the church, coming alive in encounters with new selves, remain subject to radical critique. Doctrines are not the "thing in itself"; they are not God. They need to be constantly restructured and rewritten in relation to new encounters with God's Otherness and, as we now know, in relation to new insights into the limits of the powers that be. In this way doctrines can never become the support of the powers that be no matter how benevolent their goals; they are always the critique of such powers, even in the church. A new theological focus on doctrine, far from being a conservative move, may thus lead to one of the most powerful critiques of the structures of exclusion.

Here the notion of truth is reshaped once again. Truth is tied not so much to the way things are as to the always surprising and challenging encounters with the divine Other. For that reason nobody can create a secure storehouse of truth. Truth can never be contained completely in documents or other traditional forms. Even the contextual nature of truth of which the turn to the self has reminded us is further qualified here: The context that matters is not our own but God's.

Theology turning to language and the text has rediscovered the power of doctrine and of the Bible. Language and texts are not mere reflections of reality, as conventional theories of representation claim. Words actually do something; they accomplish things. Turning our attention to language and the text, we begin to understand better how doctrines shape the church and theological thought. Theology cannot be done from a neutral position outside these doctrinal frameworks but is always already shaped by them.

Problems develop, however, when doctrines are justified just because they shape the church at present or because they have shaped the church in the past as part of its operative tradition. The biggest problem we need to face today is not that doctrines are vanishing in the life of the church but that doctrines, even though they may seem perfectly orthodox on the surface, serve masters other than God. Doctrines, not because they do not really matter in the life of the church but precisely because they are so powerful, must always be part of self-critical theological reflection.

An approach to the doctrines of the church that is aware of their power will want to make sure that those doctrines truly serve God and not other gods. In this paradigm—and this must come as a major surprise for many of those who want to pursue the turn to the texts and traditions of the church—theology becomes more rather than less critical. We need to take a closer look at how doctrines, even those considered orthodox, function in our own time. Which doctrines actually end up supporting the structures of exclusion and which provide resistance and alternatives? A hierarchical vision of God, for example, can easily be misused for projecting and justifying social power structures. Why else would following Jesus' lead in addressing God as "Abba" be such a revolutionary concept? In Rom. 8:15 and in Gal. 4:6 Paul relates this term to overcoming our slavery to the way things are, to the principalities and powers that outrank humanity in the great chain of being.

By sorting out the masters served by the texts of the church—keep in mind that nobody can serve two masters (Matt. 6:24)—the power of the doctrines of the church can be put to new use. Which doctrines speak most clearly against the gods of the global economy? Which doctrines provide true alternatives and shape new structures of accountability? Truth, in this context, is tied to what doctrines do. Here is a powerful new paradigm that revitalizes theological reflection at a time when theological awareness of the power of the church's doctrines is low. What is lacking in much of contemporary theology, whether liberal or conservative, is an understanding of how our lives are often shaped not primarily by the truth claims that we profess but by the doctrines operative in our lives, often at an unconscious level. What difference does it make if I profess that "Jesus is Lord" if the operative definition of lordship is shaped by the power of an economy that favors the strong over the weak? No wonder the main focus of theology turning to language and the text is not on representative notions of truth.

Finally, the turn to others broadens our understanding of doctrine further. A powerful set of doctrines grows out of the lives of people at the margins as they walk with God. Mary's song of praise in the Gospel of Luke is generated by the fact that God "has looked with favor on the lowliness of his servant" and that "the Mighty One has done great things for me" (Luke 1:48, 49). In the words of Frederick Herzog, "the true 'creeds' of today are bled out of the sufferings of the martyrs in the church of the oppressed."[27]

Problems develop, of course, when marginality becomes another absolute guarantee for the truth of doctrine. This may be less a problem for marginalized people themselves, whose lives are never stable and who know that suffering and oppression are no virtues in and of themselves. But theologians who follow the turn to others, trained in mainline theological methods, need to be aware of this trap.

Many biblical themes have grown precisely out of such settings. The doctrine that has perhaps most often been misused as justification for the way things are, the doctrine of creation, originally grew out of the suffering and oppression of the people of Israel in the Babylonian exile. This doctrine has nothing to do with the relaxed setting of speculation where philosophers discover at their own pace *was die Welt im Innersten zusammenhält* ("that which holds the world together at its core")[28] or where people take a stroll through nature on a sunny day. Instead, it has to do with the need of people under pressure—people who have lost control but not their will to resistance—to understand who is in charge. If these histories are lost or if doctrines are disconnected from real-life struggles, which today include those who struggle and often die at the front lines of the global market system, doctrines are easily turned into the pillars of the status quo. For this reason theology cannot negotiate doctrines in the secure environment of the ivory towers.

The new openness to encounters with the Other which is created in the encounter with others also produces new perspectives on the traditions of the church and alternative images of the self. When students and faculty at Perkins School of Theology started to go to West Dallas, a desolate area of town marked by poverty and racial marginalization, we began to realize various things. Meeting God in West Dallas, in the context of the encounter with other people, can change your life: the autonomous self of modernity is transformed. In this context new relations to the traditions of the church developed, eyes were opened to important themes in the Bible, and new interest in theology and doctrine was generated. No wonder we met resistance from certain other faculty and students precisely at this point: who would worry about a little charity where it does not hurt?

In the process another vision of truth develops. Truth has to do with openness and listening, with being shaped by rather than with being in control over the subject matter. The turn to others does not copy the classical liberal turn to the self. Marginalized people are not substitutes for the controlling position of the self. At the same time, truth does not become a relativistic concept either. Not unlike modern foundationalism, postmodern relativism is the privilege of those who are in control. Once modern claims of universality and identity break down, those in charge have the luxury to withdraw into their gated communities and churches where they can make their own rules, and thus the pluralistic play of difference becomes fun. The popular song by the group R.E.M. describes the attitude: "It's the end of the world as we know it, and I feel fine."[29]

Truth, shaped in the turn to others, is fully aware of human relativity but does not buy into relativism, that is, that anything goes. Relativism cannot be overcome by denying relativity, only by acknowledging it. In this sense the view from the underside produces a broader perspective, going directly against the logic of the powers of exclusion. The Hispanic cleaning woman, for example, has a broader perspective on life than the academic theologian or the CEO for whom being fluent in two or more languages, knowing how to behave in radically different social-economic contexts, and how to raise kids in a multicultural perspective is still a luxury rather than a matter of survival.

Truth, therefore, is that which is able to give an account of the complexity of life, reaching all the way into those areas where "no one has gone before" (at least very few systematic theologians and other members of the professional managerial classes). Truth needs to take into account that which hurts, and it is this pain which affects the humanity and "selfhood" of all of us, whether we know it or not, that pulls things together again.[30] A phrase in one of the stanzas of a famous poem and hymn by James Russell Lowell ("Once to Every Man and Nation") expresses the dynamic in more traditional terms: "Truth forever on a scaffold, wrong forever on a throne."

In sum, at a time when much of life is determined by exclusivist structures and those in power do everything to remain in control, theology—however orthodox or conceptually precise—is no safe haven. Theology does not remain unaffected by the way power is distributed in our societies, and not even a theology that is conceived purely at a desk or in the libraries is off the hook. In this context the theological turn to others helps bundle and focus the other three theological turns.

A crucial point to recognize is that this new concern for repressed others is not just imposed on us by our context. Unlike Tillich's method of correlation, this concern for others is not formulated "as if one had not received the theological answers." Many of the biblical texts themselves display this concern for those who are other. Through the incarnation the divine Other is also among those others, a human being who does not belong among the high and the mighty and is ultimately nailed to a cross by both the ecclesiastical and political powers that be.[31] As liberation theologians such as Gutiérrez and others have pointed out for decades, theology needs to opt for the poor not because the poor are good but because God is good. In other words, theology turns to others not simply because the situation demands it but because God's own logic pushes us in this direction. The turn to the Other, to the God who acts in solidarity with the non-persons, inspires the turn to others; vice versa, without following this turn to others, the turn to the Other cannot be carried through.

Here the task of theology is no longer primarily the critique of the doctrines of the church in light of the questions of the modern world (as in more liberal theologies), nor is it simply the collection of and commentary on a selection of divine truths (as in more orthodox theologies). Theology becomes a lens that helps us to discern who we are in light of who God is and who our fellow human beings are, in dialogical and self-critical relation with the doctrines of the church.[32]

Common Interests: Resisting the Powers of Exclusion

What would the social location of a new, more self-critical mode of theology look like? Recently, I overheard a student express the common misperception that liberation theology (and by implication any theology that tries to take others seriously) would promote a God who cares for the poor but not for the rich. What logic drives such a statement? According to the logic of global capitalism, funds are always limited. If there is too much concern for the poor, the rich might lose out. In the context of the United States this argument is most common in the debate about taxes. There is a major concern, shared not only by wealthy people but also by many in the lower classes, that the rich are being treated unfairly if they have to contribute more than a flat rate. According to this logic, any concern for people who are different from those in charge, whether in terms of race, class, gender, or even sexual orientation, can only be seen as pursuing special-interest deals that threaten the social fabric. In this view turns to others promote special interests that, when applied to theology, severely inhibit our perception of the divine Other and the canonical texts of the church, and undermine a healthy concern for the self.

But now we are beginning to develop a different logic. In the introduction to this book I pointed to a strange reversal: what has often been seen as common interest looks more and more like special interest. The universals promoted by those in control are not universally valid for everybody. The problems that theology once assumed were the problems of all humanity, questions of anxiety and meaninglessness, for example, turn out to be the problems of specific elite groups that have little to do with the rest of humanity. What has been dismissed as special interest, on the other hand, is becoming more and more relevant to all of us.

The apostle Paul knew that if one member suffers, all suffer together (1 Cor. 12:26). Unlike the various perspectives of privilege which feel they can afford to tend to their own context (Paul resists the same thing when he says that "the eye cannot say to the hand, 'I have no need of you,' nor again the head to the feet, 'I have no need of you,'" 1 Cor. 12:21), the view from the underside of suffering always reflects the whole body. Suffering can ultimately not be limited to one member only. The turn to others reminds us of a deeper level of pain, a common concern that is often repressed by those who can afford it. While the powers that be tend to assume that the suffering and pain of people on the margins is something that will eventually be cured by the system, we need to realize that the suffering and pain of those who are repressed first points to the truth about ourselves.[33] The death of 35,000 children every day is not a matter of special interest but is part of the collectively repressed truth about those who benefit from the global economy. The pain in our inner cities is part of the repressed truth of those who have joined the flight to the suburbs. We are all in this together. Put another way, we cannot be fully human without others, without taking a deep look at what has been repressed and pushed into the recesses of our social unconscious all this time. The extreme forms of pain at the margins affect us all. The interest of the repressed is common interest.

In this case gaining a better understanding of others and of what keeps us apart, namely, the structures of exclusion, becomes a prime theological mandate. In a society where differences in class structures are hardly addressed, it may come as a surprise to find that class structures do indeed play a major role in North American life. Our neighborhoods are, for the most part, strictly divided by class. People in the same neighborhood usually share the same income levels, the same education, the same educational opportunities for their children, the same infrastructure, and even the same churches. No wonder middle-class America as a whole was never too concerned about the deterioration of the inner cities: the problems of the cities seemed to be detached from those of the suburbs. At present there is little motivation for people in the suburbs to connect with people in the city other than a sense of charity, which often remains a one-way street. We have built our freeways and thoroughfares around the ghettoes so that many middle-class people are not even aware of their existence.

Modern systematic theology has for the longest time been developed in the theological centers of Berlin (Schleiermacher), Basel (Barth), and New Haven (Lindbeck). Theology turning to others introduces a new perspective. Feminist theology, for example, began by taking a much-needed look at the situation of women in those same settings, thus broadening the narrow horizons of those at the top. More recently feminist theologians have taken the next steps by considering the lives of women in the ghettoes of those settings as well as in out-of-the-way places such as Appalachia and other marginalized contexts around the globe. The potential for a common-interest theology starts with the underside, not with universals.

In the North American context many of the best theological schools have been conceived as places that would care about matters of context. But for decades most of the schools' contextual interests related mainly to middle- and upper middle-class settings, without much awareness of the limitations of these perspectives. Only recently have some started to broaden their horizons to include lower-class and minority settings. In the process they have encountered not only new theological questions but also the Otherness of God. Meeting God at the margins can change one's life.

In all this the challenge is not simply to align with particular marginalized groups but, as feminist theorist Rosemary Hennessy has put it, to occupy "more fully our own uneven positions within the late capitalist social arrangements."[34] What is our own place as theologians in the social system, and how can we face its challenges? Encountering others, we cannot help but wonder, Who put those others in place? This may be the hardest lesson for those of us who are in positions of control. The good guy/bad guy scheme no longer works. We need to understand the ambiguity of our own position. The turn to others, therefore, does not render obsolete the turn to the self but leads back to it, radically transforming it in the process. Mainline theology needs to understand how we are part of the problem and how resistance can be formed. The primary issue is not first of all advocacy, in the form of doing things for others in ways that leave the self intact, but self-critique.

The Church of the Future

When asked which commandment is the most important, Jesus answered: "The first is, 'Hear, O Israel: the Lord our God, the Lord is one; you shall love the Lord your God with all your heart, and with all your soul, and with all your mind, and with all your strength.' The second is this, 'You shall love your neighbor as yourself'" (Mark 12:29-31). The way the Second Commandment is interpreted in the church shows where we are and where we need to be going. To love one's neighbor as oneself is often interpreted as yet another rule Christians must follow. According to this rule, we have to sincerely try to love our neighbor and to practice charity. Such an effort often ends up as a one-way street. There is no mutual relation between the self and others. What matters most is whether the rules are met and the neighbor is taken care of.

Liberal churches often try to address this problem by turning things around. In order to love one's neighbor, it is said, one has first to love oneself. That is assumed to be the meaning of the "as yourself" part of Jesus' commandment. Here the one-way street is overcome to a certain degree since a self that loves itself is in a better position to relate to the neighbor than a self that merely follows the rules. Something always comes back in return, the liberals claim. But the relationships that develop on this basis often do not lead to the next level. The relation to the neighbor ends where it began: helping others makes people feel good about themselves. In neither of these models that are commonly found in the churches at present (following a rule of first loving oneself), models that parallel the split of conservatives and liberals, are the structures of exclusion really challenged.

An alternative way of interpreting Jesus' commandment to love one's neighbor as oneself, a way deeply rooted in the logic of the Old Testament, grows out of understanding that the neighbor is a part of oneself: "Love your neighbor as *being part* of yourself."[35] In other words, the self is not fully human without others. Here the self and others enter into a relationship that becomes mutual. In the relation to the neighbor the self is challenged, transformed, and opened up. Others, as the early Methodist tradition understood, no longer are merely the object of our service or a prop for the self but become a means of grace, a channel through which God enters our lives. Here a sense develops that the relation with human others opens up a new range of encounters with the divine Other.[36] The love of neighbor and the love of God can no longer be separated. In learning to love our neighbors as being part of ourselves, we can also learn to love God in new ways, and at this point new ways of "loving oneself" can also be explored.

When Delores Williams invites black women to "*love themselves*" at first this sounds a lot like the old liberal turn to the self. But we must not forget the different context.[37] Black women, having lived in the positions of otherness for centuries, might help us understand the true importance of the turn to the self and what it means to love oneself. The kind of self-love at stake here has nothing to do with the self-indulgence of the modern self. The self-love that passes through the turn to others has to do with resistance to the dominant images of the self.

It is now clear how the structures of exclusion distort not only theological thinking but also the nature of the church. We are beginning to understand what it means that, as Herzog has put it, "The church cannot be built from within."[38] Especially liberal and postliberal theologies are challenged by this move. The turn to others, where it teaches us respect for and points us back to the Other, reminds us that the church cannot be grounded primarily in the pious self or in the linguistic communities shaped by the text.

In the new model things are tied together no longer in the religious genius of the self or in the community of the church. But the turns to the Other and others cannot become substitute centers either. The church cannot be centered on any of these elements to the exclusion of others. At the heart of the church—and here the various Christian denominations agree—lie encounters with God that take place through all of these elements.

The Holy Communion table is one of those locations in the life of the church where the various elements come together. In the presence of Christ as Other in bread and wine (elements that respond to real hunger), however the various denominations interpret the details of this presence, the texts of the church are engaged by reading the scriptures and celebrating the liturgy, others are encountered in the people who celebrate communion together, and the self is reshaped. This experience of wholeness at Holy Communion is subverted, however, where the structures of exclusion interfere: where the encounter with others is missing because people at the margins are locked out of the church or patronized by it, where the church forgets to engage those texts that provide challenges, and where the church seeks to secure the benefits of Christ's presence and the elements of bread and wine for an elite group.[39]

Perhaps the crisis of contemporary theology has not so much to do with the failure as it does with the success of the more powerful mainline churches. We are not yet aware of the need to open up, of the need for a self-critical perspective. Douglas John Hall suspects that "churches that can seem to be successful without any depth of theological awareness are very likely to suspect and reject any theology that probes to the roots of both cultic and cultural convention."[40] Much of theology is sucked into this vicious circle, complaining about loss of relevance while continuing with business as usual. In this context self-centeredness becomes a major problem. Without a more self-critical attitude, the church will end up turning with the successful entrepreneurial self around itself.

Reactivating Theology: Between God and the Excluded

Theology is still commonly defined as "critical reflection on the witness of the church." Yet our understanding of "critical reflection," largely inherited from modern theology, is changing. While in modern theology it has usually been very clear who the author of the critique is, namely, the theologian who understands himself [sic] as coherent and unified self, this arrangement is more and more open to debate. Postmodern critics are not the only ones raising questions. For people at the margins, this turns out to be a life-and-death issue. Taking into account the blind spots of modernity, having to do with a deeply ingrained self-centeredness, the self-critical approach for which I am arguing implies a major shift. Theology as a whole is driven out of its secure position when it starts to pay attention to that which is repressed, especially when the repressed are real people, their children, and their environmental "habitats." Only when this happens can the various theological modes begin to recognize in which ways they are complementary.

The search for a theological middle road is as useless as trying to find a perfect system since both efforts pursue hegemonic dreams that are unable to break out of the structures of exclusion. Theology as self-critical reflection on the witness of the church depends on new non-hegemonic forms of listening to the various elements that produce this witness, identifying the sources of authority more clearly, and developing new awareness of their blind spots and unconscious desires. In this context the effort to pay attention to the cracks and fissures of the church's witness, of learning how to read between the lines, is not aimed at doing away with this witness but at revitalizing it and providing opportunities for creating more faithful relationships to God.[41]

Here theology no longer offers a critique from a secure position but needs to include itself into the critique. In this way it begins a process in which it constantly reforms and redefines its boundaries in relation to the "least of these" and God, who is the ultimate source of authority. What the Protestant Reformation has said of the church is also true of theology: it always needs to be reformed.

The close relation between God and others that shapes up in this connection is characteristic of the new paradigm. A well-known passage from 1 John 4:20 illustrates the common thread that is woven throughout this book. "Those who say, 'I love God,' and hate their brothers or sisters, are liars; for those who do not love a brother or sister whom they have seen, cannot love God whom they have not seen." Claims to love God, more specifically theological claims to respect God and to be open to God, can easily turn into lies, not necessarily premeditated scams but those more dangerous ideological tendencies of which we are not even aware. Claims to love God are only real, the writer of 1 John says, if they are tied to love for brothers and sisters. In our context we might say that without developing respect and openness for others at a time when social and other forces try to pull us deeper and deeper into the circles of exclusion, theology will hardly be able to make good on its well-intentioned attempts to become more open to God. Only in this light does another definition of theology make sense that understands its task as focusing on the reflection of God's presence and action in our lives.[42] In the ego's era the self has a hard time listening to anything but its own voice. But replacing the authority of the self with other authorities, such as the authority of the text, leads to similar results since authority is perceived in terms of control.

In this approach theological views "from below" (from humanity) and "from above" (from God) can no longer be played off against each other. The view "from below," no longer determined by those who are in control, does not compete with the view "from above." Instead, it opens up to it and prepares us for new encounters with God's Otherness which escape us where we think about the "from above" perspective in terms of control. Vice versa, the view "from above," the view from the God of Jesus Christ, invites us to embrace the view "from below" in radical ways at the points where Godself joins in the suffering of those who are under unbearable pressure. Without this dialectic, even views "from below" usually end up as justifications of the status quo, whatever it may be.

Theology that grows out of these dynamics will not have to worry about relevance. Becoming aware of its blind spots and realizing how it is sucked into the powers that be—in our case the structures of exclusion that have come to determine the contemporary scene all the way into the churches—theology will have to explore its rootedness in God in ways that develop new theological guidelines that put up resistance and explore alternatives. Such theology cannot be perceived as yet another fad, for as long as exclusion and oppression continue to shape our world and the way we think, there will be need for resistance.

While this type of theology will need to start at home, beginning with a self-critical assessment of its own structures and the structures promoted by the church, it will also be woven into the fate of the globe as a whole, in touch with those who suffer everywhere as a result of the expansion of the globalizing market structures. Here lies our future at a time when much of the polarization within theology and our churches has become self-serving.

Notes

Introduction

1. From the Latin American perspective, José Comblin (*Called for Freedom: The Changing Context of Liberation Theology,* trans. Phillip Berryman [Maryknoll, N.Y.: Orbis, 1998], xiii) observes that over the past thirty years there has been a shift from a situation of oppression to one of exclusion. Hugo Assmann (*Crítica à Lógica da Exclusão* [São Paulo: Paulus, 1994]) also points to exclusion as the main problem. Gustavo Gutiérrez ("Liberation Theology and the Future of the Poor," in *Liberating the Future: God, Mammon, and Theology,* ed. Joerg Rieger [Minneapolis: Fortress Press, 1998], 109) talks about the various dimensions of exclusion. Exclusion is also a central issue in recent feminist theology. See *Horizons in Feminist Theology: Identity, Tradition, and Norms,* ed. Rebecca S. Chopp and Sheila Greeve Davaney (Minneapolis: Fortress Press, 1997). Mary McClintock Fulkerson's essay in this book reminds us that awareness of the structures of exclusion is central in feminist theology. Who we are is constituted not just by what is visible on the surface but also by what is excluded, repressed, or rejected. The Lacanian perspective that I will introduce in chapter 5 takes up such insights and develops them further. I have developed this argument, initially in relation to Jacques Lacan's use of the terms *metaphor* and *metonymy,* in my book *Remember the Poor: The Challenge to Theology in the Twenty-First Century* (Harrisburg, Pa.: Trinity, 1998).

2. This was an important concern for parts of political theology which understood that the challenge was not to "politicize" theology artificially but to realize how everything, theology included, was politicized already. For a recent account of the impact of economic structures on theological thinking by leading international theologians, see Joerg Rieger, ed., *Liberating the Future.* The challenge of economic structures is also addressed in Ulrich Duchrow, *Alternatives to Global Capitalism: Drawn from Biblical History, Designed for Political Action* (Utrecht: International Books with Kairo Europe, 1995).

3. The relation of others and the Other is addressed in Joerg Rieger, *Remember the Poor.* See also "Whaling Our Way into the Twenty-First Century," in *Theology from the Belly of the Whale: A Frederick Herzog Reader,* ed. Joerg Rieger

(Harrisburg, Pa.: Trinity, 1999), and "The Means of Grace, John Wesley, and the Theological Dilemma of the Church Today," *Quarterly Review* (winter 1997–1998), 377–93.

4. No wonder that, as Robert McAfee Brown has observed, "systematic theology is not leading the list of human concerns these days. . . . The front lines in the human battles do not seem to be theological libraries and seminar rooms" (Brown, "Liberation as Drama," *Christianity and Crisis* 50, no. 4 [March 19, 1990], 76). From a South African perspective, the verdict is even stronger: "Theology as pursued in the West has become a joke" (Bonganjalo Goba, "A Black South African Perspective" in *Doing Theology in a Divided World,* ed. Virginia Fabella and Sergio Torres [Maryknoll, N.Y.: Orbis, 1985], 58).

5. Ronald Goetz, "Confessions of an Academic Liberationist: Riding the Tiger of Liberation," in *Standing with the Poor: Theological Reflections on Economic Reality,* ed. Paul Plenge Barker (Cleveland: Pilgrim, 1992), 73.

6. Data from the National Center for Children in Poverty in 1998. In 1996 poverty and near-poverty affected almost half of all young children in the U.S. (43 percent) (*News and Issues* 8, no. 1 [spring 1998]). See also the publication of the Council of Bishops of the United Methodist Church, *Children and Poverty: An Episcopal Initiative* (Nashville: United Methodist, 1996), which reports that between 1979 and 1989, child poverty in the U.S. increased by 21 percent while the Gross National Product grew by 25 percent. Preschool vaccinations lag behind those in some Third World countries.

7. Reported in the *Dallas Morning News* (July 1, 1999), 4A. The study is titled "Homeless Children: America's New Outcasts." The percentage figure was reported in a 1998 survey, quoted in the *North Texas United Methodist Reporter* (December 25, 1998).

8. U.S. numbers can be found in Bread for the World, "Background Paper," 148 (January 2000). International numbers are in the United Nations, *Human Development Report* (New York and Oxford: Oxford Univ. Press, 1998).

9. The 1999 numbers are reported in an editorial by Geneva Overholser, "Income Disparity Will Build Resentments," *Dallas Morning News* (October 19, 1999), 11A. For the other numbers, see Robert B. Reich, *The Work of Nations: Preparing Ourselves for Twenty-First Century Capitalism* (New York: Knopf, 1991), 7, 223.

10. Ernesto Cortes Jr., "Justice at the Gates of the City: A Model for Shared Prosperity" (unpublished paper, Industrial Areas Foundation, 1998), 2. According to U.S. law, the responsibility of corporate managers is not to the workers but to shareholders, and therefore to capital. Jon P. Gunnemann, "Capital Ideas: Theology Engages the Economic," in *Religion and Values in Public Life* (The Center for the Study of Values in Public Life at Harvard Divinity School) 7, no. 1 (fall 1998), 6.

11. Robert B. Reich ("The New Power," *The American Prospect* [November 23, 1999], 80) points out that the new power centers, for instance, big institutional investors and venture capitalists, are less visible than the old power centers, such as corporations, labor unions, government, and the military.

12. Reich, *Work of Nations,* 302–3. In "We Are All Third Wayers Now" (*The American Prospect* [March/April 1999], 51), Reich demands that "the winners must agree to apply a portion of their added booty to equipping the losers." Yet the whole thing thus becomes a "moral crusade," a scenario that leaves the powerful in charge and can be solved if they only put their minds to it.

13. *Dallas Morning News* (May 2, 1999), 9C: "A decade ago Dallas had only one

such development . . . today it has more than 75." Approximately one-third of all new communities in Southern California are now gated.

14. Reich, *Work of Nations*, 227.

15. Kevin Bales, *Disposable People: New Slavery in the Global Economy* (Berkeley: Univ. of California Press, 1999), 4. The common denominator of the new slaves is no longer race but poverty. Contemporary slaveholders exploit poverty and the dynamics of the global economy that tears down older support systems based on relationships and family ties. "Without work and with increasing fear as resources diminish, people become desperate and life becomes cheap" (ibid., 12). In the historical forms of slavery in the U.S., by contrast, a slave used to be a sizable investment that was cared for. Slaves were worth three to six times the average yearly wage of a worker (ibid., 16).

16. Ibid., 237.

17. The so-called working rich like Gates have surpassed the category of the "kings, queens, and dictators," led by the Sultan of Brunei with $30 billion (*Dallas Morning News* [June 21, 1999], 1D, 4D).

18. *Human Development Report*, 30. The report estimates that $40 billion a year would be needed, compared to $1 trillion in assets owned by the world's 225 richest people.

19. William Wolman and Anne Colamosca, *The Judas Economy: The Triumph of Capital and the Betrayal of Work* (Reading, Mass.: Addison-Wesley, 1997), ix, 9, 24.

20. Michèle Barrett and Mary McIntosh (*The Anti-social Family* [London: Verso, 1982], 47) show how "the family embodies the principle of selfishness, exclusion and pursuit of private interest and contravenes those of altruism, community and pursuit of the public good. Society is *divided into* families and the divisions are deep, not merely ones of slight antipathy and mild distrust." Emphasis in original.

21. Donna Landry and Gerald MacLean, *Materialist Feminisms* (Oxford: Blackwell, 1993), xii.

22. "Never before has so much Wall Street expertise been handed out to so many so fast" (Wolman and Colamosca, *Judas Economy*, 4).

23. The report appeared in the *Dallas Morning News* (June 1, 1999), 7A. More than seven hundred doctors were shown videos of patients describing identical symptoms. The patients were eight actors, an older and younger black woman, a black man, a white woman, and a white man who were dressed in hospital gowns and used the same scripts. Each also had the same insurance and occupation. Major medical organizations such as the American Medical Association are looking for solutions. The original study was published in the *New England Journal of Medicine* 340, no. 8 (February 25, 1999) by Kevin A. Schulman et al., under the title "The Effect of Race and Sex on Physicians' Recommendations for Cardiac Catheterization."

24. See David Harvey, "What's Green and Makes the Environment Go Round?" in *The Cultures of Globalization,* ed. Fredric Jameson and Masao Miyoshi (Durham, N.C.: Duke Univ. Press, 1998), 327–28. Harvey points out that "ecosystems tend to both instantiate and reflect . . . the social processes and systems that gave rise to them" (ibid., 335).

25. Introduction to *Liberation Theologies, Postmodernity, and the Americas*, ed. David Batstone et al. (London and New York: Routledge, 1997), 5. The essays in the book assume that postmodernity, the Americas, and Christianity are all part of the coordinates of the postmodern. For more specific analyses, see ibid., 8–9.

26. Martin Schwab, in the preface to Manfred Frank's *What Is Neostructuralism?* (trans. Sabine Wilke and Richard Gray [Minneapolis: Univ. of Minnesota Press, 1989], xiv), points out that the French critique of modern and rationalist thought after World War II is a collective effort, unparalleled at present, which amounts to nothing less than a "theory of our age." Derrida's work makes us face the difficulties of life and keeps us honest, as John D. Caputo (*Radical Hermeneutics: Repetition, Deconstruction, and the Hermeneutic Project* [Bloomington and Indianapolis: Indiana Univ. Press, 1987], 4, 6) puts it.

27. Jacques Derrida, "Structure, Sign and Play," in *Critical Theory since 1965*, ed. Hazard Adams and Leroy Searle (Tallahassee: Univ. Press of Florida, 1986), 84. Derrida argues that we have fooled ourselves into believing in the presence of something beyond the text. This has led to a false sense of security. No Archimedean points are left and there is no "referent" outside of the text or the system to be interpreted, be it "metaphysical, historical, psychobiographical, etc." (Jacques Derrida, *Of Grammatology*, trans. Gayatri Chakravorti Spivak [Baltimore: Johns Hopkins Univ. Press, 1976], 158).

28. Jean Baudrillard, *America*, trans. Chris Turner (New York: Verso, 1989, c1988).

29. Fredric Jameson, "The Cultural Logic of Late Capitalism," in Fredric Jameson, *Postmodernism, or the Cultural Logic of Late Capitalism* (Durham, N.C.: Duke Univ. Press, 1991), 6.

30. Ibid., 18.

31. David Harvey, *The Condition of Postmodernity: An Enquiry into the Origins of Cultural Change* (Oxford: Blackwell, 1990), 357. Nevertheless, Harvey also reminds us that "these changes, when set against the basic rules of capitalistic accumulation, appear more as shifts in surface appearance rather than as signs of the emergence of some entirely new postcapitalist or even postindustrial society" (ibid., vii).

32. For the differentiation between contextual and liberation theologies along these lines, see Joerg Rieger, "Developing a Common Interest Theology from the Underside," in Joerg Rieger, ed., *Liberating the Future*.

33. Woody White, in his annual open letter to Martin Luther King Jr., *Interpreter* 43, no.1 (January 1999), 9.

34. See the contextual approaches of many of the great theologians of this century, including Rudolf Bultmann and Paul Tillich.

35. The Asian janitors at my school, for instance, need to be aware of the perspectives and values of their employers and must speak our language. Those of us in charge at the school, on the other hand, are under no particular pressure to expand our own cultural horizons.

36. See Joerg Rieger, *Remember the Poor*; and Joerg Rieger, ed., *Liberating the Future*.

37. Alister E. McGrath, *Christian Theology: An Introduction* (Oxford: Blackwell, 1994), 155.

Chapter 1

1. In his method of correlation, questions of the self are closely related to the answers of revelation. But the questions enjoy a certain autonomy: Tillich claims that the theologian "must participate in man's finitude, which is also his own,

and in its anxiety as though he had never received the revelatory answer of 'eternity.'" Paul Tillich, *Systematic Theology,* vol. 2 (Chicago: Univ. of Chicago Press, 1957), 15.

2. "Taste for the Infinite," *Time* 91, no. 10 (March 8, 1968), 45–46. John Macquarrie, *Thinking about God* (New York: Harper & Row, 1975), 158–59. Lately the Schleiermacher seminar at the American Academy of Religion, always well attended and drawing an international crowd, has served as the clearinghouse for Schleiermacher studies. In the German context, there is hardly a Protestant theological faculty that does not offer a course on Schleiermacher.

3. Revisionist theology parallels Schleiermacher's work where it seeks to establish correlations between questions of human existence in general and the "religious classics," as, for example, in the early work of Roman Catholic theologian David Tracy. Another revisionist theologian, Schubert M. Ogden (*Existence and Faith* [Nashville: Abingdon, 1989], 10) celebrates the continuing influence of liberal theology, manifest in the historical-critical method and in the central role of the "modern cultural situation." More recent work of the revisionists goes beyond Schleiermacher in a better understanding of the implications of history and social location. See David Tracy, *On Naming the Present: Reflections on God, Hermeneutics, and Church* (Maryknoll, N.Y.: Orbis, 1994).

4. See the argument of Henry Steele Commager, *The Empire of Reason: How Europe Imagined and America Realized the Enlightenment* (New York: Oxford Univ. Press, 1982).

5. René Descartes, *Discourse on Method,* trans. John Veitch, Religion of Science Library, 38 (La Salle, Ill.: Open Court, 1952), 34.

6. Immanuel Kant, "What Is Enlightenment?" in *The Philosophy of Kant: Immanuel Kant's Moral and Political Writings,* ed. Carl J. Friedrich (New York: Random House, 1977), 132.

7. See, for example, Stephen Toulmin, *Cosmopolis: The Hidden Agenda of Modernity* (New York: Free Press, 1990). Toulmin relates the modern quest for certainty to the chaotic situation of seventeenth-century Europe, particularly to the violent clashes of religious positions in the wars of religion. Since political solutions could not stop the killing, the hope was that rational methods would make a difference (ibid., 55). It is often forgotten that most of Descartes's adult life falls into the time of the Thirty Years War.

8. Locked away in his study so that no external influences could disturb him, Descartes concludes: "I observed that, whilst I thus wished to think that all was false, it was absolutely necessary that I, who thus thought, should be somewhat; and as I observed that this truth, I think, hence I am, was so certain and of such evidence, that no ground of doubt, however extravagant, could be alleged by the Skeptics capable of shaking it, I concluded that I might, without scruple, accept it as the first principle of the Philosophy of which I was in search" (*Discourse on Method,* 35).

9. The history of liberal theology turns around this relationship, since the possibility of theology now depends on it. The most well-known example of this focus is Paul Tillich's method of correlation, relating existential human questions and religious answers. See his *Systematic Theology,* vol. 1 (Chicago: Univ. of Chicago Press, 1951).

10. Friedrich Schleiermacher, *The Christian Faith,* ed. H. R. Mackintosh and J. S. Stewart (Edinburgh: T. & T. Clark, 1986), 52.

11. Friedrich Schleiermacher, *On Religion: Speeches to Its Cultured*

Despisers, trans. John Oman (Louisville: Westminster John Knox, 1994), 31, 44.

12. Schleiermacher, *Christian Faith*, 26. See also B. A. Gerrish, *Tradition and the Modern World: Reformed Theology in the Nineteenth Century* (Chicago: Univ. of Chicago Press, 1978), 41. Gerrish explains that "Schleiermacher's theology rests not so much on 'psychologism' (Brunner) as on a 'sociology of the religious consciousness' (Troeltsch)."

13. Schleiermacher, *Christian Faith*, 16. Emphasis in original.

14. Cf., for example, Hans W. Frei, "Barth and Schleiermacher: Divergence and Convergence," in *Barth and Schleiermacher: Beyond the Impasse*, ed. James O. Duke and Robert F. Streetman (Philadelphia: Fortress Press, 1988).

15. This is the meaning of the German term *schlechthinig*, translated as "absolute."

16. Paul Tillich, too, subscribes to a "principle of identity," which he already finds in Schleiermacher. This principle is a reaction to "the principle of detachment and separation in the Enlightenment," the split between subject and object. Paul Tillich, *Perspectives on 19th and 20th Century Protestant Theology*, ed. Carl E. Braaten (New York: Harper & Row, 1967), 94. This principle "gave Schleiermacher the possibility of creating a new understanding of religion" (ibid., 95).

17. Schleiermacher, *On Religion* (trans. Oman), 43.

18. See Roger Haight, *An Alternative Vision: An Interpretation of Liberation Theology* (New York: Paulist, 1985).

19. Schleiermacher assumes that piety and reason share in the same foundation. See also Christian Albrecht, *Schleiermachers Theorie der Frömmigkeit: Ihr wissenschaftlicher Ort und ihr systematischer Gehalt in den Reden, in der Glaubenslehre und in der Dialektik* (Berlin: de Gruyter, 1994), 317.

20. Friedrich Schleiermacher, *Hermeneutics: The Handwritten Manuscripts*, ed. Heinz Kimmerle, trans. James Duke and Jack Forstman (Missoula, Mont.: Scholars, 1977), 182. Cf. the "Academy Addresses," ibid., 175–76; both grammatical and psychological interpretation aim at an "immediate understanding" (ibid., 192).

21. Schleiermacher, *Hermeneutics*, 150.

22. Schleiermacher, *On Religion* (trans. Oman), 36.

23. Schleiermacher, *Christian Faith*, 26, 27. Emphasis in original.

24. In *The Christian Faith*, he makes this argument in terms of the common presence of the feeling of absolute dependence, "for there can hardly exist a man in whom another would recognize no religious affection whatever as being in any degree similar to his own" (ibid., 28).

25. Ibid., 35.

26. Ibid., 37.

27. Ibid., 386.

28. Hans-Georg Gadamer (*Truth and Method* [New York: Seabury, 1975], 162–63) has made an even stronger case for Schleiermacher's hermeneutics, arguing that it is essentially the "art of avoiding misunderstandings."

29. Schleiermacher, *Christian Faith*, 434. Here Schleiermacher discusses the difference between a "magical" and an "empirical" view of the Christ event; the latter is the problem of liberalism and the former the problem of orthodoxy.

30. A famous example of this critique is Gustaf Aulén, *Christus Victor: An Historical Study of the Three Main Types of the Idea of Atonement*, trans. A. G. Herbert (New York: Macmillan, 1969).

31. Schleiermacher, *Christian Faith*, 126.

32. Ibid.

33. Schleiermacher, *On Religion* (trans. Oman), 43.

34. Schleiermacher, *Christian Faith*, 20, 21.

35. Schubert M. Ogden, *Faith and Freedom: Toward a Theology of Liberation*, rev. ed. (Nashville: Abingdon, 1989), 31. A similar definition of ideology is given in Schubert M. Ogden, *The Point of Christology* (Dallas: SMU Press, 1982), 94: Ideology "functions to justify the interests of a particular group or individual by representing these interests as the demands of disinterested justice." For another definition of ideology that can at times be found in the theological literature, although it is less helpful since it overlooks that ideological matters are not just irrelevant but dangerous, see Dorothee Sölle, *Political Theology*, trans. and with an introduction by John Shelley (Philadelphia: Fortress Press, 1974), 23. Sölle defines ideology as "a system of propositional truths independent of the situation, a superstructure no longer relevant to praxis, to the situation, to the real questions of life."

36. See Yorick Spiegel, *Theologie der bürgerlichen Gesellschaft: Sozialphilosophie und Glaubenslehre bei Friedrich Schleiermacher* (Munich: Chr. Kaiser, 1968), 257.

37. Schleiermacher, *Hermeneutics*, 112.

38. Gadamer, *Truth and Method*, 171.

39. God's work in Christ, for example, is adapted to the needs of the modern self. See the description of the priestly office of Christ: "For if we wish to assert the reality of human moral nature in Christ, we must not ascribe to Him, even in this connection, any other rules of conduct than such as we have to recognize as valid for us all; otherwise there would be a danger that His life would cease to be an example, and consequently that it would cease to be an ideal" (Schleiermacher, *Christian Faith*, 462).

40. Quoted in Charles M. Wood, *Theory and Religious Understanding: A Critique of the Hermeneutics of Joachim Wach*, American Academy of Religion Dissertation Series, 12 (Missoula, Mont.: Scholars, 1975), 47.

41. Schleiermacher, *Christian Faith*, 76.

42. Ibid., 433. For a critique of the overemphasis of individualism in the interpretation of Schleiermacher, see Spiegel, *Theologie der bürgerlichen Gesellschaft*, 133–34.

43. Friedrich Schleiermacher, *Brief Outline on the Study of Theology*, trans. Terrence N. Tice (Richmond, Va.: Westminster John Knox, 1966), 72.

44. John E. Thiel, *Imagination and Authority: Theological Authorship in the Modern Tradition* (Minneapolis: Fortress Press, 1991), 44.

45. This point is emphasized by Thiel, *Imagination and Authority*, 53–54; and Frei, "Barth and Schleiermacher: Divergence and Convergence." See also Anthony Thiselton, *New Horizons in Hermeneutics* (Grand Rapids, Mich.: Zondervan, 1992), 232.

46. Friedrich Schleiermacher, "Rezension von Joachim Heinrich Campe: Historisches Bilderbüchlein oder die allgemeine Weltgeschichte in Bildern und Versen," in *Kritische Gesamtausgabe*, erste Abteilung, vol. 3, ed. Hans-Joachim Birkner et al. (Berlin and New York: de Gruyter, 1988), 435.

47. Ibid., 435.

48. The editor of Schleiermacher's *Hermeneutics*, Heinz Kimmerle, finds that "the question of the discovery of the linguistic sense (of the word in a sentence) shifts more and more to the question of what special (individual) thinking lies at

the base of a linguistic expression." Introduction to Schleiermacher, in *Hermeneutics*, 20.

49. Gadamer, *Truth and Method*, 166.

50. Friedrich Schleiermacher, "Gedanken," in *Kritische Gesamtausgabe,* erste Abteilung, vol. 3, 283.

51. Martin Redecker, *Schleiermacher: Life and Thought*, trans. John Wallhausser (Philadelphia: Fortress Press, 1973), 207.

52. Quoted in Redecker, *Schleiermacher: Life and Thought*, 90.

53. Schleiermacher, *Christian Faith*, vii–viii.

54. The famous German explorer Alexander von Humboldt is a contemporary and acquaintance of Schleiermacher. Cf. Marie-Louise Pratt, *Imperial Eyes: Travel Writing and Transculturation* (New York: Routledge, 1992).

55. Schleiermacher, *Zur Siedlungsgeschichte Neuhollands*, in *Kritische Gesamtausgabe,* erste Abteilung, vol. 3, 279.

56. Schleiermacher, "Gedanken," 331.

57. See Spiegel, *Theologie der bürgerlichen Gesellschaft*, 173–74. Spiegel (ibid., 21–22) shows the parallels to Adam Smith's reflections on mutual exchange in the economic realm.

58. Theology is for the leaders of the church only: "Theology is not the special responsibility of everyone who belongs to a particular Church, except as they take part in the leadership of the Church" (Schleiermacher, *Brief Outline*, 20). Schleiermacher denies, however, that the clergy would form necessarily a "special class." See Schleiermacher, *Christian Faith*, 619, and Spiegel, *Theologie der bürgerlichen Gesellschaft*, 174.

59. See Johannes Bauer, *Schleiermacher als patriotischer Prediger: Ein Beitrag zur Geschichte der nationalen Erhebung vor hundert Jahren* (Giessen: Töpelmann, 1908), 217, 238.

60. Spiegel (*Theologie der bürgerlichen Gesellschaft*, 162) argues that Schleiermacher was the first one to initiate this focus on middle-class intellectuals. Tillich puts great emphasis on "the situation," but his focus is limited by the horizon of existentialism, posing the typical middle-class questions of that time, questions of nonbeing, finitude, anxiety, guilt, meaninglessness, and despair (*Systematic Theology*, vol. 2, 28).

61. See Spiegel, *Theologie der bürgerlichen Gesellschaft*, 219, 25.

62. See Dieter Schellong, "Bürgertum und christliche Religion: Anpassungsprobleme der Theologie seit Schleiermacher," *Theologische Existenz heute* 187 (Munich: Chr. Kaiser, 1975), 35.

63. Schleiermacher, *Christian Faith*, 450.

64. Schellong, "Bürgertum und christliche Religion," 33.

65. On this basis the Founding Fathers reasoned "that to secure these Rights, Governments are instituted among Men, deriving their just Powers from the Consent of the Governed, that whenever any Form of Government becomes destructive of these Ends, it is the Right of the People to alter or to abolish it, and to institute new Government, laying its Foundation on such Principles, and organizing its Powers in such Form, as to them shall seem most likely to effect their Safety and Happiness."

66. See Schellong's reference to an observation by G. F. W. Hegel ("Bürgertum und christliche Religion," 9). For the tension between the self and others, see also Joerg Rieger, *Remember the Poor*.

67. Cf. Spiegel, *Theologie der bürgerlichen Gesellschaft*, 233, in agreement with Jürgen Habermas. For the argument that Schleiermacher's speeches (in *On Religion*) imply a theory of two classes, see also Trutz Rendtorff, *Kirche und Theologie: Die systematische Funktion des Kirchenbegriffs in der neueren Theologie* (Gütersloh: Gütersloher, 1966), 116. Redecker (*Schleiermacher: Life and Thought*, 92) points out that politically Schleiermacher is in favor of a constitutional monarchy with constitution and parliament, connecting his acceptance of the Prussian monarchy with his democratic ideals. Schleiermacher rejects the more radical French Revolution.

68. While Schleiermacher sees the need to learn from women along those lines, he also thinks that only men are in a position to integrate the spiritual and the sensual. See the essays of Robert F. Streetman and Sheila Briggs in *Schleiermacher and Feminism: Sources, Evaluations, and Responses*, ed. Iain G. Nicol, Schleiermacher Studies and Translations 12 (Lewiston: Edwin Mellen Press, 1992).

69. Herbert Marcuse (*Reason and Revolution: Hegel and the Rise of Social Theory* [New York: Humanities Press, 1954], 14–15) sees the early roots of this development already in the Reformation: "There arose a realm of beauty, freedom, and morality, which was not to be shaken by external realities and struggles; it was detached from the miserable social world and anchored in the 'soul' of the individual. This development is the source of a tendency widely visible in German idealism, a willingness to become reconciled to the social reality."

70. See Susan Brooks Thistlethwaite, "On Becoming a Traitor: The Academic Liberation Theologian and the Future," in Joerg Rieger, ed., *Liberating the Future*, 17. Thistlethwaite, referring to an argument Frederick Herzog had made earlier, points out that Schleiermacher is more an enemy of liberation theology than Barth, not only because he forgets that God has two natures, love and justice, but because he divorces ideals of freedom and equality from the reality of the poor.

71. Bauer, *Schleiermacher als patriotischer Prediger*, 208, 212.

72. Reich, *The Work of Nations: Preparing Ourselves for Twenty-First Century Capitalism* (New York: Knopf, 1991), 76, 223.

73. This report was part of the 1998 *United Methodist Reporter* series on churches helping the less fortunate.

74. Schleiermacher, *Hermeneutics*, 42.

75. See Reinhold Rieger, *Interpretation und Wissen: Zur philosophischen Begründung der Hermeneutik bei Friedrich Schleiermacher und ihrem geschichtlichen Hintergrund* (Berlin: de Gruyter, 1988), 334.

76. Schleiermacher, *Hermeneutics*, 43.

77. Anthony C. Thiselton, *Interpreting God and the Postmodern Self: On Meaning, Manipulation, and Promise* (Grand Rapids, Mich.: Eerdmans, 1995), 51.

78. Manfred Frank, "Das 'wahre Subjekt' und sein Doppel: Jacques Lacans Hermeneutik," in Manfred Frank, *Das Sagbare und das Unsagbare: Studien zur neuesten französischen Hermeneutik und Texttheorie* (Frankfurt: Suhrkamp, 1980), 133–34.

Chapter 2

1. William C. Placher ("Being Postliberal: A Response to James Gustafson," *Christian Century* [April 7, 1999], 390) notes that the neoorthodox revolution never really reached many of the churches. According to Peter Berger's (*The Sacred*

Canopy: Elements of a Sociological Theory of Religion [Garden City, N.Y.: Doubleday, 1967], 165) analysis in the late sixties, its sociological roots were shallow. Gabriel Fackre ("Reorientation and Retrieval in Systematic Theology," *Christian Century* 108, no. 20 [June–July 1991], 654) reports Barth's popularity.

2. As reported by the PBS program "Religion & Ethics News Weekly," referenced in *United Methodist Newscope* 27, no. 3 (January 15, 1999), 4. Other names on that list include Billy Graham, Pope John Paul II, Martin Luther King Jr., and Mother Teresa.

3. See Vladimir Lossky, *Orthodox Theology: An Introduction*, trans. Ian and Ihita Kesarcody-Watson (Crestwood, N.Y.: St. Vladimir's, 1989), 23; Jean-Luc Marion, *God without Being*, trans. T. A. Carlson (Chicago: Univ. of Chicago Press, 1991). See also the introduction to Marion's book by David Tracy.

4. For a postmodern perspective, see Walter Lowe, *Theology and Difference: The Wound of Reason* (Bloomington: Indiana Univ. Press, 1993), 6–9, who notes at least in passing what is usually neglected by others who reflect on the postmodern setting: the economic dimension. See also Isolde Andrews, *Deconstructing Barth: A Study of the Complementary Methods in Karl Barth and Jacques Derrida* (Frankfurt: Peter Lang, 1996). Douglas John Hall (*Remembered Voices: Reclaiming the Legacy of "Neo-Orthodoxy"* [Louisville, Ky.: Westminster John Knox, 1998], 136) argues that the critical and prophetic legacy of neoorthodoxy has not been claimed in North America. See also Bruce McCormack, *Karl Barth's Critically Realistic Dialectical Theology: Its Genesis and Development 1909–1936* (Oxford: Clarendon, 1995), who has recovered Barth's theological critique of the North American context.

5. Karl Barth, *Protestant Theology in the Nineteenth Century: Its Background and History* (Valley Forge, Pa..: Judson, 1973), 82.

6. This is no longer the "red pastor of Safenwil" but the "mature" Barth of *Church Dogmatics* (Karl Barth, *Church Dogmatics,* vol. 2, bk. 1, ed. G. W. Bromiley and T. F. Torrance, trans. T. H. L. Parker et al. [New York: Charles Scribner's Sons, 1957], 386). Cf. Karl Barth, *Church Dogmatics,* vol. 3, bk. 4, ed. G. W. Bromiley and T. F. Torrance, trans. A. T. Mackay et al. (Edinburgh: T. & T. Clark, 1961), 544.

7. See Karl Barth, *Dogmatics in Outline* (New York: Harper & Row, 1959), 7. After World War II Germany was destroyed physically, psychologically, and spiritually. The Germans had to learn it the hard way: don't be too optimistic about the intrinsic goodness of humanity; trusting in one's own powers can go terribly wrong.

8. Karl Barth, "Christian's Place in Society," in *The Word of God and the Word of Man*, trans. Douglas Horton (New York: Harper & Row, 1957), 272.

9. Karl Barth, *Church Dogmatics,* vol. 1, bk. 1, ed. G. W. Bromiley and T. F. Torrance, trans. G. W. Bromiley (Edinburgh: T. & T. Clark, 1975), 29.

10. Barth, *Dogmatics in Outline*, 36.

11. Barth, *Protestant Theology in the Nineteenth Century*, 426. While Schleiermacher's theology is one of the main targets of Barth's critique, Barth's real concern is tied to its history of effects. See Karl Barth, *The Theology of Schleiermacher: Lectures at Göttingen, Winter Semester of 1923–24*, ed. D. Ritschl, trans. G. W. Bromiley (Grand Rapids, Mich.: Eerdmans, 1982), 194, 211.

12. Barth, *Church Dogmatics,* vol. 1, bk. 1, 6. Barth explains that "the question of truth, with which theology is concerned throughout, is the question as to the agreement of the Church's distinctive talk about God with the being of the Church. The criterion of past, future, and therefore present Christian utterance is

thus the being of the Church, namely, Jesus Christ" (ibid., 4). Cf. "Does Christian utterance derive from Him? Does it lead to Him? Is it conformable to Him?" (ibid.).

13. Ibid., 30–32.

14. Ibid., 29.

15. See, for instance, the parallel to Derrida's insistence on the notion of difference in his essay titled "Différance," in *Margins of Philosophy*, trans. Alan Bass (Chicago: Univ. of Chicago Press, 1982). Derrida maintains that there are only differences without positive terms.

16. Karl Barth, *The Epistle to the Romans*, trans. Edwyn C. Hoskyns (New York: Oxford Univ. Press, 1968), 463. John E. Thiel ("Barth's Early Interpretation of Schleiermacher," in *Barth and Schleiermacher: Beyond the Impasse*, ed. James O. Duke and Robert F. Streetman [Philadelphia: Fortress Press, 1988], 19) notes that Barth struggled against an illusory notion of peace that he found in the church, the factory, and the university of his time.

17. Barth, *Protestant Theology in the Nineteenth Century*, 471. Barth talks about the dialectic of the ellipse in Schleiermacher, which is always tempted to collapse the two foci. The notion of peace is the theme of Schleiermacher's later sermons and related to his work on *Dialectics*.

18. There is a close relation between narcissism and aggressivity. For an analysis of this connection, see Joerg Rieger, *Remember the Poor: The Challenge to Theology in the Twenty-First Century* (Harrisburg, Pa.: Trinity, 1998), 24, 26.

19. Lately North American scholars have come to understand this point as well. For a forceful critique of Hans Urs von Balthasar's famous thesis of a major shift between Barth's *Epistle to the Romans* and his *Church Dogmatics*, cf. McCormack, *Karl Barth's Critically Realistic Dialectical Theology*. The relation of *Romans* and *Church Dogmatics* is also affirmed by others such as Friedrich-Wilhelm Marquardt, *Theologie und Sozialismus: Das Beispiel Karl Barths* (Munich: Chr. Kaiser, 1972), 29; cf. Barth's own comments, quoted ibid., 337.

20. Cf. Karl Barth, *The Humanity of God* (Richmond, Va.: John Knox Press, 1960). Here Barth talks about the difference between his early emphasis on God as Wholly Other and his greater appreciation of humanity later. Yet the critique introduced early on still sets the stage: "He who may not have joined in that earlier change of direction, who still may not be impressed with the fact that God is God, would certainly not see what is now to be said in addition as the true word concerning His humanity" (ibid., 42).

21. Karl Barth, *Anselm: Fides Quarens Intellectum. Anselm's Proof of the Existence of God in the Context of His Theological Scheme*, ed. D. Y. Hadidan, trans. I. W. Robertson (London: SCM, 1960), 29. The comment about the importance of the book is made by Barth in 1958, ibid., 11.

22. Ibid., 18. This goes against the interpretation of Hans W. Frei ("Eberhard Busch's Biography of Karl Barth," in *Karl Barth in Re-View: Posthumous Works Reviewed and Assessed*, ed. H.-M. Rumscheidt, Pittsburgh Theological Monograph series, vol. 30 [Pittsburgh: Pickwick, 1981], 113), who seems to assume that with *Anselm* Barth gives priority no longer to the dialectic but to the analogy in order "to help state the mutual fitness, through God's grace, of God and humanity."

23. My interpretation obviously goes against the "domesticated Barth" of North American neoorthodoxy. The best example for a new approach is

McCormack's book. For a brief overview of the various camps of the interpretation of Barth in Germany, see Bertold Klappert, "Zum Streit um die Münchener und Berliner Barth-Deutung," in *Mit unsrer Macht ist nichts getan* (Frankfurt/Main: Haag und Herrchen, 1993), 193–98.

24. Barth, *Church Dogmatics*, vol. 1, bk. 1, 34. In the U.S. we tend to get stuck in the dualism of theological liberalism and more conservative theological positions that focus on the texts of the church (fundamentalism, etc.). See, for example, the argument of Nancey Murphy, *Beyond Liberalism and Fundamentalism: How Modern and Postmodern Philosophy Set the Theological Agenda* (Valley Forge, Pa.: Trinity, 1996). Murphy's argument is built on the diametrical opposition of those two positions, which allows her to introduce postmodern points of view as a third way. But Barth already provided an alternative.

25. Barth, *Church Dogmatics*, vol. 1, bk. 1, 41, emphasis mine. See also ibid., 265.

26. This seems to be the misunderstanding at the heart of Ronald F. Thiemann's article "On Speaking of God—the Divisive Issue," in *Barth and Schleiermacher: Beyond the Impasse*. Thiemann (ibid., 112) claims that "because Barth believed the first-order language of the Christian tradition to be roughly coherent, he was unwilling to grant to philosophy or theology the explanatory role Schleiermacher assigned to philosophical theology."

27. Ibid.

28. Barth, *Church Dogmatics*, vol. 1, bk. 1, 41.

29. Barth, "Christian's Place in Society," 291–93. Unlike Schleiermacher, Barth does not like the notion of religion.

30. Cf., for example, Mark I. Wallace, *The Second Naiveté: Barth, Ricoeur, and the New Yale Theology* (Macon, Ga.: Mercer Univ. Press, 1995).

31. Karl Barth, *Church Dogmatics*, vol. 1, bk. 2, ed. G. W. Bromiley and T. F. Torrance, trans. G. W. Bromiley (Edinburgh: T. & T. Clark, 1975), 725.

32. Karl Barth, *Das Wort Gottes und die Theologie: Gesammelte Vorträge* (Munich: Chr. Kaiser, 1925), 134. Translation mine; the English translation in *The Word of God and the Word of Man*, 150, is not very accurate.

33. Karl Barth, *Church Dogmatics*, vol. 4, bk. 3, ed. G. W. Bromiley and T. F. Torrance, trans. G. W. Bromiley (Edinburgh: T. & T. Clark, 1975), 821. This sort of thing is especially problematic when the gospel is transformed into an object of the church.

34. Barth, *Dogmatics in Outline*, 40.

35. Barth, *Church Dogmatics*, vol. 1, bk. 1, 10. Emphasis mine.

36. Barth, *Epistle to the Romans*, 33. Cf. the parallel to Søren Kierkegaard's reflections on the difference between an apostle and a genius, as referred to in Barth, *Church Dogmatics*, vol. 1, bk. 1, 112.

37. Barth, *Dogmatics in Outline*, 36–37. Here a new relation of subject and object begins. The position of humanity as subject and God as object shifts. The "subject" (humanity) is assimilated by the "object" (God). See Barth, *Church Dogmatics*, vol. 1, bk. 1, 244–45.

38. Barth, *Church Dogmatics*, vol. 1, bk. 1, 4. At this point, there can be no question about the consistency of *The Epistle to the Romans* and *Church Dogmatics*. Barth, *Church Dogmatics*, vol. 1, bk. 2, 886: "Dogmatics certainly has a basis, foundation, and centre. But . . . this centre is not something which is under our control, but something which exercises control over us."

39. Barth, *Epistle to the Romans*, 12.

40. See, for example, Barth, *Dogmatics in Outline*, 38. The Bible does not identify the center, but tells "the story of God" and "narrates His deeds and the history of this God in the highest, as it takes place on earth in the human sphere." For the reference to source and norm, see Barth, *Anselm*, 33.

41. This could easily be overlooked in statements such as the following (Barth, *Anselm*, 25–26): "Anselm always has the solution of his problems already behind him (through faith in the impartial good sense of the decisions of ecclesiastical authority), while, as it were, they are still ahead." Nevertheless, keep in mind that Barth does not want to see this in terms of the liberal Protestant, pre–Vatican II Roman Catholic debate addressed above. Cf. ibid., 24.

42. Karl Barth, *Evangelical Theology: An Introduction,* trans. Grover Foley (Garden City, N.Y.: Doubleday, 1964), 77. German: *Einführung in die evangelische Theologie* (Zurich: Theologischer Verlag, 1970), 97.

43. Barth, "Christian's Place in Society," 285. The image of the "bird in flight" is on 282.

44. Barth, *Church Dogmatics*, vol. 1, bk. 1, 175. Where McCormack (*Karl Barth's Critically Realistic Dialectical Theology*, 465) follows the English translation of *Church Dogmatics* and understands *welthaft* as secular, I would argue that we need to translate it as "worldly," since Barth seems to mean to include the whole of human reality, even the "religious" aspects.

45. Barth, *Dogmatics in Outline*, 24.

46. Barth, "Christian's Place in Society," 277.

47. Barth, *Evangelical Theology*, 94. Barth's talk about an "analogy of faith" (*Church Dogmatics*, vol. 1, bk. 1, 244) needs to be seen against this background. Barth's analogy of faith is developed in opposition to liberal theology's insistence on the analogy of being (see, for example, Paul Tillich's reference to the analogy of being in *Systematic Theology*, vol. 1 [Chicago: Univ. of Chicago Press, 1951], 131) and does not try to provide a basis for yet another theology of identity. In *Dogmatics in Outline*, 21, Barth points out that unbelief does not need to be taken all that seriously either.

48. Barth, *Anselm*, 170–71.

49. Ibid., 41.

50. Ibid., 48.

51. Paul Tillich, *Perspectives on 19th and 20th Century Protestant Theology*, ed. Carl E. Braaten (New York: Harper & Row, 1967), 91.

52. Barth, *Church Dogmatics*, vol. 1, bk. 1, 11. Or, as he defines it elsewhere, as "that which ought to be valid in the Church as reproducing the Word of God" (Barth, *Dogmatics in Outline*, 13).

53. Barth, *Dogmatics in Outline*, 13.

54. Barth, *Church Dogmatics*, vol. 4, bk. 3, 79.

55. Ibid. This is Barth's response to Ludwig Feuerbach and the question of truth. Truth, as Feuerbach started to realize, must be figured out in relation to praxis. Cf. Marquardt, *Theologie und Sozialismus*, 291.

56. Barth, *Church Dogmatics*, vol. 2, bk. 1, 272. At the same time, God's life and our lives cannot be separated. Cf. Karl Barth, *Klärung und Wirkung*, ed. Walter Feurich (Berlin: Union, 1966), 283: God as living God means (1) that God is at work in real ways and (2) that God is at work "not only in the souls of individual people or in the distant heaven, but above all and first of all in life, precisely in the 'real' life of human beings on earth."

57. See Frederick Herzog, *God-Walk: Liberation Shaping Dogmatics* (Maryknoll, N.Y.: Orbis, 1988).

58. Markus Barth, "Current Discussions on the Political Character of Karl Barth's Theology," in *Footnotes to a Theology: The Karl Barth Colloquium of 1972*, ed. H.-M. Rumscheidt (Waterloo: Corporation for the Publication of Academic Studies in Religion in Canada, 1974), 88. This is Barth's response to Marquardt, *Theologie und Sozialismus* stating his agreement.

59. Karl Barth, *Church Dogmatics*, vol. 2, bk. 1, 258. Cf. Karl Barth, *How I Changed My Mind* (Richmond, Va.: John Knox, 1966), 48: "The abstract, transcendent God, who does not take care of real man ('God is all, man is nothing!') . . . existed, not in *my* head, but only in the heads of many of my readers and *especially* in the heads of those who have written reviews and even whole books about me." Emphasis in original.

60. Barth, *Die Kirchliche Dogmatik*, vol. 2, bk. 1 (Zollikon/Zurich: Evangelischer Verlag, 1946), 304. Translation mine; the official translation in *Church Dogmatics*, vol. 2, bk. 1, 271 is problematic.

61. Barth, *Dogmatics in Outline*, 38.

62. See Barth, *Church Dogmatics*, vol. 2, bk. 1, 83–84. Cf. Marquardt, *Theologie und Sozialismus*, 19.

63. Barth, *Church Dogmatics*, vol. 2, bk. 1, 84.

64. Barth, *Evangelical Theology*, 79. See also Barth, *Dogmatics in Outline*, 5.

65. Barth (*Dogmatics in Outline*, 60) wants to "bracket" the *Weltanschauung*, even if it is a Christian one, since Christians "are once for all dispensed from attempting, by starting from ourselves, to understand what exists, or to reach the cause of things and with or without God to reach a general view."

66. Barth, *How I Changed My Mind*, 86.

67. For comments on Barth's language, see Dieter Schellong, "Karl Barth als Theologie der Neuzeit," in *Theologische Existenz heute,* 173, ed. Karl Gerhard Steck and Dieter Schellong (Munich: Chr. Kaiser, 1973); and Hans Frei ("Eberhard Busch's Biography of Karl Barth," 109), who talks about the compelling, engrossing quality of Barth's writings: "But then, as one tries to restate it afterwards the material dies on one's hands. It can be done, but there is nothing as wooden to read as one's own or others' restatements of Barth's terms." George Hunsinger (*How to Read Karl Barth: The Shape of His Theology* [New York: Oxford Univ. Press, 1991], ix) concludes that "Barth's view of theological truth is multidimensional. Truth is at once miraculously actualized and yet textually stabilized, objectively efficacious and yet existentially authenticated, unique in kind and yet habituated in the midst of the ordinary."

68. Barth, *Church Dogmatics*, vol. 1, bk. 2, 725. The reference to the "supreme question" can be found in Barth, *Epistle to the Romans*, 9.

69. Werner Jeanrond, *Theological Hermeneutics: Development and Significance* (New York: Crossroad, 1991), 137. For this reason Jeanrond classified Barth as neoorthodox.

70. Barth, *Evangelical Theology*, 79.

71. Quoted in Eberhard Busch, *Karl Barth: His Life from Letters and Autobiographical Texts*, trans. John Bowden (Grand Rapids, Mich.: Eerdmans, 1994), 466; see also 466–94.

72. This theme is repeated over and over in the work of Gustavo Gutiérrez. For a recent reference, see "Liberation Theology and the Future of the Poor," 102.

73. In *Dogmatics in Outline*, 9, Barth defines the task of theology thus: "Dogmatics is the science in which the Church . . . takes account of the content of its proclamation critically, that is, by the standard of Holy Scripture and under the guidance of its Confessions." Earlier Barth had been careful to point out that the standard was closely tied to the reality of Christ. Structuring the *Dogmatics in Outline* around the Apostles' Creed, however, makes a similar statement.

74. Cf. Lowe, *Theology and Difference*; Marion, *God without Being*; Joerg Rieger, *Remember the Poor*.

75. Barth, *Epistle to the Romans*, 277.

76. See Dieter Schellong, "Bürgertum und christliche Religion: Anpassungsprobleme der Theologie seit Schleiermacher," *Theologische Existenz heute* 187 (Munich: Chr. Kaiser, 1975), 98.

77. Karl Barth, *Protestant Thought: From Rousseau to Ritschl*, trans. H. H. Hartwell (New York: SCM, 1959), 16–17. In *Protestant Theology in the Nineteenth Century*, 41–42, Barth describes the absolutist tendencies of modernity. The middle-class revolutionaries are just as absolutist as the princes before them, assuming godlike powers for themselves (ibid., 48f., 54).

78. Barth, *Protestant Theology in the Nineteenth Century*, 82.

79. Ibid., 38.

80. Barth, *Church Dogmatics*, vol. 2, bk. 1, 141; German: *Die Kirchliche Dogmatik*, vol. 2, bk. 1, 157. In an interesting study of Barth and liberation theology (Sabine Plonz, *Die herrenlosen Gewalten: Eine Relektüre Karl Barths in befreiungstheologischer Perspektive* [Mainz: Matthias-Grünewald, 1995], 353), Sabine Plonz comes to the conclusion that the most important contribution of Barth's theology is precisely his critique of the middle class.

81. Barth, *Church Dogmatics*, vol. 2, bk. 1, 386–87. See also Barth's little-known essay "Poverty," printed in the Swiss paper *Atlantis* in 1949 and published in English in *Against the Stream: Shorter Post-War Writings 1946–52* (New York: Philosophical Library, 1954), 243–46. In this essay Barth points out that God is "here and now always to be found in the company of the hungry, the homeless, the naked, the sick, the prisoners," and concludes that "for that reason those who are rich most cleave to [the poor], if they would be close to [God]" (ibid., 246).

82. Marquardt, *Theologie und Sozialismus*, 111, 117. Timothy J. Gorringe's *Karl Barth against Hegemony* (Oxford: Oxford Univ. Press, 1999) is one of the few English works to take up and further develop Marquardt's concern in constructive fashion. Gorringe reaffirms that Barth's theology "was a refusal of hegemony" and an affirmation of a God "who can in no circumstances ever be colonized or be the subject of any hegemony" (ibid., 4–5).

83. See Hall, *Remembered Voices*, 139.

84. Barth, *Epistle to the Romans*, 277.

85. See the quotation in Marquardt, *Theologie und Sozialismus*, 179.

86. Adolf von Harnack, assuming that the matter would not deserve a careful scholarly article, published fifteen embarrassing questions. Even though he did not name Barth, it was clear who was addressed. Harnack's questions and Barth's response are now published in Karl Barth, *Theologische Fragen und Antworten*, Gesammelte Vorträge, vol. 3 (Zollikon: Evangelischer Verlag, 1957), 7–8.

87. Barth, *Einführung*, 81–82. Translation mine; for the official translation, see Barth, *Evangelical Theology*, 62–63.

88. Barth, *Evangelical Theology*, 73.

89. Barth, *Church Dogmatics*, vol. 2, bk. 1, 387.

90. Helmut Gollwitzer, "Kingdom of God and Socialism in the Theology of Karl Barth," in *Karl Barth and Radical Politics*, ed. and trans. George Hunsinger (Philadelphia: Westminster, 1976), 106.

91. Barth was not at the meeting in Barmen, but he was instrumental in developing the draft. For an English translation see *Barth, Barmen, and the Confessing Church Today*, ed. James Y. Holloway (Lewiston: Mellen, 1995).

92. Barth, *Dogmatics in Outline*, 33. Barth talks about 1933, the year before the Barmen Declaration was drafted, but his comments refer to the whole era. Yet Barth also argues that theology can only do a service to politics if it first clarifies its own business. See Barth, preface to *Church Dogmatics*, vol. 1, bk. 1, xvi (written in 1932). Even the cause of German liberation, he argues, will be better served by this way of proceeding. This is how we need to understand Barth's insistence, in 1933, to continue to do theology as "if nothing had happened" and without specifically addressing the context (Karl Barth, "Theologische Existenz heute," *Theologische Existenz heute* 219, ed. Hinrich Stoevesandt [Munich: Chr. Kaiser Verlag, 1984], 26). Barth resists the "reality" of the context.

93. This is the form of the quotation verified by Niemöller's widow. See Peter Novick, *The Holocaust in American Life* (New York: Houghton Mifflin, 1999), 221. Novick shows how contemporary U.S. interests from Vice President Al Gore to the Republican Party have misused the quotation by variously omitting Communists, Social Democrats, and trade unionists, adding Catholics and moving the place in which the Jews are mentioned.

94. Barth, *Humanity of God*, 60. The reference to gloomy theology is on 62.

Chapter 3

1. The importance of the postliberal theological mode is reflected in the space given to it by the *Christian Century*, which in 1998–1999 published numerous discussions and debates on the postliberal point of view. The October 14, 1998, issue appeared under the general theme "The Making of a Postliberal," dedicating eight pages and the work of two authors to the theme. In the issues of March 24–30, April 7, and April 14, 1999, James Gustafson and William C. Placher addressed postliberalism. The postliberal mind-set is, of course, promoted not only by the Yale Divinity School but also by other academic contexts and influential individuals such as James Wm. McClendon, Jr., Nancey Murphy (McClendon's wife) ("Introduction," in *Theology without Foundations: Religious Practice and the Future of Theological Truth*, ed. Stanley Hauerwas, Nancey Murphy, and Mark Nation [Nashville, Tenn.: Abingdon, 1994], 25), hints at the fact that McClendon saw certain things earlier. The list of contributors to this book shows the range of positions related to the postliberal perspective. "Radical orthodoxy" is promoted by the contributors to a book of the same title: *Radical Orthodoxy: A New Theology*, ed. John Milbank, Catherine Pickstock, and Graham Ward (New York: Routledge, 1999). What all of these approaches share in common is expressed by the editors of *Radical Orthodoxy* as the attempt "to reclaim the world by situating its concerns and activities within a theological framework" (ibid., 1). Milbank proposes a more radical "postliberal" approach, connected to a "fideistic realism" (ibid., 22, 32).

2. Richard John Neuhaus, "Is There Theological Life after Liberalism? The Lindbeck Proposal," *Dialog* 24, no. 1 (winter 1985), 72.

3. Frei is said to have paid tribute to *The Nature of Doctrine* as the most important work in theology to come out of Yale since H. Richard Niebuhr's *The Meaning of Revelation* (Gordon E. Michalson, "The Response to Lindbeck," *Modern Theology* 4, no. 2 [January 1988], 111).

4. A standard definition of postliberal theology goes like this: "The quest, initiated in recent years by the most interesting American followers of Karl Barth, to get beyond all forms of modernism in theology; either a *cul de sac* or the harbinger of a new theological age (too soon to tell)" (Jeffrey Stout, *Ethics after Babel: The Languages of Morals and Their Discontents* [Boston: Beacon, 1988], 301). John E. Thiel (*Imagination and Authority: Theological Authorship in the Modern Tradition* [Minneapolis: Fortress Press, 1991], 27) argues that the work of Hans Frei, George Lindbeck, Ronald Thiemann, and Stanley Hauerwas bears a "family resemblance to Barth's descriptive theology."

5. George A. Lindbeck, "Scripture, Consensus, and Community," in *Biblical Interpretation in Crisis: The Ratzinger Conference on Bible and Church*, ed. Richard John Neuhaus (Grand Rapids, Mich.: Eerdmans, 1989), 94. See also George A. Lindbeck, "The Church's Mission to a Postmodern Culture," in *Postmodern Theology: Christian Faith in a Pluralist World*, ed. Frederick B. Burnham (San Francisco: Harper & Row, 1989), 51.

6. George A. Lindbeck, "Confession and Community: An Israel-like View of the Church," *Christian Century* (May 9, 1990), 496.

7. George A. Lindbeck, *The Nature of Doctrine: Religion and Theology in a Postliberal Age* (Philadelphia: Westminster, 1984), 20, 21.

8. George A. Lindbeck, "Review Symposium on Jeffrey Stout," *Theology Today* (April 1989), 59. Lindbeck adds the aspect of language to Schleiermacher's triad of knowing, feeling, and doing, once seen as comprehensive of all human reality.

9. Lindbeck, *Nature of Doctrine*, 34.

10. Lindbeck, "Church's Mission to a Postmodern Culture," 38–40.

11. Ibid., 52.

12. Lindbeck, *Nature of Doctrine*, 83; emphasis mine. Lindbeck, with reference to Peter Berger and Thomas Luckmann, defines elsewhere: "Religion, whatever else it may be or do, provides an *overarching integrating and legitimating frame of reference* for the socially constructed worlds that human beings inhabit" (ibid., 27, n.10); emphasis mine.

13. George A. Lindbeck, "Barth and Textuality," *Theology Today* 43, no. 3 (October 1986), 361, 365.

14. Lindbeck, "Barth and Textuality," 372. Barth distinguishes three forms of the word of God. The first two forms, Bible and the proclamation of the church, are God's word only if God actually speaks through them. The third form of the word of God is the word as revelation.

15. Barth, *Church Dogmatics*, vol. 1, bk. 1, 10, 112.

16. Lindbeck, "Barth and Textuality," 373. Not unlike classic Protestant orthodoxy, Lindbeck emphasizes the unity of the three modes.

17. Jesus' reaffirmation of the commandments to love God and neighbor is well known, but there are other passages such as 1 John 4:20 that are also concerned with keeping God and other together. For my interpretation of those texts, see chapter 6.

18. David Tracy, preface to Jean-Luc Marion, *God without Being* (Chicago: Univ. of Chicago Press, 1991). Elsewhere Tracy reminds postliberal theology of his own attempts to relate Schleiermacher's romantic paradigm to more recent understandings of language: David Tracy, "Lindbeck's New Program for Theology: A Reflection," *The Thomist* 49, no. 3 (July 1985), 464.

19. Lindbeck, "Scripture, Consensus, and Community," 96. See also Lindbeck, *Nature of Doctrine*, 136.

20. Lindbeck, *Nature of Doctrine*, 21.

21. Ibid., 77.

22. Ibid., 17.

23. Ibid., 79. The reference to "popular attitudes" is on 89, n.14.

24. Ibid., 80, 107. See also Hans W. Frei, *Types of Christian Theology*, ed. George Hunsinger and William C. Placher (New Haven: Yale Univ. Press, 1991), 20: "Theology . . . is the grammar of the religion, understood as a faith and as an ordered community life." As such it is closer to the social sciences than to philosophy (ibid., 21).

25. William C. Placher ("Being Postliberal: A Response to James Gustafson," *Christian Century* [April 7, 1999], 392) quotes a similar comment by Hans Frei: "I am looking for a way that looks for a relation between Christian theology and philosophy that disagrees with a view of certainty and knowledge which liberals and evangelicals hold in common."

26. Lindbeck, "Barth and Textuality," 368.

27. Ibid.

28. George A. Lindbeck, review of *Biblical Hermeneutics in Historical Perspective: Studies in Honor of Karlfried Froelich on His Sixtieth Birthday*, ed. Mark S. Burrows and Paul Rorem, *Modern Theology* 10 (January 1994), 103.

29. George A. Lindbeck, "Atonement and the Hermeneutics of Intratextual Social Embodiment," in *The Nature of Confession: Evangelicals and Postliberals in Conversation*, ed. Timothy R. Phillips and Dennis L. Okholm (Downers Grove, Ill.: InterVarsity, 1996), 221, 222.

30. Ibid., 246.

31. Ibid., 222–23. In this way Lindbeck takes up an insight that is becoming more and more prominent in the postmodern academy, namely, that theory follows praxis.

32. Ibid., 227.

33. From a slightly different perspective, Terrence Tilley (*Postmodern Theologies: The Challenge of Religious Diversity* [Maryknoll, N.Y.: Orbis, 1995], 150) talks about telling stories to calm our terror in the postmodern world where all other foundations have crumbled. At the same time, Tilley ("Incommensurability, Intratextuality, and Fideism," *Modern Theology* 5, no. 2 [January 1989], 105) wonders why the "new Yale theology" has "left one cow sacred." By positing a "pure" text, the Bible has been removed from the cultural-linguistic dynamics. Tilley argues for a "dirty" or "contextual intratextuality" which presumes that no privileged framework is available.

34. Lindbeck, "Atonement and the Hermeneutics of Intratextual Social Embodiment," 230.

35. Ibid., 223.

36. Ibid., 224. Even the fundamentalists developed a rationalistic hermeneutics, which starts with a theory of inerrancy and inspiration.

37. Ibid., 223–24.

38. Lindbeck, *Nature of Doctrine*, 74.

39. Ibid., 68.

40. Ibid., 69.

41. Lindbeck, "Review Symposium on Jeffrey Stout," 59.

42. Lindbeck, quoting Clifford Geertz, in *Nature of Doctrine*, 115. According to Lindbeck, the notion of "thick description" is used by Geertz, following Gilbert Ryle.

43. Ibid., 117.

44. Roger E. Olson, "Back to the Bible (Almost)," *Christianity Today* (May 30, 1996), 32.

45. "To say, as Lindbeck does, that 'intrasystematic truth' is a *necessary* condition of ontological truth gives a religion an odd sort of veto power over assertions." Charles M. Wood, review of *The Nature of Doctrine: Religion and Theology in a Postliberal Age*, by George A. Lindbeck, *Religious Studies Review* 2, no. 3 (July 1985), 237.

46. Lindbeck, "Scripture, Consensus, and Community," 97.

47. Ibid., 88. Modernity, by contrast, has stressed the text as yet another variable.

48. Lindbeck, "Church's Mission to a Postmodern Culture," 41. Here is another parallel to the thought of Jacques Derrida, who in "Structure, Sign and Play in the Discourse of the Human Sciences" (in *Critical Theory since 1965*, ed. Hazard Adams and Leroy Searle [Tallahassee: Florida State Univ. Press, 1989], 90–91) points out the significance of play for deconstruction. But Derrida is clearer than Lindbeck that play means to give up any security and to reject the attempt to define a center.

49. Ernst Käsemann, "Begründet der neutestamentliche Kanon die Einheit der Kirche?" in *Exegetische Versuche und Besinnungen*, vol. 1 (Göttingen: Vandehoeck & Ruprecht, 1960), 221.

50. Kathryn Tanner, *Theories of Culture: A New Agenda for Theology* (Minneapolis: Fortress Press, 1997), 158. The reference to theology as a culture-specific activity and to Lindbeck can be found on 64, and 183, n.7.

51. Ibid., 158.

52. Ibid., 48, 159, 175.

53. Lindbeck, "Atonement and the Hermeneutics of Intratextual Social Embodiment," 247.

54. Liberal theology is seen as the fundamental problem of modernity, and Lindbeck claims that the Christian supporters of both Nazism and Stalinism were grounded in liberal theological positions. Lindbeck, *Nature of Doctrine*, 126.

55. Ibid., 22, 25. What is changing is the intellectual climate: "For the first time since the Renaissance and Reformation the regnant outlook in the intellectual high culture is not opposed to treating a classic, whether Christian or non-Christian, as a perspicuous guide to life and thought" (Lindbeck, "Church's Mission to a Postmodern Culture," 51).

56. George A. Lindbeck, "Ecumenical Imperatives for the Twenty-First Century," *Currents in Theology and Mission* 20, no. 5 (October 1993), 361–62.

57. Lindbeck, "Church's Mission to a Postmodern Culture," 49.

58. See C. C. Goen (*Broken Churches, Broken Nation: Denominational*

Schisms and the Coming of the American Civil War [Macon, Ga.: Mercer Univ. Press, 1985]), who argues that the split of the churches contributed to the split of the nation.

59. Lindbeck, "Ecumenical Imperatives for the Twenty-First Century," 363–64.

60. George A. Lindbeck, "Theologians, Theological Faculties, and the ELCA Study of Ministry," *Dialog* 28, no. 3 (summer 1989), 202.

61. Lindbeck's long commitment to ecumenical dialogue goes back to the Second Vatican Council, where he was an observer for the Lutheran World Federation. Hans W. Frei ("Epilogue," in *Theology and Dialogue: Essays in Conversation with George Lindbeck*, ed. Bruce D. Marshall [Notre Dame: Univ. of Notre Dame Press, 1990], 277) sees this as one of the fundamental concerns of Lindbeck: how to account for doctrinal reconciliation without doctrinal change. In "Confession and Community: An Israel-like View of the Church," 493, Lindbeck states that, even more than his teaching at Yale, the ecumenical movement has been the context of his thinking.

62. See, for example, George A. Lindbeck, "Two Kinds of Ecumenism: Unitive and Interdenominational," *Gregorianum* 70, no. 4 (1989), 656. Elsewhere Lindbeck argues that "when it is work not worship which unites, human need rather than God's glory becomes central, and justification by service replaces justification by faith" (George A. Lindbeck, "The Meaning of *Satis Est*, or Tilting in the Ecumenical Wars," *Lutheran Forum* 26, no. 4 [November 1992], 23). Lindbeck equates worship with faith and confession. In other words, early confession/doctrine is concerned with God's glory; service is concerned merely with human need.

63. Lindbeck, "Ecumenical Imperatives for the Twenty-First Century," 364.

64. Lindbeck explicitly dismisses many of these models, arguing that "those circles in which popular, serious Bible reading is most widespread—conservative Protestant, charismatic, Cursillo, base communities—are often fundamentalist and almost always precritical in their hermeneutics" ("Two Kinds of Ecumenism: Unitive and Interdenominational," 659).

65. Lindbeck, "Church's Mission to a Postmodern Culture," 45–47.

66. Lindbeck, *Nature of Doctrine*, 127.

67. Lindbeck, "Confession and Community: An Israel-like View of the Church," 495.

68. Lindbeck, *Nature of Doctrine*, 128. Lindbeck nevertheless resists the Christendom perspective. Christianity is not to seek cultural and social power. The church must not strive to program the culture; this can only be a by-product of the church's faithfulness (Lindbeck, "Church's Mission to a Postmodern Culture," 54).

69. Lindbeck, "Atonement and the Hermeneutics of Intratextual Social Embodiment," 235–36.

70. The advertising industry is perhaps the most prominent example. But powerful church leaders also at times attempt to tie into the popular faith expressions of the people. The debates around the Latin American Bishops' Conference in Puebla are one example. See Joerg Rieger, *Remember the Poor: The Challenge to Theology in the Twenty-First Century* (Harrisburg, Pa.: Trinity, 1998), 56–57, 191.

71. D. Z. Phillips, "Lindbeck's Audience," *Modern Theology* 4, no. 2 (January 1998), 153.

72. Mark Ellingsen, *A Common Sense Theology: The Bible, Faith, and American Society* (Macon, Ga.: Mercer Univ. Press, 1995), 191.

73. Ibid., 55. Ellingsen finds himself in agreement with the work of Robert Bellah, Allan Bloom, and Christopher Lash.

74. Ibid., 77.

75. Ibid., 154; reference to a 1993 Gallup Poll. This position, it is claimed, can still do justice to 44 percent who doubt that the Bible is accurate in all details.

76. Ibid., 12 and n. 20.

77. See, for example, Olson, "Back to the Bible." See also Olson, "Postconservative Evangelicals Greet the Postmodern Age," *Christian Century* (May 3, 1995), 481.

78. Timothy R. Phillips and Dennis L. Okholm, *The Nature of Confession: Evangelicals and Postliberals in Conversation*, ed. Timothy R. Phillips and Dennis L. Okholm (Downers Grove, Ill.: InterVarsity, 1996), 11, 20. Lindbeck himself realizes that for the postliberal research project to have "a real future as a communal enterprise of the church, it's more likely to be carried on by evangelicals than anyone else" (Lindbeck, "Atonement and the Hermeneutics of Intratextual Social Embodiment," 253).

79. Theophus Smith, "Ethnography-as-Theology: Inscribing the African American Sacred Story," in *Theology without Foundations*, 119, 120.

80. Lindbeck's approach has also been related to other more radical approaches such as the work of Sharon Welch and Cornel West; see Gordon Michalson, "The Response to Lindbeck," *Modern Theology* 4, no. 2 (January 1988), 118, n. 7. But Welch's own comments about the difference between intratextual positions such as Lindbeck's and her own intertextual position are clear. See her *A Feminist Ethic of Risk* (Minneapolis: Fortress Press, 1990), 123–24: "Unlike theorists who argue that the prerequisite of solid moral reasoning is a cohesive community with a shared set of principles, norms, and mores, I argue that material interaction between multiple communities with divergent principles, norms, and mores is essential for foundational moral critique." In other words, self-critique is not possible within a closed community.

81. Amy Plantinga Pauw, "The Word Is near You: A Feminist Conversation with George Lindbeck," *Theology Today* 50, no. 1 (April 1993), 45, 49, 50.

82. Ibid., 46.

83. Ibid., 51–52.

84. Kathryn Tanner, "Social Theory Concerning the 'New Social Movements' and the Practice of Feminist Theology," in *Horizons in Feminist Theology: Identity, Tradition, and Norms,* ed. Rebecca S. Chopp and Sheila Greeve Davaney (Minneapolis: Fortress Press, 1997), 189–90. Tanner argues for a tradition that is "self-critical, pluralistic, and flexible." See also Kathryn Tanner, "Theology and the Plain Sense," in *Scriptural Authority and Narrative Interpretation*, ed. Garrett Green (Philadelphia: Fortress Press, 1987), 75.

85. See Robin W. Lovin, "Religion, Civil Rights, and Civic Community," in *Religion, Race, and Justice in a Changing America*, ed. Gary Orfield and Holly Lebowitz Rossi (New York: Century Foundation, 1999), 82.

86. Anthony B. Robinson, "Beyond Civic Faith," *Christian Century* (October 14, 1998), 934–35.

87. Copenhaver puts his finger on an important issue: "I have not lost interest in ministering to a hurting world. But determination is not enough to sustain compassion" (Martin B. Copenhaver, "Formed Reformed," *Christian Century* [October 14, 1998], 938). Copenhaver's essay parallels that of Robinson (both are

under the headline "The Making of a Postliberal"; the Robinson quote is from "Beyond Civic Faith," 936.)

88. Herb Miller, "Managing Lifeboats," *North Texas United Methodist Reporter* (January 22, 1999), 4.

89. Copenhaver, "Formed Reformed," 938.

90. Rebekah Miles, "The Faith behind the Confessions: Postmodern Assumptions behind the United Methodist Confessing Movement," *Quarterly Review* (winter 1997–1998), 341, 343.

91. Justo González writes from a North American Hispanic context and Gustavo Gutiérrez from Peru. See Justo González, *Mañana: Christian Theology from a Hispanic Perspective* (Nashville, Tenn.: Abingdon, 1990), 86; and Gustavo Gutiérrez, *We Drink from Our Own Wells: The Spiritual Journey of a People*, trans. Matthew J. O'Connell (Maryknoll, N.Y.: Orbis, 1984), 34.

92. Lindbeck, "Atonement and the Hermeneutics of Intratextual Social Embodiment," 240.

93. Lindbeck, "Barth and Textuality," 374.

94. Cf. Robert Samuels, *Between Philosophy and Psychoanalysis: Lacan's Reconstruction of Freud* (New York: Routledge, 1993), 89.

95. Gustavo Gutiérrez, *The Power of the Poor in History*, trans. Robert R. Barr (Maryknoll, N.Y.: Orbis, 1983), 113.

96. Tanner, *Theories of Culture*, 168.

Chapter 4

1. Toril Moi ("Feminism, Postmodernism, and Style: Recent Feminist Criticism in the United States," *Cultural Critique* [spring 1988]) reminds postmodernist feminists that an "abstract, ontological feminization of Otherness" will not liberate the oppressed because it does not take seriously the situation of women.

2. Recently more attention has been given to the interrelationships of the three modes. See, for example, John E. Thiel, *Imagination and Authority: Theological Authorship in the Modern Tradition* (Minneapolis: Fortress Press, 1991); Hans W. Frei, *Types of Christian Theology*, ed. George Hunsinger and William C. Placher (New Haven: Yale Univ. Press, 1992); and David Tracy, *On Naming the Present: Reflections on God, Hermeneutics, and Church* (Maryknoll, N.Y.: Orbis, 1994).

3. In the North American context liberation theology has commonly been related to the modern turn to the self. See Roger Haight, *An Alternative Vision: An Interpretation of Liberation Theology* (New York: Paulist Press, 1985); and Peter C. Hodgson, *New Birth of Freedom: A Theology of Bondage and Liberation* (Philadelphia: Fortress Press, 1976). Lately, however, there have also been arguments for relating liberation theology to the turn to the tradition. See Terrence Tilley, *Postmodern Theologies: The Challenge of Religious Diversity* (Maryknoll, N.Y.: Orbis, 1995); and Richard Shaull, *The Reformation and Liberation Theology: Insights for the Challenges of Today* (Louisville, Ky.: Westminster John Knox, 1991). The relation to the turn to the Other has been less frequent, but the work of Frederick Herzog, *God-Walk: Liberation Shaping Dogmatics* (Maryknoll, N.Y.: Orbis, 1988) referring to notions such as theopraxis, christopraxis, and spiritpraxis, has taken up this concern.

4. I take a first step in this direction in my book *Remember the Poor: The*

Challenge to Theology in the Twenty-First Century (Harrisburg, Pa.: Trinity, 1998).

5. For a dialogue of such perspectives, see Joerg Rieger, ed., *Liberating the Future: God, Mammon, and Theology,* (Minneapolis: Fortress Press, 1998).

6. Male study of feminist thought is not strictly done from the outside, but from the other side: we need to understand not just what sexism does to women but what it does to men, to those who benefit from sexist structures. Rebecca S. Chopp ("Feminist and Womanist Theologies," in *The Modern Theologians: An Introduction to Christian Theology in the Twentieth Century*, ed. David F. Ford [Cambridge, Mass.: Basil Blackwell, 1997], 402) formulates the challenge of the feminist perspective for theology in the form of a question: "Is feminist theology a special language only for a few, or is it an important language for all Christians?" This chapter responds to Chopp's question, exploring the importance of the feminist approach for Christian theology as a whole.

7. One of the early texts is Jacqueline Grant, *White Women's Christ and Black Women's Jesus: Feminist Christology and Womanist Response* (Atlanta, Ga.: Scholars, 1989). See also Ada María Isasi-Díaz, *Mujerista Theology: A Theology for the Twenty-First Century* (Maryknoll, N.Y.: Orbis, 1996). For a discussion of various shapes of feminist theory and their relation to human nature and politics, see Alison M. Jaggar, *Feminist Politics and Human Nature* (Totowa, N.J.: Rowman and Littlefield, 1988).

8. For the effects of the global market on various modes of liberation theology, see the essays in Joerg Rieger, ed., *Liberating the Future.* Already in the eighties Angela Y. Davis (*Women, Race, and Class* [New York: Vintage, 1983]) explored the interdependencies of race, sex, and class.

9. Particularly the latest visions promote a closer look at the specific shape of women's marginality, beyond the liberal feminist emphasis on equality and the romantic feminist emphasis on feminine essence. See, for example, Rebecca S. Chopp's account in *The Power to Speak: Feminism, Language, God* (New York: Crossroad, 1991), 107.

10. See Joerg Rieger, "Developing a Common Interest Theology from the Underside," in *Liberating the Future: God, Mammon, and Theology,* ed. Joerg Rieger (Minneapolis: Fortress Press, 1998).

11. Sandra Harding, "The Instability of the Analytical Categories of Feminist Theory," *Journal of Women in Culture and Society* 11, no. 4 (1986), 649. Harding argues that feminist thought must not replicate modern thought's reliance on Archimedean points—replacing the liberal notion of experience with women's experience, for instance—but must move forward by embracing the instability of analytical categories.

12. Mary McClintock Fulkerson, *Changing the Subject: Women's Discourses and Feminist Theology* (Minneapolis: Fortress Press, 1994), 325.

13. For a recent example, cf. R. R. Reno, "Feminist Theology as a Modern Project," *Pro Ecclesia* 5, no. 4 (1996).

14. Rosemary Radford Ruether, *Sexism and God-Talk: Toward a Feminist Theology* (Boston: Beacon, 1993), xviii. Cf. Rita Nakashima Brock, "What Is Feminist? Strategies for Change and Transformations of Consciousness," in *Setting the Table: Women in Theological Conversation*, ed. Rita Nakashima Brock, Claudia Camp, and Serene Jones (St. Louis: Chalice, 1995), 6: "Feminist thinking began with women's awareness of a mismatch between our lives and the social, cultural, and religious expectations, stereotypes, and attitudes imposed on us."

Letty M. Russell (*Household of Freedom: Authority in Feminist Theology* [Philadelphia: Westminster John Knox, 1987], 18) points out that for this reason feminist theologians take "the *via negativa* and describe the contradictions of our past and present social, political, economic, and ecclesial experiences. But at the same time, we live out of a vision of God's intention for a mended creation. . . . In an important sense Christian feminists only have this future."

15. Marian Ronan ("Reclaiming Women's Experience: A Reading of Selected Christian Feminist Theologies," *Cross Currents* 48, no. 2 [summer 1998]) describes how the commonly used phrase "theologizing from the base of women's experience" became more and more problematic for her, living in the diversity of New York City. Chronicling the progress in the debates on women's experiences, Ronan describes a second step in the development of the focus on women's experience that is more aware of historical differences, even though at this stage there are still parallels to what I have called the turn to the self. It is only in a third step that feminist theologians such as Mary McClintock Fulkerson, Rebecca S. Chopp, and Sharon Welch develop women's experience in terms of more complex structures, inviting a self-critical perspective.

16. Consuelo del Prado, "I Sense God in Another Way," in *Through Her Eyes: Women's Theology from Latin America,* ed. Elsa Tamez (Maryknoll, N.Y.: Orbis, 1989), 140.

17. María Pilar Aquino, *Our Cry for Life: Feminist Theology from Latin America* (Maryknoll, N.Y.: Orbis, 1993), 151, 153.

18. The subaltern study groups explore specific phenomena of subordination and oppression. A closer look at the actual situation of the people must now verify the postmodern lesson that "the subaltern is not one thing" but rather a "mutating, migrating subject." The analysis of otherness and difference is opened up beyond the traditional concern for the plight of one oppressed group to other groups as well. See for instance the Latin American Subaltern Studies Group's "Founding Statement," *Boundary 2* 20, no. 3 (fall 1993), 121.

19. Laura E. Donaldson, *Decolonizing Feminisms: Race, Gender, and Empire-Building* (Chapel Hill: Univ. of North Carolina Press, 1992), 138. Donaldson (ibid., 11) critiques the colonialist impulse to reduce the other to the same and its manifestations in feminism. In this regard the debates around the notion of "postcolonialism" have explored new ground. See, for example, *Postcolonialism and Scriptural Reading,* ed. Laura E. Donaldson, *Semeia* 75 (Atlanta, Ga.: Scholars, 1996).

20. Rebecca S. Chopp, "Theorizing Feminist Theology," in *Horizons in Feminist Theology: Identity, Tradition, and Norms,* ed. Rebecca S. Chopp and Sheila Greeve Davaney (Minneapolis: Fortress Press, 1997), 226.

21. Susan B. Thistlethwaite, *Sex, Race, and God: Christian Feminism in Black and White* (New York: Crossroad, 1989), 2. Emphasis in original.

22. Ibid., 43, 44. Thistlethwaite points out that black women have understood that.

23. Ibid., 22.

24. Ibid., 91.

25. Delores S. Williams, *Sisters in the Wilderness: The Challenge of Womanist God-Talk* (Maryknoll, N.Y.: Orbis, 1993), xi, xii. She relates her method to Anselm of Canterbury's "faith seeking understanding."

26. Ibid., 108.

27. Ibid., 12.

28. Isasi-Díaz, *Mujerista Theology,* 3. "What passes as objectivity in reality merely names the subjectivity of those who have the authority and/or power to impose their point of view. So instead of objectivity what we should be claiming is responsibility for our subjectivity. All theology has to start with self-disclosure" (ibid., 77).

29. Ibid., 5.

30. Ibid., 67–69.

31. Ibid., 81, 83 n.5.

32. Fulkerson, *Changing the Subject*, 311.

33. Mary McClintock Fulkerson, "*Theologia* as a Liberation *Habitus:* Thoughts toward Christian Formation for Resistance," in *Theology and the Interhuman: Essays in Honor of Edward Farley,* ed. Robert R. Williams (Valley Forge, Pa.: Trinity, 1995), 174.

34. Sheila Briggs ("'Buried with Christ': The Politics of Identity and the Poverty of Interpretation," in *The Book and the Text: The Bible and Literary Theory,* ed. R. Schwartz [Cambridge, Mass.: Basil Blackwell, 1990]) points out the dangers of identity politics, since everybody unites in themselves different identities. Even an emphasis on community that does not pay attention to the fragmentation of real life leads to hegemony. Briggs argues that any form of "sameness" supports cultural hegemony.

35. Fulkerson, *Changing the Subject,* 348.

36. For a list of names of the second generation, see, for example, the contributors to *Horizons in Feminist Theology.*

37. Fulkerson, *Changing the Subject,* 359, 354. At the national meeting of the American Academy of Religion in 1998, Laura E. Donaldson pointed out, from a Native American perspective, that we need to rethink the role not only of the colonizers but of the colonized as well, in order to avoid the disappearance of their history into the victim complex. Too often the situation of the colonized is seen as uniform and monolithic—a situation where time stands still. Donaldson tells the history of independent Cherokee women.

38. Rey Chow ("Where Have All the Natives Gone?" in *Displacements: Cultural Identities in Question,* Theories of Contemporary Culture, vol. 15, ed. Angelika Bammer [Bloomington: Indiana Univ. Press, 1994], 133) cautions: "As we challenge a dominant discourse by 'resurrecting' the victimized voice/self of the native with our readings . . . we step, far too quickly, into the otherwise silent and invisible place of the native and turn ourselves into living agents/witnesses for her."

39. This is one of the main points in Joerg Rieger, *Remember the Poor.*

40. Fulkerson, *Changing the Subject,* viii. Emphasis in original.

41. Ruether, *Sexism and God-Talk,* 13. Ruether accepts that "human experience is the starting point and the ending point of the hermeneutical circle" (ibid., 12).

42. Ruether, *Sexism and God-Talk,* xvi. She understands that this "cross-cultural" and "multivocal" dialogue has put her own work into its appropriate context, "as the work of one feminist theologian among others, functioning in an Anglo-American Christian context." Sheila Davaney ("The Limits of the Appeal to Women's Experience," in *Shaping New Vision: Gender and Values in American Culture,* ed. Clarissa W. Atkinson, Constance H. Buchanan, and Margaret R. Miles [Ann Arbor, Mich.: UMI Research Press, 1989], 31–49) is one of the first white feminists to point out that white women have made a mistake similar to white men

by universalizing their own experience. Cf. Sheila Greeve Davaney, "Problems with Feminist Theory: Historicity and the Search for Sure Foundations," in *Embodied Love: Sensuality and Relationship as Feminist Values,* ed. Paula M. Cooey, Sharon A. Farmer, and Mary Ellen Ross (San Francisco: Harper & Row, 1987), 79–95. Thistlethwaite (*Sex, Race, and God*) is also concerned with this issue and develops it further in relation to black women.

43. Mary McClintock Fulkerson, "Sexism as Original Sin: Developing a Theacentric Discourse," *Journal of the American Academy of Religion* 59, no. 4 (winter 1991), 656 n.6.

44. Williams, *Sisters in the Wilderness,* 108–9. This type of experience, Williams suggests, broadens black theology's vision of experience and promotes constructive interaction of other liberation perspectives (ibid., 158, 160).

45. See also Joerg Rieger, *Remember the Poor,* 75–88.

46. Graham Ward, review of *Changing the Subject: Women's Discourses and Feminist Theology* by Mary McClintock Fulkerson, in *Modern Theology* 11, no. 4 (October 1995), 478.

47. Russell, *Household of Freedom,* 20.

48. Fulkerson, *Changing the Subject,* 370.

49. See ibid., 383.

50. Ibid., 384 n.31. At this point, Fulkerson's critique of Sharon Welch's neglect of God's transcendence is more crucial than the brief footnote acknowledges, since theologians, part of the "professional managerial class," are in special need of the critique a theo/acentric perspective delivers.

51. Ibid., 384.

52. Ibid., 395.

53. Ibid., 336. Already the pioneers of feminist theology, such as Ruether and the early work of Mary Daly—even though strongly influenced by modern theology—rely more fully on "appropriation of the memory of the Christian community."

54. Mary McClintock Fulkerson, "Contesting the Gendered Subject: A Feminist Account of the Imago Dei," in *Horizons in Feminist Theology,* 115: "If there is insight in telling Christian stories, it might be that they can invite us to move ceaselessly toward the discovery of new 'outsides,' new strangers and the conditions that support them."

55. Fulkerson, *Changing the Subject,* 358, reference to Rebecca S. Chopp.

56. Ibid.

57. See Mary McClintock Fulkerson, "Theological Education and the Problem of Identity," *Modern Theology* 5 (October 1991), 477.

58. Mary McClintock Fulkerson, "Toward a Materialist Social Criticism," in *Changing Conversations: Religious Reflection and Cultural Analysis,* ed. Dwight N. Hopkins and Sheila Greeve Davaney (New York: Routledge, 1996), 55. In *Changing the Subject,* 91, Fulkerson promotes a "materialist" approach that pays "consistent attention to the particular and the changing relations that constitute reality." The term "materialism," in this context, does not appeal to stuff out there; the point is rather to widen the attention to the way everything participates in structures of power and interest.

59. Fulkerson, "*Theologia* as a Liberation *Habitus,*" 164. "We must be able to see the ways our discourse *produces* the other as a result of where *we* are" (Fulkerson, *Changing the Subject,* 381, 382). Emphasis in original.

60. While Davaney ("Limits of the Appeal to Women's Experience") has challenged the notion of truth from the perspective of white feminist theology, some feminist theologians such as Marjorie Suchocki and Pamela Young continue to look for moral or metaphysical foundations. See, for example, Pamela Dickey Young, "Feminist Theology: From Past to Future," in *Gender Genre and Religion: Feminist Reflections*, ed. Morny, Joy and Eva K. Neumaier-Dargyay (Waterloo, Ontario: Wilfred Laurier Univ. Press, 1995), 78.

61. Chopp, *Power to Speak*, 28. See also Fulkerson, *Changing the Subject*, 67.

62. Isasi-Díaz, *Mujerista Theology*, 70, 72. In this context the differences between *mujeristas* and womanists must not be forgotten. While both value popular Christian traditions, the role of experience in relation to the authority of the Bible is different. In the mainly Roman Catholic context of current *mujerista* theology, the Bible is not as central as in the black community. Isasi-Díaz claims that in *mujerista* theology the starting point is not the Bible but Hispanic women's experience and struggle for survival. Nevertheless, in this context room is created for the biblical text to raise questions (ibid., 149, 164).

63. Fulkerson sees herself as problematizing the knowledge of truth but not the possibility of truth. See, for example, *Changing the Subject*, 373, reference to Donna Haraway. Acknowledging multiple points of view does not mean to reject truth, but here a sense develops in which multiple visions are necessary in order to broaden the horizon.

64. Susan L. Secker, "Women's Experience in Feminist Theology: The 'Problem' or the 'Truth' of Difference," *Journal of Hispanic/Latino Theology* 1, no. 1 (1993), 56.

65. Rebecca S. Chopp, *Saving Work: Feminist Practices of Theological Education* (Louisville, Ky.: Westminster John Knox, 1995), 80, 81.

66. Ibid., 82, 83. When Chopp then moves on to the topics of "ethics" and "praxis," this might be mistaken for the liberal emphasis on the autonomous self and its "just do it" mentality. But what is at stake is the development of new selves in resistance to the modern self.

67. Mary Gerhart, "Framing Discourse for the Future," in *Gender Genre and Religion*, 14.

68. Fulkerson, *Changing the Subject*, 120.

69. Ibid., 138–39.

70. Fulkerson observes a similar problem: "From the position of a feminist analytic, 'community' is a false unity and needs to be contested as such, lest it be allowed to replace the universal subject in relation to the text" (ibid., 150).

71. Ibid., 150.

72. Ibid., 154, 164.

73. Cf. Stephen B. Bevans, *Models of Contextual Theology* (Maryknoll, N.Y.: Orbis, 1992), 64.

74. Fulkerson, *Changing the Subject*, 370; the term goes back to Richard Hays.

75. Sheila Greeve Davaney, "Changing Conversations: Impetuses and Implications," in *Changing Conversations*, 255. For attention to such ordinary sites of meaning, see also the other essays in that volume.

76. Chopp, *Saving Work*, 56.

77. Paula Cooey, "Bad Women," in *Horizons of Feminist Theology*, 152. For the danger of romanticization, see also Joerg Rieger, *Remember the Poor*.

78. Cooey, "Bad Women," 142–43, 150.

79. Jeanette Rodríguez, "Experience as a Resource for Feminist Thought," *Journal of Hispanic and Latino Theology* 1, no. 1 (1993), 71.

80. Secker, "Women's Experience in Feminist Theology," 65.

81. Fredric Jameson, "Third-World Literature in the Era of Multinational Capitalism," *Social Text* 15 (fall 1986), 85.

82. Fulkerson, *Changing the Subject,* 390.

83. Mary McClintock Fulkerson, "Changing the Subject: Feminist Theology and Discourse," *Literature and Theology* 10 (June 1996), 133.

84. Fulkerson, *Changing the Subject,* 294. See also her essay "Changing the Subject," 140.

85. Mary McClintock Fulkerson ("Gender—Being It or Doing It? The Church, Homosexuality, and the Politics of Identity," *Union Seminary Quarterly Review* 47, no. 1–2 (spring 1994), 33) refers to the work of Michel Foucault and Judith Butler. Both liberal and conservative positions on homosexuality, for instance, seem to share the assumption that sexuality is at the core of the self and the convergence of gender with sex (ibid., 37–38).

86. Ibid., 40.

87. Chopp, *Saving Work,* 51.

88. Marjorie Procter-Smith, *In Her Own Rite: Constructing Feminist Liturgical Tradition* (Nashville, Tenn.: Abingdon, 1990), 171, reference to poet Muriel Rukeyser.

89. Conversation with the German pastor and theologian Brigitte Enzner-Probst, May 1999. See also Teresa Berger, *Sei gesegnet meine Schwester: Frauen feiern Liturgie* (Würzburg: Echter, 1999); and *idem, Women's Ways of Worship: Gender Analysis and Liturgical History* (Collegeville, Minn.: Liturgical, 1999).

90. Procter-Smith, *In Her Own Rite,* 147.

91. Ibid., 148.

92. Ibid., 53.

93. Ibid., 164. This spirituality includes the political.

94. Frederick Herzog (*Liberation Theology: Liberation in the Light of the Fourth Gospel* [New York: Seabury, 1972], 222) has reminded us that the church must not become the thing itself: "The liberation church is not a matter of being realized here and there in beautifully visible groups. As soon as we begin to point to the holy few . . . we have surrendered our theological integrity." We need to learn to focus beyond ourselves, "to the place where we can see God doing his thing, quiet, unobtrusive, inconspicuous—where we least expect it." For good reasons, one of the epigraphs in my book *Remember the Poor* reminds us that "the poor do not exist."

95. Against Thiel, *Imagination and Authority*, 27–29. Cf. Antonio Gramsci's notion of the organic intellectual and my interpretation in the final chapter of *Remember the Poor*.

96. Sharon Welch, *A Feminist Ethic of Risk* (Minneapolis: Fortress Press, 1990), 150.

Chapter 5

1. The point of Lacan's model of reflection is, therefore, not to find an Archimedean point that is always the same. But he continues to search for truth—as that which moves people and the factors that produce it. "More than any other

rhetorical theory, Lacan's model provides the means for explaining how a given text [subject matter] *moves* people." Emphasis in original. (Mark Bracher, "On the Psychological and Social Functions of Language: Lacan's Theory of the Four Discourses," in *Lacanian Theory of Discourse: Subject, Structure, and Society,* ed. Mark Bracher et al. [New York: New York Univ. Press, 1994], 126). Emphasis in original.

2. Jacques Lacan, "The Agency of the Letter in the Unconscious," in *Jacques Lacan. Écrits: A Selection,* trans. Alan Sheridan (New York: Norton, 1977) 165. For the term "ego's era," see Jacques Lacan, "Function and Field of Speech and Language in Psychoanalysis," *Écrits,* 71. Lacan has discovered these structures in his practical work as a psychoanalyst. See Shoshana Felman, *Jacques Lacan and the Adventure of Insight* (Cambridge, Mass.: Harvard Univ. Press, 1987). According to Lacan, part of the genius of Freud lies in the fact that he did not block out evidences and experiences derived from his praxis; this led the way into new reflection. Cf. Jacques Lacan, "The Agency of the Letter in the Unconscious, or Reason since Freud," *Écrits,* 167; and Felman, *Jaques Lacan and the Adventure of Insight,* 24.

3. For further exploration of the aggressivity of the modern self, closely related to its narcissism, see Joerg Rieger, *Remember the Poor,* 24ff.

4. See, for example, the bestseller by Christopher Lasch, *The Culture of Narcissism: American Life in an Age of Diminishing Expectations* (New York: Norton, 1978). See also Charles Taylor, *Sources of the Self: The Making of the Modern Identity* (Cambridge, Mass.: Harvard Univ. Press, 1989).

5. For additional aspects of this problem, see also Joerg Rieger, *Remember the Poor,* 23–28.

6. Lacan introduced the four discourses in his 1969–1970 seminar "L'envers de la psychanalyse." The established text of this seminar is now available in French as *Jacques Lacan, Le séminaire Livre XVII. L'envers de la psychanalyse,* ed. Jacques-Alain Miller (Paris: Éditions du Seuil, 1991). I will quote this text as *L'envers de la psychanalyse.* Translations are mine unless otherwise indicated.

7. These suggestions led to the hostility of a large number of students. Cf. Marcelle Marini, *Jacques Lacan: The French Context,* trans. A. Tomiche (New Brunswick, N.J.: Rutgers Univ. Press, 1992), 63.

8. Cf. Nestor A. Braunstein, "The Transference in the Four Discourses," *Prose Studies* 11, no. 3 (December 1988), 51.

9. Those deeper levels are not foundations that are a priori, given, or untouchable; the deeper levels are produced by repressions, by that which is foreclosed from the surface level. At a time when postmodern theory stresses the surface level in terms of "metonymy," Lacan maintains the importance of "metaphor," that which is repressed below the surface. See Joerg Rieger, *Remember the Poor,* 78, including nn. 6 and 7. A similar dynamic has been explored by feminist thinkers. See Rosemary Hennessy, *Materialist Feminism and the Politics of Discourse* (New York: Routledge, 1993), 93, whose "symptomatic reading" promotes an exploration of what has been repressed and reappears in the form of symptoms. For the Lacanian interpretation of the symptom, see Joerg Rieger, *Remember the Poor,* 83–84.

10. Mark Bracher, "Lacan's Theory of the Four Discourses," *Prose Studies* 11, no. 3 (December 1988), 45.

11. Fredric Jameson ("Imaginary and Symbolic in Lacan," in *The Ideologies of Theory: Essays 1971–1986,* vol. 1 [Minneapolis: Univ. of Minnesota Press, 1988],

114) interprets the discourse of the self as "a commitment to existential authenticity, to the obedience of Hegel's 'law of the heart,' and to a repudiation of the letter for the 'spirit' when the latter can be identified within us as true meaning and as what we instinctively 'know' and recognize."

12. Walter Rauschenbusch (*A Theology for the Social Gospel* [Nashville, Tenn.: Abingdon, 1978], 3) notes that "the impulse to social service" is the most important and most religious element in the lives of many in the student population, even for ministerial students, where "there is an almost impatient demand for a proper social outlet." It is not surprising to hear him talk about "our determination to establish God's kingdom on earth" (ibid., 8).

13. This is the point at which Lacan leaves behind any philosophical dialectics of the Hegelian kind; this is the place of the "real." See my use of the Lacanian "real" in *Remember the Poor,* chapter 3.

14. "The being of man not only cannot be understood without madness, but it would not be the being of man if it did not carry madness within it as the limit of its liberty" (Lacan, quoted in Anthony Wilden's commentary in Jacques Lacan, *Speech and Language in Psychoanalysis,* trans. and commentary by Anthony Wilden [Baltimore: Johns Hopkins Univ. Press, 1981], 136, n.116).

15. Lacan, *Speech and Language in Psychoanalysis*, 43.

16. Lacan also includes organic stimuli into the functions of the self. The neurotic finds support "either in the natural functions of the subject" or "in the images which organize at the limit of the *Umwelt* and of the *Innenwelt,* their relational structuring" (Lacan, *Speech and Language in Psychoanalysis,* 43). This includes the imaginary order. See Joerg Rieger, *Remember the Poor,* 23–24.

17. Jameson, "Imaginary and Symbolic in Lacan," 112.

18. Ellie Ragland-Sullivan, *Jacques Lacan and the Philosophy of Psychoanalysis* (London: Croom Helm, 1986), 264.

19. Lacan, *L'envers de la psychanalyse,* as translated by Bracher, "Lacan's Theory of the Four Discourses," 37. There is apparently a typographical error in Bracher's text.

20. Ragland-Sullivan, *Jacques Lacan and the Philosophy of Psychoanalysis,* 76.

21. Braunstein, "Transference in the Four Discourses," 54. Braunstein examines how Lacan's earlier reflections on transference are related to the theory of the four discourses.

22. Cf. ibid., 58.

23. Schleiermacher, *On Religion: Speeches to Its Cultured Despisers*, trans. John Oman (Louisville: Westminster John Knox, 1994), 37.

24. Friedrich Schleiermacher, *On Religion: Speeches to Its Cultured Despisers,* trans. Richard Crouter (New York: Cambridge Univ. Press, 1988; 1999), 136. One of the differences between religion and "metaphysics and morals" is that the latter two "see in the whole universe only humanity as the center of all relatedness, as the condition of all being and the cause of all becoming." In contrast, "religion wishes to see the infinite, its imprint and its manifestation, in humanity no less than in all other individual and finite forms" (Schleiermacher, *On Religion* [trans. Crouter], 102). A similar issue is discussed somewhat later in the 1821 version of the second speech; see *On Religion* (trans. Oman), 36.

25. Churches are trying to make use of this. For instance: following up on new visitors by thanking them for attending their church, a suggestion recently made in a church newsletter.

26. In *The Christian Faith* Schleiermacher plays down the importance of the Old Testament.

27. See Bracher, "Lacan's Theory of the Four Discourses," 35.

28. Hans Frei argues that, after 250 years of neglect of the "classical themes of communal Christian language modeled by the Bible," Barth had to "recreate a universe of discourse" (Frei, "Eberhard Busch's Biography of Karl Barth," in *Karl Barth in Re-View: Posthumous Works Reviewed and Assessed*, ed. H.-M. Rumscheidt, Pittsburgh Theological Monograph series, vol. 30 [Pittsburgh: Pickwick, 1981], 111).

29. Jameson, "Imaginary and Symbolic in Lacan," 114.

30. Karl Barth, *Church Dogmatics,* vol. 1, bk. 1, ed. G. W. Bromiley and T. F. Torrance, trans. G. W. Bromiley (Edinburgh: T. & T. Clark, 1975), 199, 208, 222.

31. For Lacan's comments, see Lacan, *L'envers de la psychanalyse,* 101–2, 178, translated in Bracher, "On the Psychological and Social Functions of Language," 121.

32. Ragland-Sullivan, *Jacques Lacan and the Philosophy of Psychoanalysis,* 305.

33. Juliet Mitchell and Jacqueline Rose, eds, *Feminine Sexuality: Jacques Lacan and the école freudienne,* trans. Jacqueline Rose (New York: Norton, 1982), 161, n.6, footnote to Lacan, "A Love Letter." The wisdom of a popular joke makes a similar point. Asked why Barth had to die before he could finish *Church Dogmatics,* God responds, "He knew too much!"

34. To be sure, I am not following the standard evangelical critique that Barth is still a modernist because he does not fully embrace "classical orthodoxy" and denies "any stable foundation." See R. Albert Mohler Jr., "The Integrity of the Evangelical Tradition and the Challenge of the Postmodern Paradigm," in *The Challenge of Postmodernism: An Evangelical Engagement,* ed. David S. Dockery (Wheaton, Ill.: Bridge Point, 1995), 76.

35. Lacan, *Speech and Language in Psychoanalysis,* 43.

36. Ibid., 130, n.102, commentary by Wilden.

37. Braunstein, "Transference in the Four Discourses," 54.

38. Ragland-Sullivan, "Limits of Discourse Structure," 75.

39. Cf. Lacan, *L'envers de la psychanalyse,* 218; cf. Bracher, "On the Psychological and Social Functions of Language," 122.

40. Braunstein, "Transference in the Four Discourses," 56.

41. Nestor Braunstein, "Con-jugating and Playing-with the Fantasy," in *Lacanian Theory of Discourse,* 152.

42. There remains a certain ambiguity in Lindbeck's work. He seems to move back and forth between Bible (more strongly emphasized in *The Nature of Doctrine*) and creed. Elsewhere he points out that his starting point is "neither biblicistic nor experiential and certainly not individualistic, but dogmatic: it commences with the historical Christian communal confession of faith in Christ," starting with the ancient trinitarian and christological creeds (Lindbeck, "Confession and Community: An Israel-like View of the Church," *Christian Century* (May 9, 1990), 494.

43. According to Ferdinand de Saussure, the father of structuralism, language (made up of differential relations between signified and signifier without positive terms) is what creates reality and meaning. Post-structuralism goes one step further and focuses virtually exclusively on the signifier, thus putting even more emphasis on language than Saussure did.

44. Cf. Braunstein, "Transference in the Four Discourses," 51.

45. Lindbeck, *The Nature of Doctrine: Religion and Theology in a Postliberal Age* (Philadelphia: Westminster, 1984), 126.

46. Braunstein, "Transference in the Four Discourses," 52.

47. Lacan, *L'envers de la psychanalyse,* 220; see also Bracher, "On the Psychological and Social Functions of Language," 116. That production happens both in relation to the self (even though culture does not want to admit that even the cultural virtuosity of its leaders is produced) and in relation to the master signifiers.

48. Lacan, *L'envers de la psychanalyse,* 179, referred to in Bracher, "On the Psychological and Social Functions of Language," 114.

49. Cf. Bracher, ibid., 115.

50. Jameson, "Imaginary and Symbolic in Lacan," 114.

51. Cf. Mark Bracher, *Lacan, Discourse, and Social Change: A Psychoanalytic Cultural Criticism* (Ithaca: Cornell Univ. Press, 1993), 56. Bracher nevertheless sees this as somewhat oppressive since it is still aimed at subordinating the students.

52. James Buckley, "Doctrine in the Diaspora," *The Thomist* 49, no. 3 (1985), 457.

53. Miroslav Volf, "Theology, Meaning, and Power: A Conversation with George Lindbeck on Theology and the Nature of Christian Difference," in *Nature of Confession,* 56f.

54. Lacan, *Speech and Language in Psychoanalysis,* 44. The previous quotation is on 62.

55. Ibid., 45.

56. Ragland-Sullivan, *Jacques Lacan and the Philosophy of Psychoanalysis,* 285.

57. Lacan, *Speech and Language in Psychoanalysis,* 44.

58. Ibid., 45.

59. Braunstein, "Transference in the Four Discourses," 55.

60. Ibid.

61. Ibid.

62. Bracher, "On the Psychological and Social Functions of Language," 117.

63. "The analyst is not the possessor of a diploma but the site of a listening attention in which he or she is constantly surprised, reimplicated" (Stephen Heath, "Difference," *Journal of the Society for Education in Film and Television* 19, no. 3 [1978], 52, n.1).

64. See Mikkel Borch-Jacobsen, *Lacan: The Absolute Master* (Stanford: Stanford Univ. Press, 1991), 5–8.

65. Jacques Lacan, "Seminar 20, *Encore*" (1972–1973), in *Feminine Sexuality,* 144. It is important to note that Lacan's discussion of sexuality is not an argument as to what women or men essentially are but an analysis of existing identifications and power structures and the modes of their construction in the ego's era (against Alice A. Jardine, *Gynesis: Configurations of Woman and Modernity* [Ithaca: Cornell Univ. Press, 1985], 107, 116).

66. Cf. Jacqueline Rose, "Introduction II," in *Feminine Sexuality,* 50: "As negative to the man, woman becomes a total object of fantasy (or an object of total fantasy), elevated into the place of the Other and made to stand for its truth. . . . this is the ultimate form of mystification."

67. Rose, "Introduction II," 48. Lacan's statement can be found in Jacques Lacan, "Seminar of 21 January 1975," in *Feminine Sexuality,* 167. Cf. Jacques Lacan, *Television,* trans. Denis Hollier, Rosalind Krauss, and Annette Michelson; *A*

challenge to the psychoanalytic establishment, trans. Jeffrey Mehlman; ed. Joan Copjec (New York: Norton, 1990), 38: "But the fact that she doesn't exist doesn't stop me from making her the object of one's desire."

68. Lacan, "Seminar 20, *Encore,*" 143–44, 152.

69. Fulkerson, *Changing the Subject: Women's Discourses and Feminist Theology* (Minneapolis: Fortress Press, 1994), 390. "The decentering of the feminist subject had to do with the removal of a false sense of the power and self-determination of the woman subject, a process crucial to the discernment of the social conditions of oppression" (Mary McClintock Fulkerson, "Theological Education and the Problem of Identity," *Modern Theology* 5 [October 1991], 475).

70. Lacan, *L'envers de la psychanalyse,* quoted and translated in Marini, *Jacques Lacan,* 64.

71. Cf. Braunstein, "Transference in the Four Discourses," 51.

72. Cf. Bracher, *Lacan, Discourse, and Social Change,* 73.

73. Cf. Lisa Isherwood, "Methodology," in *An A to Z of Feminist Theology,* ed. Lisa Isherwood and Dorothea McEwan (Sheffield, England: Sheffield, 1996), 138–39. Here feminist theology is seen as growing in part out of process theology, seen as congenial to feminist theology because of its emphasis on experience.

74. Bracher, *Lacan, Discourse, and Social Change,* 67. Bracher goes too far when he states that the "master signifiers are produced by the subject rather than imposed upon the subject from the outside" (Bracher, "On the Psychological and Social Functions of Language," 124). The self that we are talking about here is not the autonomous Cartesian self but the divided self whose relationship to the other elements can no longer be neglected.

75. I deal with this misunderstanding in *Remember the Poor.*

76. Rebecca S. Chopp, "Feminist and Womanist Theologies," in *The Modern Theologians: An Introduction to Christian Theology in the Twentieth Century*, ed. David F. Ford (Cambridge, Mass.: Basil Blackwell, 1997), 393.

77. Jameson, "Imaginary and Symbolic in Lacan," 115.

78. Braunstein, "Con-jugating and Playing-with the Fantasy," 151, 152.

79. At the same time, there is also a danger of overemphasizing the tradition in the position of the truth. Yet if the tradition is part of a larger process, it cannot be treated as absolute either.

80. Mary McClintock Fulkerson, "Contesting Feminist Canons: Discourse and the Problem of Sexist Texts," *Journal of Feminist Studies in Religion* 7, no. 2 (fall 1991), 57.

81. Unlike earlier feminists and liberationists, Fulkerson has built in a recognition of different selves, objects of desire, and master signifiers. See, for example, Fulkerson, "Contesting Feminist Canons," 69–70.

82. This brings us back to an earlier observation in Lacan, *Speech and Language in Psychoanalysis,* 69.

83. Bracher, "On the Psychological and Social Functions of Language," 123.

84. Unpublished transcript of Lacan, "L'envers de la *psychanalyse,*" 177, first part.

85. Unpublished transcript of Lacan, "L'envers de la *psychanalyse,*" 176, referred to in Bracher, "Lacan's Theory of the Four Discourses," 47; this is omitted in the established version in *L'envers de la psychanalyse.*

86. Bracher, "On the Psychological and Social Functions of Language," 126.

87. Rita Nakashima Brock, "What Is Feminist? Strategies for Change and

Transformations of Consciousness," in *Setting the Table: Women in Theological Conversation*, ed. Rita Nakashima Brock, Claudia Camp, and Serene Jones (St. Louis: Chalice, 1995), 12–13.

88. This overemphasis of the position of the analyst can be found in the psychoanalytical traditions that Lacan opposes, particularly Heinz Hartmann's ego psychology. Bracher seems to see the Lacanian analyst in a somewhat similar power position, since he does not really question the analyst's limits and dependencies (Bracher, "On the Psychological and Social Functions of Language," 123–28).

89. Braunstein, "Transference in the Four Discourses," 56.

90. Ibid., 57.

91. My colleague Danna Nolan Fewell keeps reminding me that in the Deuteronomic reform of the Old Testament the monarchy, building up the military, was quite concerned that each family and village took care of their own poor. Who is interested in the proliferation of charity in the contemporary ecclesial scene of the U.S.? What about the newly coined term "compassionate conservatism"?

92. Fulkerson, "*Theologia* as a Liberation *Habitus:* Thoughts toward Christian Formation for Resistance," in *Theology and the Interhuman: Essays in Honor of Edward Farley,* ed. Robert R. Williams (Valley Forge, Pa.: Trinity, 1995), 176.

93. Ibid., 172, 175.

94. Bracher, *Lacan, Discourse, and Social Change,* 68.

95. See Charles M. Wood, *Vision and Discernment: An Orientation in Theological Study* (Atlanta, Ga.: Scholars, 1985), pulling together the notions of authenticity, truth, and fittingness.

96. Lacan, interview in *Scilicet,* translated in Marini, *Jacques Lacan,* 63.

97. Jameson, "Imaginary and Symbolic in Lacan," 111.

98. Cf. Marini, *Jacques Lacan,* 64, 65. Another paradigm that I am not able to take up follows the position of the repressed "a," and how it gets pushed around: $ represses the other; S1 desires the other; S2 wants to do something for the other, and so on. Yet even in this model not all problems are solved once the other is put into the place of authority.

99. Lacan, *L'envers de la psychanalyse,* quoted and translated in Ragland-Sullivan, "Limits of Discourse Structure," 81.

100. Bracher, *Lacan, Discourse, and Social Change,* 78.

101. Tracy shows two interrelated aspects of the postmodern vision, pointing out that after an earlier turn to language and narrative we now have to deal with a growing concern for the other (David Tracy, "Theology and the Many Faces of Postmodernity," *Theology Today* 51, no. 1 [April 1994], 108). Yet he neglects to ask, Who put the other in place? and, What keeps the other in place? The other appears to be out there, simply overlooked by modernity and finally rediscovered by postmodernity. Tracy forgets that already modernity discovered the other, trying to co-opt otherness for its own purposes in various colonialist enterprises. We must not repeat that mistake in a different form.

Chapter 6

1. Irving Greenberg, quoted in Frederick Herzog, "New Birth of Conscience," in *Liberating the Future: God, Mammon, and Theology,* ed. Joerg Rieger (Minneapolis: Fortress Press, 1998), 149.

2. In the field of biblical studies Gary A. Phillips and Danna Nolan Fewell ("Ethics, Bible, Reading as If," in *Bible and Ethics of Reading,* ed. Danna Nolan Fewell and Gary A. Phillips, *Semeia* 77 [Atlanta, Ga.: Scholars, 1997], 1–20) have recently reminded us of the life-and-death character of reading biblical texts.

3. Paul Tillich, as we have seen in chapter 1, starts theology with the questions of humanity. But he never gets much beyond a fixed set of questions, the questions of middle-class existentialism.

4. Another parallel between feminist theology and Barth is the critique of the modern self. See Serene Jones, "This God Which Is Not One," in *Transfigurations: Theology and the French Feminists,* ed. C. W. Maggie Kim et al. (Minneapolis: Fortress Press, 1993), which relates Barth and postmodern French feminist thought. No doubt the concern for otherness and difference is a common feature here (ibid., 110). But—and Jones reminds us that this question should not be overlooked despite all the parallels—why does Barth's God end up male?

5. The Old Testament concern for the widows, the strangers, and the orphans sets the stage for Jesus' own concern for those at the margins and reminds us that such a concern must not be spiritualized prematurely.

6. A new awareness of the Other can help us to find a new approach to language and text of the church since, according to the Lacanian model, the Other takes up the place of the repressed truth in this discourse.

7. From a European perspective, for instance, it is difficult to understand how important references to God are for politicians and other public figures in the U.S.

8. According to the Lacanian paradigm, the turn to language and the text can also help to gain new insights into the turn to the other since language and text are the repressed elements in this discourse.

9. Hal Foster, *The Anti-Aesthetic: Essays on Postmodern Culture* (Port Townsend, Wash.: Bay, 1983), xi–xii.

10. Karl Barth, *Church Dogmatics,* vol. 1, bk. 1, 112.

11. This is where identity politics—where each group fights for its own needs—becomes a problem. Hall makes a commonly accepted point: "When the critical cutting edge of the Christian movement . . . falters and fragments into identity- and issue-theologies, victory is ceded to the most reactionary . . . elements within the churches" (Douglas John Hall, *Remembered Voices: Reclaiming the Legacy of "Neo-Orthodoxy"* [Louisville, Ky.: Westminster John Knox, 1998], 136, reference to Todd Gitlin's book on the culture wars).

12. Such texts include a broad range of material, beginning with ancient stories, such as Hagar and Ishmael in the Book of Genesis, and continuing in the faith expressions of women, diverse expressions of popular religion around the world, and the challenges of the prophets both ancient and new.

13. Gustavo Gutiérrez, "Church of the Poor," in *Born of the Poor: The Latin American Church since Medellín,* ed. Edward L. Cleary, O.P. (Notre Dame: Univ. of Notre Dame Press, 1990), 16.

14. I develop the idea of unity in difference in "Whaling Our Way into the

Twenty-First Century," in *Theology from the Belly of the Whale: A Frederick Herzog Reader,* ed. Joerg Rieger (Harrisburg, Pa.: Trinity, 1999), 9–10.

15. Mary McClintock Fulkerson, "Contesting the Gendered Subject: A Feminist Account of the Imago Dei," in *Horizons in Feminist Theology,* 115.

16. At Perkins School of Theology I have recently begun to experiment with new forms of spiritual formation that bring together experiences of students working alongside marginalized people with spiritual disciplines and theological reflection.

17. For biblical parallels, see the Psalms, the Gospels, 1 Corinthians, and many other texts.

18. The critiques of Ludwig Feuerbach are well-known examples.

19. In "Whaling Our Way into the Twenty-First Century," 7–8, I talk about this as "trialectic theology," taking up a term coined tongue-in-cheek by Frederick Herzog.

20. In the United Methodist tradition, which is my own, these four elements are also known as the "quadrilateral." Other theologians from various different contexts have picked up the four elements in their own ways. See, for example, Frederick Herzog, *God-Walk*; Lisa Sowle Cahill, *Between the Sexes: Foundations for a Christian Ethics of Sexuality* (Philadelphia: Fortress Press, 1985); and Alister E. McGrath, *Christian Theology: An Introduction* (Oxford: Blackwell, 1994).

21. Karl Barth, "Concluding Unscientific Postscript on Schleiermacher," in *The Theology of Schleiermacher: Lectures at Göttingen, Winter Semester of 1923–24,* ed. D. Ritschl, trans. G. W. Bromiley (Grand Rapids, Mich.: Eerdmans, 1982), 278. See also B. A. Gerrish, *Tradition and the Modern World: Reformed Theology in the Nineteenth Century* (Chicago: Univ. of Chicago Press, 1978), 39. Cf., for example, the following passage in Schleiermacher, *The Christian Faith*, ed. H. R. Mackintosh and J. S. Stewart (Edinburgh: T. & T. Clark, 1986), 573: "As no one can attain the new life except in and through the fellowship, he has his share in the Holy Spirit, not in his personal self-consciousness viewed by itself, but only in so far as he is conscious of his being part of this whole—that is, he shares the Spirit as a common consciousness."

22. Barth's ultimate critique of Schleiermacher, that "*the Word is not so assured here in its independence in respect to faith as should be the case if this theology of faith were a true theology of the Holy Spirit*" still stands as a fundamental critique. Karl Barth, *Protestant Theology in the Nineteenth Century: Its Background and History* (Valley Forge, Pa..: Judson, 1973), 471. Emphasis in original. See also Dietmar Lütz, *Homo Viator: Karl Barths Ringen mit Schleiermacher* (Zurich: Theologischer Verlag Zurich, 1988).

23. Michael Welker (*God the Spirit,* trans. John F. Hoffmeyer [Minneapolis: Fortress Press, 1994]) seems to put his finger on a similar issue. In the introduction to this book he notes that "many readers may be sighing, 'Those were the days, when every theology afoot had only "two sides" (above and below, God and "the" human person, the ego and the whole, experience or transcendence) or even just one system of reference (reality in the singular, "the" modern subject, religious experience in the singular).' To that nostalgia one should calmly respond, 'Those were also the days in which evidently no forms of thought and experience could be found that enabled clear insight into the testimonies to the Spirit of God' " (ibid., xii).

24. George A. Lindbeck, "Barth and Textuality," *Theology Today* 43, no. 3

(October 1986), 374. Schleiermacher, in *Christian Faith,* 65, points out that "inasmuch . . . as the [human] reason is completely one with the divine Spirit, the divine Spirit can itself be conceived as the highest enhancement of the human reason, so that the difference between the two is made to disappear." The main difference between mere reading and reading in the power of the Spirit is, according to Lindbeck, like the difference between the reading of a book by an author who is dead and an author who controls one's future. "The utmost in objective is essential: one's future is at stake" (Lindbeck, "Barth and Textuality," 375).

25. Classic liberalism lumped together all of humanity into certain categories, be it in terms of Schleiermacher's "feeling of absolute dependence" or in terms of Tillich's existential categories of anxiety, meaninglessness, and despair. Contemporary liberalism can often be found in postmodern shapes and guises that preach pluralism.

26. Barth, *Church Dogmatics,* vol. 1, bk. 1, 165.

27. Frederick Herzog, "Reformation Today," *Christian Century* 99, no. 33 (October 27, 1982), 1079. I quote Herzog and give a further interpretation of this theme in *Theology from the Belly of the Whale: A Frederick Herzog Reader,* ed. Joerg Rieger (Harrisburg, Pa.: Trinity, 1999), 14.

28. This is the destructive fantasy of Goethe's Faust, who enters into a pact with the devil in order to "learn the things that hold / The world together at its core, / So I may potencies and seeds behold, / And trade in empty words no more" (Johann Wolfgang von Goethe, *Faust,* in *Goethe's Plays,* trans. Charles E. Passage [New York: Frederick Ungar, 1980], 225–26).

29. This is often called "ludic postmodernism." Teresa L. Ebert ("The 'Difference' of Postmodern Feminism," *College English* 53, no. 8 [December 1991], 899) has critiqued the fact that "difference in postmodern thought displaces social contradictions." She shows instead that differences are not free-floating but related to social contradictions. For this reason the "other" inscribed within the system needs to be taken more seriously. Postmodern theories are important since they point to the constructed nature of reality: the real is not given or unalterable. Nevertheless, they can also function as securing the status quo of capitalism.

30. See Joerg Rieger, "Developing a Common Interest Theology from the Underside," in *Liberating the Future: God, Mammon, and Theology,* ed. Joerg Rieger (Minneapolis: Fortress Press, 1998).

31. Here Martin Luther's distinction between a theology of the cross and a theology of glory might be helpful and appears in new light.

32. See Rieger, "Whaling Our Way into the Twenty-First Century," 14.

33. On this matter see also my discussion on Lacan and the notion of the real in Joerg Rieger, *Remember the Poor,* 83ff.

34. Rosemary Hennessy, *Materialist Feminism and the Politics of Discourse* (New York: Routledge, 1993), 65.

35. See Rieger, *Remember the Poor: The Challenge to Theology in the Twenty-First Century* (Harrisburg, Pa.: Trinity, 1998), 99–100, with reference to the work of Herzog. Emphasis in original.

36. For the connection to the means of grace, see Joerg Rieger, "Means of Grace," 377–93. The close relation between love of God and love of neighbor is maintained throughout the Bible. See, for example, Amos 5:10-15 and Matt. 18:23-35.

37. Williams, *Sisters in the Wilderness: The Challenge of Womanist God-Talk* (Maryknoll, N.Y.: Orbis, 1993), xvi. Emphasis in original.

38. Frederick Herzog, "Dual Citizens," in *Theology from the Belly of the Whale,* 298.

39. The apostle Paul faced similar problems with the Christians in Corinth when he pointed out to them that during Holy Communion "each of you goes ahead with your own supper, and one goes hungry and another becomes drunk"(1 Cor. 11:21).

40. Hall, *Remembered Voices,* 139.

41. Mark McClain Taylor ("Tracking Spirit: Theology as Cultural Critique in America," in *Changing Conversations,* 135–36) makes an intriguing suggestion that parallels what I have in mind by using the term "listening" when he defines *theology* as "tracking spirit," a metaphor which includes an active process of identifying integrative, liminal, and emancipatory manifestations of the Spirit—a much deeper process than merely "taking a look at."

42. The United Methodist *Book of Discipline* ([Nashville, Tenn.: United Methodist, 1996], 72), for example, picks up this concern when it defines *theology* as reflection "upon God's gracious action in our lives," giving "expression to the mysterious reality of God's presence, peace, and power in the world."

Index

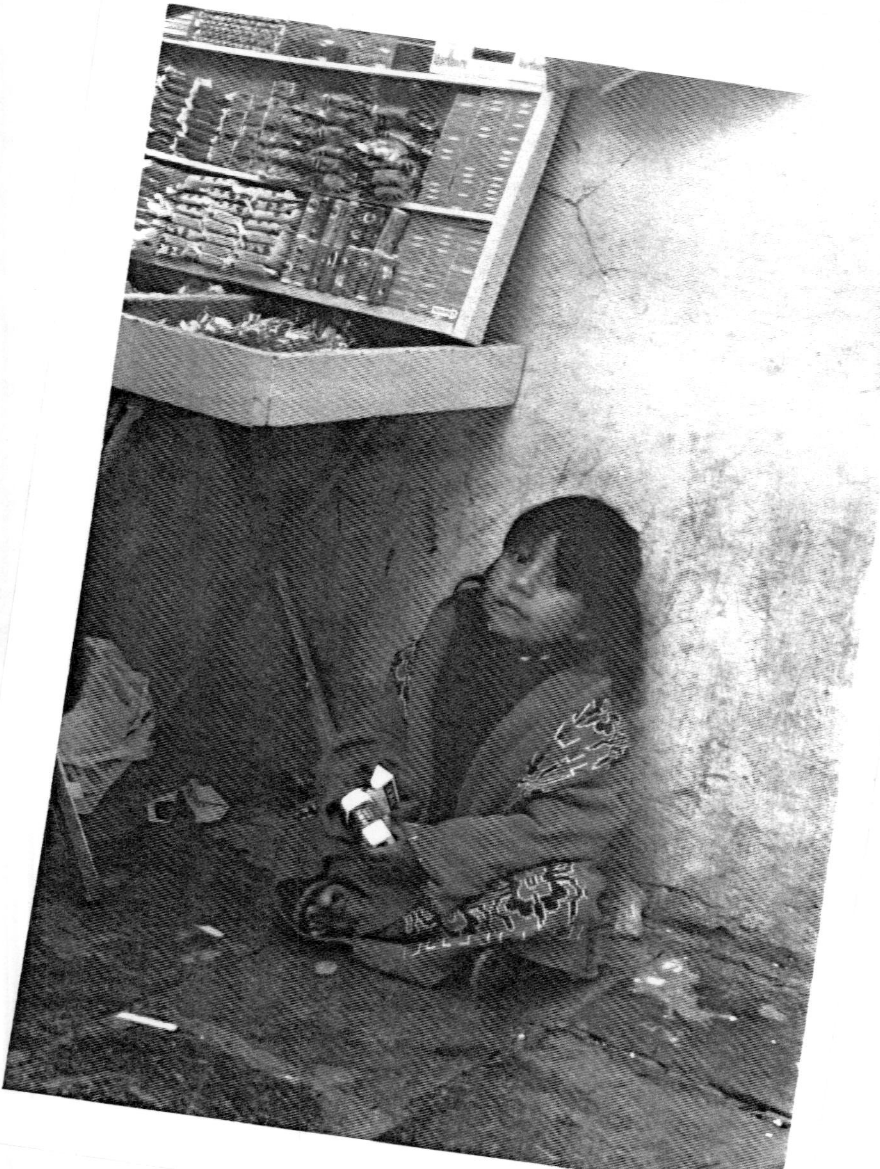